WHY YOU GET SICK
AND
HOW YOU GET WELL

WHY YOU GET SICK
AND
HOW YOU GET WELL

The Healing Power of Feelings

DR. ARTHUR JANOV

DOVE BOOKS

ISBN 0-7871-0685-2

Printed in the United States of America

Dove Books
8955 Beverly Boulevard
West Hollywood, CA 90048

Distributed by Penguin USA

Text design by Stanley S. Drate/Folio Graphics Co., Inc.

First Printing: August 1996

10   9   8   7   6   5   4   3   2   1

pour la belle France

Tout être bien portant est un malade qui s'ignore
(Every well person is a sick one who doesn't know it).

MOLIÈRE

I'm not strong enough to stand the remedies;
it's all I can do to stand the disease.

MOLIÈRE

Just because there is a problem doesn't mean
there is a solution.

PROVERB

The seeds of solution lie in the problem.

JANOV

ACKNOWLEDGMENTS

This book was years in the making. Along the way the author sought advice, editing help, criticism, and whatever else it takes to make a good book. Several people helped in this undertaking. My thanks to David Lassoff for organizing information and doing research, and to Howard Spanier, who did endless hours of copying and binding to give the book a polished look. To Wendy Campbell for improving the manuscript. Randy Malat has edited my last three books and has been indispensable in presenting ideas clearly and coherently.

Thanks to my former colleague, neurologist Dr. Michael Holden, for his input on brain function and feelings, and to my colleague of many years, Jonathan Christie (an author in his own right and a specialist in nutrition), for literally putting in months of work, suggesting alternate ideas, offering late-breaking research, discussing ideas that were not clear, and eliminating repetition and the boring parts. My thanks, too, to brain researcher Dr. Erik Hoffmann for his cutting-edge work in brainwave diagnosis. Thanks especially to my wife, France, a doctoral candidate in psychology, for reading endless drafts, offering brilliant analyses, telling me what was too technical, what wasn't technical enough, what needed fleshing out, and what needed rewriting. I must not forget Valérie Beausoleil, who kept my computer in repair and kept me up to speed with this new technology.

A special thanks is due to those who toil at Dove Books. First to Doug Field for bringing me into the publishing house and to Mary Aarons, who makes the key literary decisions at Dove. Secondly, to Marie Rowe for the excellent abridging she has done, and lastly to Lee Montgomery, who spent a good part of her life putting my manuscript together so it looks and acts like a book. Finally, thanks to my patients, who always manage to teach me something new, who contributed their stories to this book, and who made the theoretical advances therein possible.

ARTHUR JANOV, Ph.D.
The Primal Center
1205 Abbot Kinney Boulevard
Venice, California 90291
(310) 392-2003

CONTENTS

INTRODUCTION

And did you get
what you wanted from this life even so?
I did.
And what was that?
To call myself beloved.
To feel myself beloved on this earth.

Late Fragment
Raymond Carver

Why do so many people say they feel "empty" and "half alive"? Why are so many of us unenthusiastic and depressed so much of the time, even though we have a loving spouse and family, good friends, a decent job, a nice place to live, plenty of free time?

Why do we get anxious and worried in the absence of any apparent cause? What is it that makes some of us feel "trapped" or "tied down" or "suffocated" in a relationship or at work and have such a hard time maintaining intimacy or holding down a job? Why are others helpless to make decisions and solve their problems?

Why do so many people spend their lives seeking love and never finding it, going from one unsatisfying relationship to another? Why do some people have such a hard time enjoying sex? Why are some of us active in bed and others passive? Why do some masturbate chronically, have recurrent fantasies, or develop fetishes?

Why are so many of us believers—embracing irrational ideas and religions, following gurus, seeking the "meaning of life," perhaps by discovering who we were in past incarnations?

Why do many types of psychotherapy seek to help patients "understand" their problems but don't really lead to healing, compelling the patient to return for hourly sessions week after week, year after year, as if going to church? Why do professionals and laypeople believe that medications like Prozac are the most effective way to deal with the symptoms of neurosis, knowing full well that such medications cannot cure?

Why are so many people plagued by headaches, high blood pressure, bronchitis, asthma, intestinal distress, alcoholism, allergies, and other chronic health problems?

And why do many patients find that after reliving traumas which occurred early in their life, their anxiety and depression diminish, their relationships and sex lives improve, they no longer feel the urge to drink or use drugs, and discover that their migraines, high blood pressure, and other lifelong symptoms are partly or wholly alleviated?

Over the last thirty years I have learned a great deal about humans and what drives them. As trite as it may seem, what I have found is a single yet complex emotion called love. Not the romantic love of novels, but a fundamental love—the love of a parent for a child. When a child lacks love and nurturing, no matter how that lack is manifest, it creates pain, and if this pain is not "felt" or integrated into the system, it will in turn cause physical and emotional illness in later life.

It's hard to believe that there are ways to measure the pain of the lack of love, but when a child is neglected, criticized, humiliated, or ignored, there are physiological changes in internal and brain processes that are actually measurable when patients relive those pains years later.

Recent advances in research in psychology, biology, and neurology have broadened knowledge so that information from a variety of fields is being integrated into a single framework which allows us to understand human beings, their motives, their unconscious, and how their history affects them. That history, it turns out, goes as far back as the first few months of life when the pain tracts are laid down and the fetus receives pain but cannot defend against it.

Who could have ever dreamt that migraines, neurosis, phobias, and adult sexual problems could begin as early as birth because of trauma or poor oxygen supply, or that these illnesses could be reversed by reliving the early trauma? It is a powerful idea that one can undo and redo history. Nature gave us trauma yet also provided the chemicals in the brain to defend against it, storing the memory for later processing. All that is needed to unlock the mystery of physical and emotional illness is access to the unconscious feelings of hurt, of lack of love, of fear and rejection, and the "system" will do the rest. It is simply logic, a logic of feelings which have their own system of knowing.

By helping patients feel their buried feelings, we give them back their humanity and the power for transformation and choice—the freedom to choose a life outside of the program set down in childhood. It is the patient who develops insights. Everything they have to learn is just lying there in the brain, waiting for liberation.

When you read this book you'll be joining me on a journey deep into the psyche as we unlock the secrets of the unconscious.

WHY YOU
GET SICK
AND
HOW YOU
GET WELL

1

WHY YOU GET SICK

One of my patients in primal therapy had a hard time looking people in the eye. In a group session at my clinic, he kept talking about eyes, insisting that everyone in the room was staring at him with "angry eyes." I then bent over him, making my eyes look as angry as I could. This suddenly drove him into a memory of being in the crib, crying for his mother. A moment later his father appeared, furious about being bothered, and yelled at the helpless infant. After my "angry eyes" had reawakened this memory, a memory he hadn't known existed, he began crying once more, infant cries that he would not have been able to duplicate otherwise.

On another occasion, a patient began writhing on the floor, arms and legs in fetal position, breathing deeply without pause for twenty minutes. Such rapid, raspy "locomotive" breathing, organized deep within the brain, told me he was reliving his birth. I measured his core body temperature, pulse, and blood pressure, all of which were dropping rapidly enough to suggest that he was on the road to dying. Yet, beyond the unusual breathing pattern, something extraordinary was happening in terms of his physical activity: His movements were so vigorous that they somehow canceled the effects of his deep breathing.

There were no signs of the hyperventilation syndrome that ordinarily accompanies rapid breathing, nor was there dizziness, loss of consciousness, or hands frozen in a clawlike position. He was simply in the grip of a memory, a memory he was completely unaware of just a few minutes before. Instead of dying, he was on the road to living.

Meanwhile, in a biological laboratory, a single-celled amoeba is swimming in a petri dish of water. An experimenter adds some drops of india ink to the dish. The amoeba incorporates the pigment into itself and stores it in a vacuole. The water in the dish is then replaced with fresh water. The amoeba discharges the india ink granules, returns to its normal state, and goes about its business.

These three seemingly unrelated events are actually closely linked. In the one-celled amoeba's behavior and both patients' agony lie clues to the nature of mental and physical illness. We have only to ask the right questions of our observations to find the answer to the riddle that underlies so many afflictions. The right questions can lead to answers that will eventually spell out a cure. They will also lead to an understanding of the human condition: of what and who we are and what makes us behave as we do. In this book I redefine mental illness and its cure, for neurosis is not at all what we are accustomed to thinking it is. Although we tend to conceive of neurosis in terms of social behavior, its readily identifiable behavioral manifestations are merely the tip of the iceberg. Beneath the surface of neurotic behavior lie repressed traumas experienced early in life: a dramatic event such as being in an auto accident, or, more important, the hurt of not having our childhood needs met; being neglected, ignored, abused, or made to feel unloved.

Over the last three decades, we have found ways to measure the ongoing presence of early trauma. The force of a traumatic memory remains in the system, reverberating on lower brain levels and working against the body, producing symptoms wherever the body happens to be vulnerable. Early experience shapes our interests, values, motivations, and ideas. Buried memories constantly activate the system, creating disruptions that can eventually result in serious mental illness. We may suddenly find ourselves with certain afflictions or obsessions and have no idea of their origin. Back pain, insomnia, chronic immune diseases such as Epstein-Barr and chronic fatigue syndrome, depression, high blood pressure, arthritis, migraines, allergies, colitis, epilepsy, heart disease, alcoholism, addiction, anxiety, and ulcers, among other ailments, have become so prevalent that society has built new industries on relieving pain alone. Television bombards us with advertisements for ibuprofen, aspirin, sleeping pills, and other painkillers, implicitly acknowledging the pain we are all in.

In the fields of medicine and psychotherapy today, doctors continuously deal with symptoms. Just look at the *Diagnostic and Statistical Manual of Mental Disorders* (DSM-IV), a reference book used by professionals in psychology and psychiatry, which contains page after page of every conceivable variation of mental illness. And in Washington, D.C., monuments have been erected to symptoms in the form of buildings dedicated to the study of drug abuse, alcoholism, heart disease, cancer, and so on. All over the United States, experts specialize in treating colitis, ulcers, migraines, diabetes, high blood pressure, asthma, anxiety, depression, marital problems, eating disorders, and so forth. They add salt, take away salt, add thyroid, remove thyroid, speculate about the reasons for one's allergies or unhappiness, analyze dreams, and nearly always prescribe medication. *They are trying to normalize the symptom instead of normalizing the person who is exhibiting the symptom.*

Specialists typically divide human dysfunctions into physical and psychological ailments and treat them as if the two domains are separate entities despite recent evidence to the contrary. In this country, there has been an increasing trend toward treating the whole person in some areas of alternative medicine, and more and more research efforts are being devoted to theories concerning healing and the mind. In our work at the Primal Center, we have remarkable evidence that every emotional hurt has a bodily counterpart, and that the two must not be separated.

The real killer in the world today is not heart disease, cancer, stroke, or immune system failure. It is repression, the agent of neurosis. Repression limits our ability to react to events and inhibits the expression of feelings. It is the foundation of many diseases, emotional and physical, and it often literally kills. Not only does it cause us to act out and antagonize those around us without our knowing it, but it also keeps us from knowing and being ourselves and enjoying our lives.

Even though repression makes us miserable and often ill, its power has been overlooked because it is a force that is as invisible as gravity. It wraps itself around our traumatic memories and clouds our history, altering brain circuits so that we do not see what we dare not see and do not comprehend what is dangerous to know.

What causes repression? Pain. When trauma or deprivation inflicted early in life is so great that it exceeds the organism's capacity to react to it, it becomes pain. This pain, in turn, stimulates the production of repressive agents—the endorphins and other natural painkillers.

Evidence from various sources suggests that many ailments that until now have been difficult to explain may in fact all stem from the same source. The same is true for personality quirks, habits, behavior, drives, and obsessions. One powerful fact that supports the similar-source theory is that the same kinds of tranquilizers and painkillers are used to treat entirely different symptoms. Consider the "wonder drugs" known as the serotonin uptake inhibitors—Prozac, Paxil, Zoloft—which are used to treat insomnia, anorexia, depression, anxiety, and obesity, among other afflictions.

In primal therapy, we work in reverse from the conventional approach. Instead of working from symptoms to possible causes, we work from causes to symptoms. Through this method, our therapists have developed a more profound understanding of who we are, what moves us forward, and what holds us back. We have learned that what makes people sick is the key to making them well again.

Memory studies reported in neurophysiologist E. Roy John's book *Mechanisms of Memory* reveal that the same brain cells are used when an individual first sees an object and is later asked to remember that same object. Imagine what happens when whole systems are called into play in the recollection of a past traumatic event. Although this is clearly an area for future research, it supports our findings that internal reality is always present and that it is difficult for some to distinguish between internal and external reality. What one perceives as an external event may be internal and connected to an event from the past.

Primal therapy helps people deal with this internal reality. This reality has nothing to do with self-esteem, ego, self-worth, creative visualization, or image-enhancing exercises. It is basic human need, the core around which neurosis and its attendant ailments revolves. If you avoid addressing the truth of your history and your unmet needs, whether in the social or psychological sphere, symptoms will remain and you will be forced into treatment regimens that address only symptoms. When these treatments fail to neutralize the primal tide washing below your misery, you will continue to suffer. Emotionally based illnesses such as depression, anxiety, and obsessive-compulsive disorders tend to be treated with antidepressants or electroshock therapy, the latter of which is now sadly making a comeback in treating children. With physiologically based afflictions such as ulcers, treatments become more and more invasive, involving increasingly stronger drugs and often surgery. But if people could identify and experience the *source* of the pain that has attacked their system, the pain could be avoided. Addressing *need*, rather than ignoring it or drugging or shocking it into hiding, is the only way to normalize the cells and return the organism to a steady state, or homeostasis.

As in other areas of mainstream science, primal therapy's hypotheses are testable, progress predictable, and healing quantifiable. What lies in the unconscious is like nothing that most psychiatrists and psychologists have imagined. Instead of our brutal animal legacy, we find a friendly place. The deeper we delve into the unconscious, the larger the healing possibilities. We have found that there is nothing more healing than feeling: to fully experience discrete memories and emotions from early in one's life. If the therapy is done correctly so that the unconscious gradually becomes conscious in the proper sequence, each repressed memory will be integrated and its suffering component eliminated.

With the reversal of the neurotic process, we feel better and more relaxed. We have fewer migraines and lower blood pressure. Colitis, allergies, asthma, and epileptic seizures become less severe, perhaps even disappear. There is less nervous energy interfering with our concentration and compelling us to seek spiritual guidance or discover the meaning of life. We are, at last, free to live.

2

NEUROSIS: THE FOUNDATION OF ILLNESS

Neurosis is so widespread that it seems as though it has been genetically programmed into the majority of the population. We do not inherit neurosis; what we do inherit is a brain structure—shaped and formed over millions of years—that has the capacity for neurosis. This legacy has given us the ability to handle pain through repression, to compensate for the input of pain by dislocating function, and to be unaware of ourselves and what we feel and sense. In short, we survive by using mechanisms that help us avoid and divert reality when that reality is overwhelming.

When trauma created the need for a countervailing force, the brain "grew" a cortex to help us think our way out of problems. That made us smart and able to think abstractly, to live "in our heads" and convince ourselves that thinking was the way to solve our problems. It allowed us to fool ourselves into using the very tools that countermand feelings and render us internally inaccessible. And it gave us a mechanism for survival that can make us sick and even cause us to die before our time.

The human system is not liberal; it is fascist. It is unmerciful and unrelenting, and knows no pity. Its only concern is survival of the species, not of the individual. To preserve the species, we must disconnect from ourselves. Repression allows us to treat ourselves and others inhumanely because it effectively suppresses our humanity. It causes us to rear generation after generation of emotional cripples so that civilization might go on. Neurosis is not a perversion of man; it is the essence of being human. To be neurotic is not to be "sick" but to be compatible with nature's overall aim of continuing life. Without neurosis many of us would be in constant agony. We become lesser human beings with neurosis, but at least we function. We just *feel* less.

The human brain not only remembers, but it is also memory concretized, the culmination of a long history of evolution. Contrary to the popular saying, what you don't know *can* hurt you, because *the repressed memory of trauma is traumatic.* Neurosis preserves childhood in pristine form, and it is the *memory* of the deprived childhood that keeps on hurting us. Not being loved during one's childhood puts the system on alert that needs are not being fulfilled. The body pumps out stress hormones to accommodate the memory. Patients who come to the Primal Treatment Center usually have high stress hormone levels at the beginning of therapy. The body is energized to both flee and fight an unseen enemy—our feelings. Stress hormones raise the blood pressure, increase the pulse, and can ultimately lead to cardiovascular problems. The higher the stress, the lower the immune efficiency. The hormones interfere with normal functioning so that eventually we may fall ill with anything from allergies to cancer. We have found that when adult patients relive and address their unfulfilled need to be loved, their stress hormone levels drop. Until they do so, little changes. To repress childhood feelings is to move partially unconscious throughout life. As a result, a good part of our population is, in effect, sleepwalking.

The person who is driven, who feels he or she can't take a vacation, who can't sit still, who must stay on the move at all times is sick. The "big bang" of that person's childhood pain is absorbed as the years progress. One keeps on going to avoid the feeling that there was, or is, nothing one could do about one's early situation. When the brain is occupied with this continual repression, all that energy and activation has to find its way into some kind of disease. The hyperactivity that began with being left alone for hours or days right after birth, that continued with the neglect by a sick or depressed mother, that was exacerbated by a tyrannical or hostile father, may end up causing a stroke and partial paralysis at age sixty-five.

We don't *have* an imprint; we *are* the imprint. Neurosis is everywhere and nowhere, invisible at first glance yet very visible in its psychophysiologic effects, in how we behave and in our state of health. It has so many different faces that it seems as though we are dealing with a hundred diseases rather than just one. It is so labyrinthine that it is difficult to pinpoint and treat. Most doctors may find it difficult to accept the notion that a heart attack or stroke is the result of something that occurred sixty or sixty-five years earlier. But if we could put a tiny camera into the brain, similar to what neurologist Wilder Penfield did in his study of epileptics (see Chapter Fourteen), we would see the traumatic memories preserved in pristine form. Perhaps then the cause of the stroke would not be such a mystery. Indeed, some adults who experience hallucinations have shown increased limbic activity in structures of the brain such as the hippocampus and thalamus, where childhood emotions are stored, as well as the cortex, where old feelings rise and are either interpreted or squashed. The hallucinations may be an offshoot of historical imprints from some forty years earlier and are no different from the physical symptoms that may show up decades after the event.

Neurosis and its physical manifestations is a lifetime sentence from which there is only one escape: consciousness. That route is so well hidden, however, that it has evaded the gaze of countless professional eyes. We are historical beings, and any therapy that neglects that history is doomed to failure. Without history, all anyone can offer is "help," which is not a bad thing, but with history one can offer more—cure.

Unlocking the Key to Our Neurosis

Let us return to the example of the amoeba in the introduction. This microscopic, unicellular organism is quite primitive, but its behavior can tell us much about human neurosis because it is, in an evolutionary sense, the prototype for ourselves. How the amoeba handles an alien intrusion of india ink granules is a paradigm for how we handle trauma. In both cases, a stressor causes the organism to mass its defenses and alter its normal functioning. The amoeba sequesters the india ink granules in vacuoles; we repress noxious information and store it in the brain in a series of structures known as the limbic system. We survive in spite of our unmet needs; perhaps a better term for our behavior would be *survival*, not neurosis.

New information shows how similar our cells function to the amoeba. According to the April 29, 1994, issue of *Science News*, there are human cell caves, or caveolae; these are actual caves inside cell chambers that store noxious or harmful material. These caveolae can open, take in molecules from the outside, then close, very much like the amoeba. It is possible to mine these caves for their historic contents, much like what was done with ancient cave drawings found in France. For example, it was found in diabetics that the accumulation of substances altered by prolonged exposure to blood sugar could damage kidneys and other organs. The harmful substances can lodge inside the caveolae. Ultimately, they can be released by the caveolae. When my patients relive being etherized at birth and actually smell ether again, perhaps it shouldn't be dismissed.

We save ourselves by internalizing adverse circumstances such as anoxia, abandonment, and other kinds of trauma, engraving them into our brain and physiology. Repression preserves our childhood traumas like a fly in amber: the hopelessness of a young child who realizes his parents cannot love enough; the helplessness of a child sent to a foster home where she is physically and emotionally abused; the despair of a child whose mentally ill father can never be a caring, loving person; the sadness of a child whose mother stands idly by while the father criticizes and beats the child. This child grows up and takes tranquilizers or antidepressants to make up for what her parents did not do: 20 milligrams of Prozac or 10 milligrams of Xanax day after day to do the work that hugs should have done. What allows this person to come alive again is re-experiencing the neglect of early need. Feeling the lack is what makes one whole because the lack is everywhere in the system.

Current reality hasn't a chance against old, unfulfilled needs. Even when we are loved and adored in adulthood, we are still starving for love we did not get in our childhood. Even when we receive a heap of praises in the present, we tend to focus on that one slight criticism because it resonates with a past that was all too critical. In the brain, "back then" is "now." There will never be enough love in the present to change the past, never enough praise to reverse a lifetime of being berated or disapproved. Marilyn Monroe could have attested to that. She was loved by presidents, famous writers, and baseball stars, adored by millions of fans, yet she still felt unloved. Alas, no amount of reassurance was enough to stop her use of drugs and alcohol to keep the pain down. Her very early pain was horribly compounded by childhood neglect. If her history truly included incest, which has been hinted at, the combined force of the pain must have been staggering. In the end, applause from thousands is not real love; it is a symbol of love. Real love is hugs and kisses, responsibility, caring, protection, stability, and being there when the person is in need.

Every neurotic has a secret life because every neurotic has secret feelings. But neurosis holds the key to its own undoing. Our neurotic or "sick" behaviors and our physical symptoms are actually part of the road to health. When it is safe, we address our hurts and incorporate them into our system. As with the amoeba, noxious elements are safely stored for later release in the proper environment. When the amoeba is put into clean water—a safe environment—the vacuole moves to the edge of the cell membrane and discharges the india ink granules, restoring the amoeba to its normal state. Likewise, to achieve resolution and return to normal functioning, the human being must "discharge" noxious elements (rage, for example) from its limbic storehouse into consciousness, and finally out of the body. This can occur only in a warm, kind, therapeutic environment. Unfortunately, it won't happen in the conditions found in many drug treatment programs, where a patient crying about her early abuse may in turn be abused verbally; in such places "tough love" is thought to build character. In a benevolent environment, however, she would be encouraged to allow the full force of the memory of her abuse into consciousness, and to react to it with the screaming and cries of terror she had to repress at the time.

In primal therapy we unlock the door to our stored historic feelings. We have found a way to help people feel the need and trauma and connect it to consciousness. We have seen the awesome power of imprinted memory in the intensity of a primal. To see a reliving of birth anoxia or the terror of a tyrannical father, a reliving that goes on for session after session over a period of months or years, is to realize the incredible amount of repressed energy inside us. That energy must be diverted elsewhere. It makes the development of cardiovascular illness, strokes, and other symptoms less of a mystery and explains the remarkable persistence of obsessions and compulsive behavior, phobias, depression, and anxiety.

The totality of response—the original environment and the reactions to it that were aborted—must be brought out: All the smells and sights, sounds and images must return, accompanied by the same emotions. The imprint must be discharged in small fragments lest the patient be overwhelmed. Consciousness enlarges as each bit is brought up, until the entire imprint has been made conscious and the whole of its energy released. As with the amoeba, as the abuse is discharged, healing begins; the organism gradually returns to normal. Once it is fully relived, the trauma can no longer cause damage. Our history is finally put where it belongs. It becomes simply a memory, shorn of its power.

ALIETTA: THE RELIEF OF FEELING

Tonight it is as if slow death is descending upon me. Death. I have always been obsessed by it. The fear of being alone in the dark is still there. I am alone, I have always been alone, I am never going to make it alone, I need help. I am so scared. It is as if I am going to die if nobody helps me, if nobody comes. I am totally still, I don't dare move, and slowly I feel myself fall irresistibly into a powerful drowsiness. A part of me becomes totally panicked. But I don't move. My body refuses the smallest movement. I try taking a big breath of air and find that I can't breathe. The panic grows and with it my need to breathe. As I try to open my mouth, I feel it contort in a silent scream. I am choking, and I choke until I feel myself falling in a black hole. "Where are you, Mama? I need you to help me. I am dying." I have no idea how long I stayed in this narcoleptic state. It seemed like an eternity.

Suddenly, from somewhere deep inside me, I feel an overwhelming need to move, a fear of it, too, the need to scream, to shake myself out of this death. Something in me refuses to die. A part of me, still alive, is growing. I have to summon up all my willpower. It is a physical need. I have to move, I have to get out of it. I have to get out.

When I am forcing myself to move, to shake that incredibly powerful lethargy, I am screaming an inhuman scream, and my body starts moving erratically. I start kicking, my back arches violently, every part aches as my body tenses up to make me push, to crawl in weird motions that I do not understand and that are totally out of my control. I just need to do it with all my strength. It is extremely hard, but I have to do it. I keep pushing, arching, gagging. I can't breathe. I am dying again. Again, I fall into the comalike state, and again that little flame gets me out of it. As I am pushing and trying to breathe, I suddenly feel that I am making it. I can breathe; I open my eyes. From very deep in me, an explosion of amazing intensity rushes over me and grows into an unexpected bliss. I made it. I made it. I am alive. And suddenly a flash. I am born!

I remember the joy I felt. It was powerful. I was laughing. I was feeling the blood flow quickly through my body. Every part of me wanted to move, to stretch, to jump, to express the incredible joy I was now feeling. It became pure ecstasy, the ecstasy of simply being alive. I was laughing alone in my dark room and I realized I had never felt like this before. Was this what being alive felt like? How phenomenal. I had only felt pain, never joy, but now it was there and I wanted more of it. A new addiction to life was starting. It was fantastic. I was exhausted and yet I wanted to jump up and down, to feel my body move and dance. I was finally born. The insights started pouring out. Yes, birth, unmistakably so.

The agony of death, the struggle to be born, and finally coming out into this world all by myself with no help, only because of my determination not to die. That same determination has kept me alive through the worst and has kept me searching for something to save me. It led me to therapy, and here again it is only I who can do it and save myself. I know now I will make it. I had to leave my mother's womb in which I was held prisoner, slowly suffocating for too long. I had to get out of the control of her body. I had to leave my home because I couldn't stand the permanent control I was subjected to, the rigidity of a Catholic bourgeois education. I had to be able to do what I wanted because otherwise I would die. And the child I was did die slowly through all these years of repression and lack of love. But now I will get her back, and Alietta is going to live again.

I asked my mother later what had happened at my birth. At first she didn't remember, then she acknowledged the fact that she had to be given drugs to allow her to relax because I couldn't get out.

Making the Unconscious Conscious

To get well, we must first determine what makes us sick. The neurotic carries around an incredible load of repressed feelings. The person is unaware of this prison of pain, yet it directs her every waking moment. It limits her thought processes, perceptions, imagination, and choices; it directs her dreams, aspirations, values, and interests; it gets in the way of natural sexual reactivity and blocks the ability to fully experience herself as a feeling human being; and it masks itself by channeling into organs that we then treat as malfunctioning entities, or by channeling into belief systems that serve to defend the person against the same feelings that gave rise to these beliefs.

Neurosis, in short, is diabolic. We are all characters in a Eugene O'Neill play, only we are not aware of the masks we wear.

And because we are not aware of being sick or of what makes us sick, we do not know how to get well. Worse, we don't know that we *should* get well. Our neurosis has fulfilled its function of making us comfortable. We are headed for an early cardiac crisis or other catastrophic disease, but we continue blithely on, unaware of the ticking bomb inside. That bomb is loaded with horrendous screams and cries. All that noise constantly rises to the surface, keeping us from concentrating and thinking clearly, so we stuff it back down. If we keep muffling those explosions, the pressure will build and eventually we will crack.

To get well, we must return to a time when we experienced pure suffering on its own terms, with nothing to soften the blow. The return in personal time allows us to peer into the history of the human species. Evolution offered us the tool of neurosis in order to survive, and when patients agonize and writhe on the floor, unable to move their arms and hands, we know that prehuman history still resides in us. In a primal where the patient has tapped into the area of memory that cannot be captured with language, he will turn and twist like a salamander, arms and legs useless, choking and gagging perhaps, but without words. He is now completely in the grip of that primitive brain, responding as it dictates. He is more than a hundred million years away in evolutionary time, healing in that brain and no other, because that is the brain that was traumatized. His vital signs and brainwave patterns accompanying this state skyrocket systematically.

When we see this, we can disentangle some of the great scientific mysteries of the ages: What is a human being? What is neurosis? Why are people anxious and depressed? What happened in our childhood? Why did I get sick? How do I get well? The search for answers has been the very thing that has led the searchers away from the true solutions. By minutely analyzing human life, taking humans apart cell by cell, measuring this or that blood cell, this or that hormone, we have neglected the whole human being, thereby avoiding finding the unique quality of who we are and why we are that way. And by philosophizing as to what the basic nature of man is, we have been led "into our heads," away from feelings and the forces that would have provided the answers we seek. Neurosis can't be "figured out;" it has to be felt. Feelings have a logic all their own.

But because memory can be selective, how do we know that the recovered memory is real? It is often quite simple. I offer two examples from my own experience. One of my patients was reliving being starved by his mother, who put him on scheduled feedings. She was holding him in her arms but was not breast-feeding him. He was six months old. As an adult, he had the memory of looking up and seeing her earrings and wondering why she made him starve. When he went to visit his mother and described the earrings she was wearing, she was astonished. She had lost those earrings when the child was one year of age and had never discussed them. Yet his description was exact as to color and shape. In the second example, another patient was reliving his birth. He was a twin and was re-experiencing the difficulty he had getting out behind his sister. His mother had told him that that was impossible, as he was first born. He wrote to the hospital, which sent him the records confirming that he was second born.

At the Primal Center we have taken a diametrically-opposed approach to conventional treatments. We look at human beings not as a collection of symptoms or organs or cells but as whole organisms. We don't simply treat high blood pressure as a specific and isolated affliction. We see how a person's history has possibly produced that level of pressure. It usually turns out that the pressure is literal. We don't want to drug or talk or shock suffering out of existence; we want to coax it into the real feeling and trauma it is.

Primal therapy breaks down repression's invisible walls and allows people to fully respond to traumatic aspects of their childhood for the first time. No other therapy thinks the unconscious can or should be unlocked. But *there is no painless way out of neurosis.* In conventional therapy, a patient who promises to be "honest" with his therapist and bare all his "secrets" can't be honest because he doesn't know his secrets; and many of them lie deep in his cells. We know this because after primal therapy, the electrical potential of certain muscle cells is diminished. This means that in those muscle cells are fragments of hidden truths, truths that need to be expressed.

In neurosis there is no truth without pain. Awareness of self without feeling does not mean being oneself. It simply means being an objective observer of a split self. To bring the selves together involves suffering because suffering is what kept them apart. Active suffering is the first important stage in getting well. As fearful as it sounds, our patients can't wait to come to sessions and feel. Each session is another piece of hurt that comes out of the system and won't have to be felt again. There is nothing quite like having that burden lifted.

One need not be afraid of the unconscious. Therein lies only yourself—the bewildered, lost infant; the sad, innocent child; the angry, enraged preteen. In taking patients to the depths of their unconscious, we have yet to see the mysteries heretofore described in the psychiatric literature. It is not a vault of Dantéesque phantasmagoria. There are no demons from the eighteenth century, no id or shadow forces à la Freud, no mystical consciousness to aspire to, nothing that involves a transcendental process. What we find is just sad, terrified little us.

ALIETTA: FIFTEEN YEARS LATER

The insights have become deeper and more complete. After so much time I am still astonished at the power of a primal. I still have one once in a while, but the pain has finally subsided. I do not have to feel this experience so often. Only when life brings up some old unfinished pain do I have to feel this. It is very rare now. Feeling always brings clarity and simplification, and I can now deal with reality and the present, and no more with the past.

My life is now very much in order. I am no longer my father's son. I am no longer a hard-driving businesswoman. I am no longer after success, but only after fulfillment of my real self. My real self is now in command; my life is much simpler. I have found love at last, and I am able to love and be loved. I am now an artist. This is what I should have been from the beginning, for it gives me great satisfaction and peace. It is the real me. I sleep well (I was always an insomniac), I eat better, I don't drink, I am not a dope addict anymore. I am generally much healthier. I used to have infections and hemorrhages, and there was often something wrong with me. My eyesight was deteriorating rapidly. After being in therapy, I lived without my glasses for two weeks before I realized I had lost them.

Now years have passed and age has caught up with me. I am a lot softer, easier to be with, and a lot more open and warmer. I even go to parties, although I still don't like doing it that much. But it is not the crucifying experience it used to be and very often I enjoy it thoroughly. It is easier to be with people. I don't run away or pack my bags. Instead I stay and feel the feelings. I like to listen to music and grow flowers. I enjoy more stability.

My sex life is normal. For years I had to have birth primals before I could experience an orgasm because my body had been so shut off by the pain of birth that the pain always preceded the pleasure. I am more relaxed because so much tension has left me for good. My dreams are no longer symbolic. If they are painful, all I have to do is get back to the feeling contained in them and deal with it.

I feel I got what I expected from primal therapy and more. What you get here is not just therapy: It is the gift of life. I know who I am and what I am. I am no longer a mystery to myself. In fact, I am not sure I still have an unconscious. So much has surfaced and become conscious. It is a great relief. My life is in order. All these years of pain have paid off. I am finally happy.

3

The Birth of Neurosis

We are all creatures of need. These needs are not excessive: to be fed, to be kept warm and dry, to grow and develop at our own pace, to be held and caressed, and to be stimulated. These primal needs are the central reality of the infant. The neurotic process begins when these needs go unmet for any length of time.

A newborn does not know that he should be picked up when he cries or that he should not be weaned too early, but when his needs go unattended, he hurts. At first the infant will do everything in his power to fulfill his needs. He will cry, kick his legs, and thrash about to have his needs recognized. If his needs go unfulfilled, either he will suffer continuous pain until his parents satisfy him, or he will shut off the pain by shutting off his need. If his pain is drastic enough, death may intervene, as shown in studies of some institutional babies.

Because the infant cannot address the sensation of hunger (that is, he cannot go to the refrigerator) or find substitute affection, he must separate his sensations (hunger, wanting to be held) from consciousness. This separation of oneself from one's needs and feelings is an instinctive maneuver to shut off excessive pain. We call it *the split*. The organism splits in order to protect its continuity. This does not mean that unfulfilled needs disappear, however. On the contrary, they continue through life, exerting a persistent, unconscious force toward the satisfaction of those needs. But because the needs have been suppressed in the consciousness, the individual must pursue substitute gratification. Because he was not allowed to express himself as an infant, he may be compelled to try to get others to listen and understand later in life.

Not only are unattended needs separated from consciousness, but their sensations become relocated to areas where greater control or relief can be provided. Thus, feelings can be relieved by urination (later by sex) or controlled by the suppression of deep breathing. An infant who was weaned from the breast too early learns how to disguise and change his needs into symbolic ones. As an adult he may not feel the need to suckle his mother's breast, but he may be a chain smoker. His need to smoke is a symbolic need.

Symbolic satisfactions, however, cannot fulfill real needs. In order for real needs to be satisfied, they must be felt and experienced. Unfortunately, pain has caused those needs to be buried, and neurosis takes their place. What is the difference between real needs and neurotic needs? Real needs are natural needs: to grow and develop at one's own pace, for example. As a child, this means not being weaned too soon, not being forced to walk or talk too early, not being forced to catch a ball before one's neurological apparatus can do so comfortably. Neurotic needs are unnatural ones—they develop from the nonsatisfaction of real needs. We are not born into this world needing to hear praise, but when a child's real efforts are denigrated, when he is made to feel that nothing he can do will be good enough, he may develop a craving for praise. Similarly, when the need to express oneself as a child is suppressed, such denial may turn into a need to talk incessantly as an adult.

A loved child is one whose natural needs are fulfilled. Love takes his pain away. An unloved child is the one who hurts because he is unfulfilled. A loved child has no need for praise because he has not been denigrated. He is valued for *what he is,* not for what he can do to satisfy his parents' need. A loved child does not grow up into an adult with an insatiable craving for sex. He has been held and caressed by his parents and does not need to use sex to satisfy that early need. Real need flows from inside out, not the reverse. The need to be held and caressed is part of the need to be stimulated. The skin is our largest sense organ and requires at least as much stimulation as other sense organs. Disastrous consequences can occur when there is insufficient stimulation early in life. Organ systems may begin to atrophy without stimulation; conversely, with proper stimulation they may develop and grow. There must be constant mental and physical stimulation.

Unfulfilled needs supersede any other activity in the human until they are met. When needs are met, the child can feel. He can experience his body and his environment. When needs are not met, the child experiences only tension, which is a feeling of being disconnected from consciousness. Without that connection, the neurotic does not feel.

Neurosis does not begin at the instant a child suppresses his first feeling, but we might say that the neurotic *process* does. The child shuts down in stages. Each suppression and denial of need turns the child off a bit more. But one day there occurs a critical shift in which the child is primarily turned off. From that time on, he will operate on a system of dual selves: the unreal and real selves. The real self is the real needs and feelings of the organism. The unreal self is the cover of those feelings and becomes the facade required by neurotic parents in order to fulfill needs of their own. A parent who needs to feel respected because he was humiliated constantly by his parents may demand obsequious and respecting children who do not sass him or say anything negative. A babyish parent may demand that his child grow up too fast, do all the chores, and in reality become adult long before he is ready, so that the parent may continue to be the cared-for baby.

Parental need becomes the child's implicit command. The child begins struggling to fulfill his parents from almost the moment he is alive. He may be pushed to smile, to coo, to wave bye-bye, later to sit up and walk, and still later to push himself so that his parents can have an advanced child. As the child develops, the requirements become more complex. He will have to get A's, to be helpful and do his chores, to be quiet and undemanding, to say bright things, to be athletic. What he will not do is be himself. The thousands of operations that go on between parents and children that deny the natural primal needs of the child mean that the child will hurt. He cannot be what he is and be loved. These deep hurts, these primal pains, are repressed or denied by consciousness. They hurt because they have not been allowed expression or fulfillment.

Each time a child is not held when he needs to be, each time he is shushed, ridiculed, ignored, or pushed beyond his limits, more weight will be added to his pool of hurts, which I call the primal pool. One day an event will take place which, though not necessarily traumatic in itself—giving the child to a baby-sitter for the hundredth time, for instance—will shift the balance between real and unreal and bring on what we defined earlier as the split. I call that event the major primal scene. It is a time in the young child's life when she realizes, "There is no hope of being loved for what I am." The realization is not a conscious one. Rather, the child begins acting in the manner expected by his parents. He says *their* words and does their thing. He acts unreal, that is, not in accord with the reality of his own needs and desires. In a short time the neurotic behavior becomes automatic.

The more assaults on the child by the parents, the deeper the split between real and unreal. He begins to speak and move in prescribed ways, not to touch his body in proscribed areas (not to feel himself, literally), not to be exuberant or sad, and so on. The split, however, is necessary in a fragile child. It is the reflexive (i.e., automatic) way the organism maintains its sanity. Neurosis, then, is the organism's defense against catastrophic reality in order to protect its own development and psychophysical integrity.

Neurosis involves being what one is not in order to get what doesn't exist. If love existed, the child would be what he is, for that is love—letting someone be what he or she is. Thus, nothing wildly traumatic need happen in order to produce neurosis. It can stem from forcing a child to punctuate every sentence with "please" and "thank you" to prove how refined the parents are. It can also come from not allowing the child to complain or cry when he is unhappy. Parents may rush in to quell sobs because of their own anxiety. They may not permit anger—"good girls don't throw tantrums; nice boys don't talk back"—to prove how respected the parents are. The child gets the idea of what is required of him quite soon. Perform, or else. It is the hopelessness of never being loved that causes the split. The child must deny the realization that his own needs will never be filled no matter what he does. He then develops substitute needs, which are neurotic.

Let us take the example of a child who is being continually denigrated by his parents. In the schoolroom he may chatter incessantly (and have the teacher come down hard on him); in the schoolyard he may brag nonstop (and alienate the other children). As an adult, he may crave and loudly demand something as patently symbolic (to the onlooker) as the "best table in the house" in an expensive restaurant. However, getting that table cannot undo the "need" he has to feel important. Otherwise, why repeat his performance every time he eats out? Split off from the authentic, unconscious need to be recognized as a worthwhile human being, he derives the "meaning" of his existence from being recognized and catered to in fancy restaurants.

Children are born, then, with real biological needs, some of which, for one reason or another, are not fulfilled by their parents. It may be that some mothers and fathers simply do not recognize the needs of their child. Or, out of a desire not to make any mistakes, follow the advice of some august authority in child rearing and feed their child by a timetable an airline would envy, wean him according to a flowchart, and toilet train him as soon as possible.

Nevertheless, I do not believe that either ignorance or methodological zeal accounts for the bumper crops of neurosis our species has been producing since history began. The major reason I have found that children become neurotic is that their parents are too busy struggling with unmet infantile needs of their own. Thus, paradoxically, a woman may become pregnant in order to be babied—which is what she has actually needed to be all her life. Being pregnant would serve *her* need and have nothing to do with contributing a healthy human being to society. As long as she is the center of attention, she is relatively happy. Once delivered of her child, though, she may become acutely depressed. She may blame the child for depriving her of the attention she got when she was pregnant. Because she is not ready for motherhood, her milk may dry up, leaving her newborn with the same raft of early deprivations she herself may have suffered. In this way the sins of the parents are visited on the children in a seemingly never-ending cycle.

I call the attempt of the child to please his parents the struggle. The struggle begins with parents, then spreads beyond the family as the person carries his deprived needs with him wherever he goes, and those needs must be acted out. He will seek out parent substitutes with whom he will play out his neurotic drama, or he will make almost anyone, including his children, into parental figures who will fulfill his needs. If a father was suppressed verbally and was never allowed to say much, his children are going to be listeners. They, in turn, having to listen so much, will have suppressed needs for someone to hear them; this someone may well be *their* own children.

The locus of the struggle shifts from real need to neurotic need, from body to mind, because mental needs occur when basic needs are denied. But mental needs are not real needs. They are neurotic needs because they do not serve the real requirements of the organism. The fascination of seeing our names in lights or on the printed page is but one indication of the deep deprivation of individual recognition in many of us. Those achievements, no matter how real, serve as a symbolic quest for parental love. Pleasing an audience then becomes the struggle. What the neurotic does is put new labels (the need to feel important) on old unconscious needs (to be loved and valued). In time he may come to believe that these labels are real feelings and that their pursuit is necessary.

Struggle is what keeps a child from feeling her hopelessness. It manifests itself in overwork, in slaving for high grades, in being the performer. Struggle is the neurotic's hope of being loved. Instead of being himself, he struggles to become another version of himself. Sooner or later the child comes to believe that this version is the real him. The "act" is no longer voluntary and conscious; it is automatic and unconscious. It is neurotic.

Some parents unintentionally inflict irreparable damage on their children. Other forms of deprivation, such as incest, parental separation, abandonment, being sent to a foster home, or seeing a parent killed in a car crash, can be sudden and excruciating. Other damage can be less dramatic but potentially as hurtful. For example, to leave your child alone once is not necessarily damaging, but to make that child feel all alone throughout his childhood is.

Whether deprivations are sudden or gradual, they are traumas young children are not equipped to understand or explain. As they grow older, the specific pain—"I'm so lonely"—will be translated into amorphous suffering: "I feel so bad, and I don't know why."

What we generally term as *neurotic*—nervousness and anxiety, worries and fears, "lack of self-confidence" and "negative thinking patterns," obsessions and compulsions—are merely the outward signs of buried pain. As pain accumulates, repression builds in its quiet way. When we are thoroughly repressed, we lose touch with who we are. Our system finds ways to tamp down the pain and go on, but the pain is still there. Lack of love in childhood doesn't just go away as we grow up. Repressed trauma stays with us as an *imprint*, a force that is stored in our cells like the india ink stored in the amoeba's vacuole.

Because of the imprint, we go about our lives feeling lonely, anxious, empty, half-alive, depressed, desperately trying to find love but not knowing how, leaving a trail of unsatisfying relationships while wondering what it all means. Meanwhile, over time, from its hiding place, the imprint continually disrupts our physiology, perhaps causing colds and allergies during youth, wearing us down physically, making us vulnerable to chronic diseases, weakening our immune functions. At some point, the deep repression against primal pain may even cause more serious immunological disorders and cancer.

The force of repression is diabolic because it cannot be seen, tasted, felt, or palpated. That is why it is so difficult to accept. The only way we see the effects of repression is through primal therapy, when patients relive the early lack of love. We then see how the lack of touch and care has produced a memory that never leaves. When symptoms are eradicated through primal therapy, we know for sure that repressed early feelings in childhood and later symptoms in adulthood are related.

Many people, including prominent figures in psychology, doubt the theory that our bodies remember events of which we are unaware. That is what the "repressed memory syndrome" controversy is about. How is it possible that someone who is twenty or thirty or forty years old suddenly recalls that her father molested her when she was a small child? How could she have forgotten such a traumatic event? If she did not remember it for so many years, isn't it more likely that it never happened? Might she not be inventing reasons to explain her persistent unhappiness? Maybe she believes her therapist's "suggestions" that such a thing could have happened? Maybe she has embellished childhood events or made them up entirely?

The skepticism of those who have never seen a long-repressed experience rise again to consciousness, even decades later, is understandable. The sight of that pain emerging, when I first saw it in a patient, was far beyond anything I had ever seen in my seventeen years of conventional therapy practice. The pain can be so severe that a traumatic childhood event such as incest may take hundreds of relivings to finally eliminate its toxic effects from the organism. Some amputees have what's known as phantom limb pain—pain they feel in their lost limbs. Its existence suggests that something in the past, long dead and gone, can still hurt; that one can be hurt by a *memory* that is not consciously remembered.

Recent findings with transplant patients also point to the fact that actual cells may have memories of their own. One woman who had a heart and lung transplant began to develop strange cravings for beer and Chicken McNuggets. A little research brought out the fact that the person who was the donor was "addicted" to both of these. This transplant patient also began dreaming about things that were foreign to her; she dreamed about people who were evidently known to the donor. She formed a group with other transplant individuals who report similar results. This is anecdotal at best, but it seems to point again to cellular memory, memories embedded not in the brain but elsewhere in the system. It sounds credible to me because I have seen this kind of memory in my patients for decades. How else to explain fingerprint marks that appear on the feet of my patient after reliving birth? (See Chapter Thirteen.)

ALICE: THE SENSATIONS OF REJECTION

In one particular session I had begun to cry over hurting so much physically. As I sat up afterward, I felt a hand grabbing me in the exact spot on my left shoulder where I hurt. I had the distinct feeling that someone had grabbed me there. I fell into feelings and relived a scene in which my father and mother were fighting. It turned out to be the last day my father was in my life. I was very frightened and was clinging to my mother's knees. Suddenly I felt a hand grab me by the back of my shirt and literally whip me backward. I was stopped when I crashed into the bedpost. I heard my father leave the room and go downstairs. Then he drove away.

Before I started feeling, I had no idea what happened when my parents got a divorce. It was so traumatic because of the meaning of that day. I never saw my father again. It is still painful to remember that scene. The two pains in my back were recurring in exactly the two locations where my father's hand had grabbed me and in the line down my back where the bedpost engraved its knobs on my back.

After some time, the pains have finally disappeared, and they have never come back except in connection with those same feelings of my parents fighting and my father leaving me forever.

In primal therapy we have found that the stronger the emotion in an event, the stronger the memory of that event, and, paradoxically, the more likely it will not be remembered consciously. According to a *Science News* article by James McGaugh of the University of California, Irvine, "Intense feelings triggered by a stressful or emotional event help preserve memories of that experience, in large part by activating . . . [adrenergic] stress hormones responsible for storing emotionally charged information." In other words, McGaugh writes, emotional memories "spark the release of adrenergic hormones which strengthen memories of those events." He goes on to point out that stress hormones may foster intrusive memories in those with post-traumatic stress disorder, and he concludes that *the stronger the emotional experience, the more reliable the memory.* In short, stress hormones make for stronger memories.

In his book *Memory's Voice*, Dr. Daniel Alkon of the National Institutes of Health in Washington, D.C., says, "Memories in childhood . . . become doubly imprinted in the brain. They would not only be stored in networks already present in the child, they would actually be stored in the network designs they helped to create and structure." Thus, early memory can change the patterns of brain networks, and *the memory, in part, is affected by those changes.*

We have observed the corollary of this: The stronger the memory, the more it affects personality, behavior, and health, whether or not one has access to that memory. J. E. LeDoux corroborates this perspective in an article in *Scientific American:* "The emotional memory system . . . clearly forms and stores its unconscious memories of [traumatic] events," and for this reason, Ledoux adds, "trauma may affect mental and behavioral functions in later life, albeit through processes that remain inaccessible to consciousness."

To provide a better understanding of recovered memories, the next chapter looks at the physiological mechanisms by which the body represses feelings and puts them into storage while shielding us from knowing either that they exist or that they are at the root of what's wrong with our health and well-being.

4

LIFELONG EFFECTS OF EARLY TRAUMA

If basic needs are not met early in life, we cannot be normal. Yet there is a life-giving, primary need more basic than the need for nourishment, warmth, attention, affection, caring, and protection: oxygen.

A few minutes without oxygen can mean either severe brain damage or death. Living human beings clearly have a primordial need for oxygen. It, too, falls under the rubric of love. *To be loved means having all needs met, beginning with the basic physical need for oxygen.*

Unfortunately, neurosis can be born before we are. Too often during childbirth, mothers are given heavy dosages of anesthetics for pain. If a mother is given a dosage large enough to render her unconscious (relieved of the awareness of pain), the anesthetic acts directly on the survival functions of the fetus. Anesthetics interfere with access to oxygen and can quickly become life-threatening. Oxygen deprivation can also occur if the umbilical cord is constricted or becomes wrapped around the baby's neck. Oxygen is also difficult for a baby to access if the mother does not dilate properly, prohibiting the baby's egress. In some cases the umbilical cord is cut too early, allowing the much needed oxygen to remain in the placenta.

When the fetus is deprived of oxygen, its circulatory and respiratory systems shut down and its body begins to go into a frenzy. To struggle against death is a normal reaction, but in this case the struggle increases the danger. The result is fetal distress syndrome, characterized by rapid heart rate, high blood pressure, and frantic breathing. At the Primal Center we often witness patients reliving these early traumatic events, where we see excessive physiological reactions time after time. Not only are these reactions life-threatening, but if protracted, they also could be lethal, because the act of struggle consumes too much oxygen and makes the deprivation worse. The stronger the battle, the tighter the cord gets, and the greater the asphyxiation.

In a struggling fetus, though, two things can occur. Either the frenzy uses up stores of oxygen and changes the alkalinity-acidity of the blood, or *repression is called in to quell the frenzy and conserve oxygen to save the infant's life.* In either case, whatever the mechanism, unconsciousness is the result. This reaction is stamped on the baby as an "imprint" and will surface as a prototypical reaction later on in response to stress of any kind. The imprint not only shapes personality but dictates later symptoms and may even control life expectancy.

When pain is repressed, our bodies remember. The memory of anoxia, or oxygen deprivation, takes up residence in the cells, a noxious intruder like the india ink. It remains there, imprinted in the cell with the life-and-death urgency of the original event, waiting for reconnection to consciousness. For many of us it can remain buried for a lifetime, affecting our health and the way we function in the world.

Birth trauma involving anoxia can have catastrophic consequences and often results in childhood illnesses including allergies, asthma, epileptic seizures, attention deficit disorder (ADD), and sudden infant death syndrome (SIDS), commonly known as crib death. In adolescence and adulthood birth trauma can lead to depression and suicide attempts, chronic fatigue syndrome, panic attacks, phobia, paranoia, and psychosis.

Although many of us can recall being scolded or spanked at a very young age, it is hard to believe that memories extend back to birth. The *most powerful memories, though, are those that have no words*. There are no words or ideas with which to circumscribe these early traumatic experiences, no way to make them logical.

Finding the Link Between Past Trauma and Present Behavior

If birth is often so harmful, one may ask, why has it been by and large overlooked? It hasn't. Other research has also verified the lifelong effects of early oxygen deprivation and other early traumas. A study by L. Salk and colleagues, reported in the English medical journal *The Lancet,* found that respiratory distress lasting more than an hour at birth is associated with increased risk of teenage suicide. A number of studies have found that violent criminals and suicide cases experienced serious birth trauma. Writing in *Psychology Today,* Sarnoff A. Mednick reviews research findings that among a study group of 2,000 Danish males born in the same year, of the sixteen men who committed violent crimes, fifteen of them "had the most difficult conditions at birth . . . and the sixteenth had an epileptic mother." On the effects of birth trauma on psychosocial development, another study, published in the *American Journal of Obstetrics and Gynecology,* found that among 1,700 nine-year-old children studied, one-fourth of those who had been breech-born had flunked at least one grade in school and one in five needed remedial help. Other studies show that Cesarean babies are more emotionally disturbed, more fearful and restless, while at the same time more passive in response to stimulus, than babies born normally. I discuss these findings in my book *The Feeling Child.*

Research also documents how prebirth trauma can affect a child's physiological and emotional development. It's well known, for example, that a baby can be born HIV-positive. It's also well known that drug trauma can occur well before birth.

Drugs cross the placental barrier, and the fetus has difficulty detoxifying them. For example:

- A study by Davis et al. in *Advances in Neurology* of human mothers who took barbiturates during pregnancy found that the child's nervous system is permanently affected, especially the neurotransmitter systems.
- Drugs given to carrying mothers resulted in depressed responsiveness in offspring, with difficulty in mother-child bonding a direct result.
- A study reported in *Pediatrics* found that babies of mothers who smoked during pregnancy had three times the risk of dying of SIDS.
- Commonly used drugs fed to pregnant animals caused decreased brain weights in offspring, with later learning difficulties and reproductive problems.
- Sobrian has found that stress to a pregnant mother will lower the immune strength of her offspring.
- According to a 1980 article in *Science News,* researchers at Columbia University have found that stress to the mother during pregnancy can "alter the way embryonic nerve cells express their genetic potential." The intermediary role of hormones is implicated in this change. The Columbia scientists are in accord with the point made earlier that trauma in early life may change the unfolding of the genetic blueprint. When you alter genetic potential, you are altering the course of one's life and all of its implications for one's biology, psychology, behavior, and health.
- Preliminary evidence concerning homosexuality, recently reported in the British press, shows that homosexuals are twice as likely to have extra ridges on the fingertips of their left hand, whereas most heterosexuals have more ridges on the fingertips of their right hand. The authors of the study report that this may be a trait developed before birth. If this proves out, it will be one more piece of evidence that traumas before birth can alter the anatomy and physiology permanently and perhaps change the genetic unfolding and personality as well.

We also know that what happens *after* birth is crucial to development. In searching for possible links between birth complications (stimulated labor, breech birth, use of forceps, irregular birth position) and childhood rejection with later violent crime, it was found that individuals who had had both kinds of trauma were six times as prone to commit violent crimes as those who had had neither traumatic experience. "Having one factor alone," as study authors Adrian Raine, Patricia Brennan, and Sarnoff Mednick noted in the *Brain-Mind Bulletin*, "didn't increase the risk [of violent crime] very much but the two together seem almost like a chemical reaction."

In animal and human studies on the potential link between violence and brutality experienced early in life and the propensity for violence later on, the *New York Times* reported that those children with violent early childhoods tended to be violent later on. This may be due to the fact that early violence leaves "a clear mark on the chemistry of the brain," one result being that the serotonin system becomes less effective and the repression of aggressive impulses less functional. Individuals studied showed poor ability to concentrate, further indication of a faulty repressive apparatus and the fact that the body must continually process lower-level pain.

In the Salk study, sixty percent of fifty-two adolescents who had attempted suicide had three major risk factors around the time of birth: respiratory distress, chronic disease in the pregnant mother, and lack of prenatal care for the first twenty weeks of pregnancy.

A thirty-year study reported by Emmy Werner in *Scientific American* neatly sums up the effects of birth and early trauma. This investigation of children born on the Hawaiian island of Kauai was designed to assess the long-term effects of prenatal and perinatal stress. Six hundred and ninety-eight infants were enrolled in the study in 1955, and their development was closely followed by a group that included public health nurses, social workers, psychologists, and doctors. From among this group, twenty-three suffered severe pre- or perinatal complications (nine of them dying before the age of two); sixty-nine suffered moderate complications before or around birth; and one of every six children had physical or intellectual handicaps of perinatal or neonatal origin. Those children who experienced both birth trauma and childhood rejection were twice as likely than the group average to receive some form of mental health help before age ten due to learning or behavioral problems. Of the seventy children who had mental health problems by the age of eighteen, fifteen also had records of repeated delinquencies.

The central finding of the study surprised the researchers: The effects of early trauma diminished over the years *if the child-rearing was good*, meaning the child formed a close bond with at least one caretaker. This identifies a crucial need—a nurturing relationship with a parent early in life—that can make the difference between poor and good psychosocial adjustment and health later in life (though still not resolve some of the dislocations related to birth and prebirth trauma which may, in the long run, lead to physical illness). Among the group with both birth and childhood trauma, there were about three times more health problems than the overall group average. Common illnesses among the young men who were reassessed at age eighteen and later at age thirty included back problems, dizziness and fainting spells, and weight gain and ulcers. Women's health problems "were largely related to pregnancy and childbirth."

This study illustrates that birth trauma has long-lasting effects, even if these effects are not always evident. Why do we get sick? Because early trauma weakens the system and predisposes it to all manner of disease. Why don't we know it? Because early trauma is the most repressed and therefore the most easily forgotten. It is part of the mass unconsciousness.

You cannot love neurosis away. When someone's feelings are repressed, it is difficult for him to feel loved; his parents' love is beating against repression's door and cannot get in. The same will occur later with his loving spouse; her affection and support cannot fully get through to him, cannot fulfill the needs that went unmet originally.

According to a study by H. Lagercrantz and Theodore Slotkin on diminished oxygen levels during birth, reported in *Scientific American*, the researchers said, "The human fetus is squeezed through the birth canal for several hours, during which the head sustains considerable pressure and the infant is intermittently deprived of oxygen (by compression of the placenta and the umbilical cord during contractions). Then the neonate is delivered from a warm, dark, sheltered environment into a cold, bright hospital room, where some large creature holds it upside down and slaps it on the buttocks."

During the strain of birth, the fetus produces high levels of stress hormones, also known as the catecholamines (adrenaline and noradrenaline), which prepare the system for flight or fight from danger, in this case the danger of death from anoxia (low oxygen). In our studies of entering patients, their systematically high stress hormone levels indicate that they still seem to be responding to the early imprinted trauma. The catecholamines accelerate the heart rate and help shunt blood away from the peripheral organism and toward the key organs such as the heart and lungs. Interestingly, studies done on our patients found better blood flow in the peripheral vessels after one year of therapy.

As long as the stress is not excessive, stress hormones are helpful both during and after birth. Cesarean babies, who have been denied the natural birth process, tend to have far more respiratory problems later in life. During birth, the catecholamines help the absorption of lung liquid and also help to clear the alveoli of the lungs. Some patients reliving birth will bring up cupfuls of fluid. Their clearing mechanisms are evidently faulty, indicating possible birth trauma. Lagercrantz and Slotkin state: "Nearly every newborn has an oxygen debt akin to that of a sprinter after a run." This is exactly what we have found in those reliving birth. Pressure on the head is one of the major factors increasing the catecholamine levels during birth. These hormones can, in response to a cold delivery room, help produce a special heat-producing tissue called brown fat.

Being aroused at birth, as opposed to being sluggish, makes the baby far more ready to adapt.

Neurosis in the Womb

Those who say we can't have feelings before birth and can't have memories until we have words with which to remember them are ignoring evidence to the contrary. The fetus is capable of registering, coding, and storing pain. Even before birth, between the seventh and twentieth week, the nerve tracts that carry pain signals from the spinal cord to the lower centers of the brain are almost fully developed. This means there is pain perception and storage at a most rudimentary level. The problem is that the inhibitory neurotransmitter tracts are not fully operational until later on. Many of the neurotransmitter networks begin their development at thirteen weeks in the womb and continue developing until the thirtieth week. The endorphin tracts seem to be operational at about the fifteenth week. If a mother smokes or drinks, takes suppressants or tranquilizers, and is nervous or depressed during the third or fourth month of gestation, her hormonal and blood changes impact the nervous system. Trauma of this nature can skew the physiology of the fetus toward passivity or hyperactivity, depending on the kind of trauma. Because deviations and dislocation of function are determined within weeks of conception, they can easily be confused with genetic predispositions. Later, when subtle afflictions take hold, it will be almost impossible to tell where the origins lie, although more and more studies are indicating the hazards of nicotine and alcohol. Nicotine has been implicated in low birth weights and alcohol has been associated with an increased incidence of cancer in offspring.

Recent studies in medicine echo our findings in primal therapy. Vom Saal et al.'s research in mice indicates that maternal stress changes the concentrations of male and female sex hormones of the fetus. Bolon and St. Omer found that additional hormonal changes in the mother affect neurotransmitter development in the fetus and "define the organization of brain pathways" and that "alterations in maternal, fetal and neonatal biochemistry during critical periods (of development) may irreparably alter the circuitry and thus postnatal behavior of young animals." When a mother is under stress, her hormones change, particularly the stress hormones, and that in turn will alter brain circuits of the offspring in a permanent way. In some cases these very early changes are equivalent to "hardwired" circuitry and may be irreversible. Biologic warping can occur early on in womb life. My homosexual patients have told me time and again that they felt "different" from the ages of five and six on. They may be responding to basic alterations in biochemistry and nerve circuitry laid down in the first months of life after conception. When we see serious illness in someone at the age of fifty, we may be looking at something that started just weeks after conception. A basic terror can be imprinted at this early stage and may show up decades later as panic attacks that appear suddenly, without any rhyme or reason. Or, if the trauma to the mother is serious and prolonged enough, it can produce a brain dysfunction in the newborn that can later cause learning disorders and alter sex and other hormones.

The set-points for normality, then, are raised or lowered before and during birth and will follow the person throughout his or her life. Normalizing someone with this kind of early imprint may prove difficult. Predisposition toward depression may be set in the third or fourth month of womb life. When the mother is chronically depressed and her hormone changes affect the fetus, what appears to be a genetic factor may be a very early environmental factor, the mother being the baby's environment. Afflictions such as Parkinson's disease (the death of brain cells secreting dopamine) may show up at the age of sixty partly due to the very early traumas. Thus, prebirth and birth traumas may damage dopaminergic neurons; this plus a lifetime of smoking, drinking, poor nutrition, and overall life stress may increase demand on dopamine output later in life. Eventually, the supplies are exhausted.

Hence, neurosis is possible before the fetus ever interacts

with the outside world. Does the fetus feel pain? British researchers report that fetuses between twenty and thirty-four weeks of gestation showed a stress response to an invasive procedure. In one study in *The Lancet*, blood samples were drawn from forty-six fetuses by puncturing through the abdomen into the liver. *The fetuses responded with vigorous "breathing" movements and physical thrashing.* There was a 590 percent rise in the stress hormone cortisol and a 183 percent rise in the endorphins that dull pain perception. In this procedure, neither the mothers nor their unborn children received any painkillers, and the authors suggest that any therapeutic procedure on an unborn child should be accompanied by adequate anesthesia.

If an intrusive procedure makes a fetus start thrashing around, triggers a stress response, and steps up the production of internal painkillers, the fetus can clearly experience painful sensations and after the fifth month is capable of repression. That is one reason why babies of alcoholic and smoking mothers can be born deformed or subject to severe illness in the first years of life. According to the California Birth Defects Monitoring Program, babies born to mothers who have smoked during pregnancy have double the chance of being born with cleft lip and palate, an opening in the upper lip and roof of the mouth. This is important since the study indicates that one in every four women in California smokes during pregnancy. There are genetic tendencies toward cleft palate in some babies, but smoking increases the chances that it will be manifest by 800 percent. Thus, genetic tendencies are significant, but it often requires some kind of environmental stress to produce a symptom.

AARON: "I'VE GOT TO GET OUT OF HERE!"

My mother died of breast cancer shortly after my birth. She was sick while she was carrying me, and she was in deep mourning for her father, who had just died. She was married to an angry, crazy man, and she was under great stress. It must have been very difficult for her to give birth during that time. It would have been better for me if they had not made the effort to keep me alive because I was dead on arrival.

I am a child of the twentieth century, born of sick parents into a sick country, a sick world, where I have known only one law: survival. All I have done my entire life is try to survive. I never expected anything more. I died inside my mother a long time before I came into this world. The promise that every living organism feels, that everything was going to be all right, was already broken. For inside my mother, it was not all right; as a matter of fact, everything was very wrong. She was sick with cancer, grief, and anger. My development in her womb was not normal, and there was nothing I could do about it. I lived in an unfriendly environment that would not let me be.

I've always felt, "I've got to get out of here. Something awful is going to happen if I don't." That has been my feeling all my life.

Some say babies do not feel pain the way adults do. They're right. *They feel much more.* Babies have a wide-open sensory window and nothing to filter or attenuate the force of a trauma. Studies by Anand and Hickey reported in the *New England Journal of Medicine* found that babies undergoing surgery have five times the stress response of adults undergoing similar surgery. In these babies (as in the fetus study previously mentioned), hormone levels, blood pressure, and heart rate all skyrocketed. The point is that the reaction of babies to trauma is often more than they can bear. Part of the response is repressed and then held in storage for a lifetime. This excess is to be found in reverberating circuits in the brain, where it causes continuing changes in biological functioning.

The baby's response is not confined to surgery. Emotional traumas will accomplish the same thing. This is because the imprint of a trauma includes the original environment plus the original response. The original environment is held as a memory and we go on responding to it as if it were present. The response is always the same as it was originally because the overall event is still intact. We know this by observing patients reliving early life trauma. If birth anoxia were not an enduring and exact memory, how else can one account for the hundreds of our adult patients who relive the oxygen deprivation they experienced at birth, losing their breath, bringing up copious fluid, and choking, gasping, and coughing? In addition, predictable changes in body temperature, pulse, and blood pressure accompany this state. These patterns are surely the reactions that accompanied the original trauma, for they are the same changes seen in one who undergoes anoxia in the present.

The Power of Love?

Even if parents are nurturing and loving, the full impact of their love cannot get through to a child who is already repressed due to very early trauma. Again, repression is a defense that keeps dangerous information out of consciousness and physiological reactivity under control; but it also operates to keep other kinds of information, such as love, from coming in. This could partly account for differences in personality between two siblings. Both may have been hugged and kissed, but one may have had massive pain early on that set up equally massive repression. Thereafter, his experience of life will differ from his brother's or sister's.

Repression dampens inner feelings and emotions, instigating neurosis. But how does repression work? The following chapter focuses on the three levels of consciousness—instinct, emotion, and intellect—and how repression acts upon them.

5

INSTINCT, EMOTION, AND INTELLECT: CONSCIOUSNESS AND THE MECHANISM OF REPRESSION

A businesswoman goes on vacation to a tropical paradise, hoping to escape her stressful lifestyle, to forget her cares for a few days. But once there, she finds she just cannot relax. If she doesn't keep busy at something—playing backgammon, volleyball, snorkeling—she feels unsettled inside. She thinks seriously of going home.

When a person cannot feel comfortable on a quiet beach, yet cannot identify exactly what it is that's making her uneasy, where is the stress coming from? I believe it is from the primal intruder lurking below the surface of conscious-awareness. The imprint from decades ago continues to affect her and impel her behavior, though she does not feel it for what it is. How can this be? Because we possess different brain structures that process different levels of consciousness and biochemical mechanisms that mediate repression.

According to Paul Maclean of the Laboratory of Brain Evolution in Poolesville, Maryland, human beings have a "triune brain" made of up three elements: a *reptilian* brain, the (primarily) brainstem structure we share with reptiles; the *paleo-mammalian* brain, or limbic system, which we have in common with other mammals; and the *mammalian brain*, or neocortex. These three brains operate like interconnected computers, each with its own special function and memory that define *three distinct levels of consciousness* which have become a cornerstone to the diagnosis, prognosis, and access to feelings in primal therapy.

What each of these three brains does and how they interact are fundamental to understanding neurosis:

1. The first brain level to evolve, which I call *first-line consciousness*, is the instinctive level. Largely located in the brainstem and hypothalamus, it regulates vital functions.

2. The limbic system is the seat of the emotional *second-line consciousness*, where our feelings reside. It is mediated by the brain's limbic system and temporal lobe.

3. On the *third-line* or cortical level, we reason and develop ideas, integrating the input from the two lower levels, providing the meaning of experience.

The development of each level of consciousness mirrors the evolutionary development of our species. Just as hundreds of millions of years elapsed between the evolution of the first line and the arrival of the thinking cortex, a person's development of first-line consciousness far predates the time when his neocortex begins to function. This helps explain how we can experience trauma before we have words to describe what happened, and how it's possible for us to be "unconscious" of memories that affect us for a lifetime.

Instinctual Consciousness

The *first line* of consciousness involves the primitive nervous system. Although its structures are competent at birth, they actually begin processing during gestation and mediate the physiological changes in development. The first line is the visceral mind, the caretaker of sensations, and vital functions are largely under its control: breathing, cardiovascular activity, hormone output, and digestive and urinary processes. First-line consciousness preserves homeostasis, maintaining our blood pressure, heart rate, and other vital functions at appropriate levels.

Because we always respond with the highest level of neurologic functioning available to us, traumas that occur before six months of age are likely to affect these functions. Hence, if a patient presents with colitis or palpitations, we may anticipate that a first-line trauma—something that happened before the infant was six months old—is involved. This may help to explain why some people have far lower pulse, blood pressure, and body temperature than others. We have seen that early trauma can change the set-point for the body's thermostat, hormones, and much of our biology, often playing an unseen but direct role in later physical illness. Because first-line development predates emotions, we cannot cry tears when it is manifest. Nor can we speak, as language is a higher-level function that comes later. When patients relive very early traumas, there are never any words involved. The first line can, however, store the cataclysmic *sensations* of approaching death, the frenzied breathing and body movements. These memories, unseen but active physiologically, tax the organism for years and can play a role in the development of cardiovascular disease and other ailments.

First-line pains are the least accessible; it is the level from which memories are the most difficult to retrieve, perhaps because they are so difficult to get to. When they are accessed, they resolve both symptoms and suffering. It is this level that is disrupted at the beginning of life, altering hormone output, such as thyroxine. And it is in reliving this level that hormone output is finally stabilized. We know that thyroxine (secreted by the thyroid gland) begins its manufacture at about twenty weeks of fetal age. Stress by the mother can be transmitted to the fetus, making slight alterations in thyroxine set points. Later on, either as a child or an adult, one can see beginning tendencies of oversecretion or undersecretion of thyroxine. Patients who were hypothyroid, listless and lacking energy and gaining weight too easily, are often no longer hypothyroid after reliving traumas on the first line. Without access to this level, we cannot determine what incredible impact trauma on the first line has on later behavior and symptom development, how it shapes who we are and what we do.

Emotional Consciousness: How We Process Feelings

The second line, the "affective level" or "feeling mind," begins to develop at about the sixth month and continues into childhood. Over time, the infant relates to a world beyond the breast and the mother's cheek, establishing emotional attachments to parents, siblings, aunts, uncles, and pets, coding feelings on the second line. This is the level of feeling states at which individuals can enjoy music, develop images, and appreciate poetry. It's also where the strange images found in children's drawings and, later, in the paintings of artists come from.

The second line cannot do calculus, but it can dream and mix emotions with first-line sensation to form the guts and agony of experience. It can defend consciousness against the terror of a first-line trauma and convert that terror into fearful dreams of monsters trying to strangle us, or into a phobia of enclosed places. Under stress, a child may feel he or she is choking. It is the first line intruding on the second.

A traumatic event, such as incest, that occurs at the age of four or five largely involves the second line, and the suffering, feeling component of pain is stored on this level. When the second line is in operation, the child has control of the muscles of the body wall, and with that comes the ability to tense those muscles to help block anxiety, a first-line reaction. Specific, deep pain stimulates the cortex in a diffuse way so that the person feels activated without knowing why. It feels bad, and we call it anxiety. When our adult patients reliving an early second-line trauma begin to cry like an infant, indeed *as* an infant—in a way that would be impossible if they tried to do so willfully—it's a clear indication that memories from different times of life reside on different levels of consciousness.

The Intellectual Level: How Thinking Defends Us Against Feeling

The intellect, or *third line* of consciousness, begins to play an active role at about age six and goes on developing until around age twenty. Mediated by the brain's frontal lobe, the third line organizes things intellectual. Third-line consciousness integrates the lower levels, helps inhibit impulses and feelings, deals with the external world, and provides the meaning of feelings.

Necessity is the mother of invention, especially in terms of brain function. A long time ago, when our ancestors had to hide from adversity, the migration of brain cells upward and outward to form the neocortex gave them an evolutionary edge. Thanks to this evolutionary development, we have inherited the ability to speak and understand language. The neocortex deals in logic, rationality, concepts, calculation, and reality testing. It can develop ambition, plan for the future, have insights, be socially and politically aware, and have a sense of time. The neocortex finds "reasons" to explain other people's behavior and enables us to project motives onto others, have faulty perceptions, and bend logic into accord with our internal truths.

With the aid of this newly developed cortex, we became able not only to escape from saber-toothed tigers but also to figure out where to find food and warmth; we also had a way to escape from our pain-filled selves. The third line conjures up ideas to defend against both second-line and first-line trauma. The neocortex's ability to inhibit feeling permits us to make plans, to set goals and follow them through, to keep functioning even though there may be a seething cauldron of pain below. This survival mechanism allows many people who are traumatized deep down to "find God" as a way to shield themselves from pain, not knowing that their beliefs are being generated by repressed material. It makes it possible for the same person to juxtapose complex scientific information with the most irrational ideas. One may be totally logical in working out a problem in differential calculus while simultaneously believing in an all-powerful being who created the world in six days; a brain surgeon can be a Moonie. Because it is shielded from the feelings stewing at a lower level of consciousness, the rational mind cannot analyze the contradictions involved in the belief system. As we grow up, the neocortex matures, developing a greater capacity for repression.

Damage to one level will not necessarily affect another. For example, one can have the speech area of third-line consciousness damaged but still be fully feeling. One can have one's motor functions impaired but retain crystal-clear perception. Those in a coma are operating on the first line, with the two higher levels inactive. They may continue to live for months or even years in a vegetative state. They make no contact and behave at a rudimentary level, certainly with no concept of what is going on, but they are "functioning." Those who have awakened from comas report that they had perceived touch and reassurance at some level. Holding the hand of someone who is under anesthesia can help attenuate pain to some extent. The person still senses this contact even though he is "unconscious" or residing on another level of consciousness.

Each level of consciousness contributes to what we call the mind. In a normal, healthy person, these three distinct minds function as a single mental apparatus. They work in harmony for the good of the organism, allowing the person to be a feeling, thinking being with healthy emotional reactions to outside stimuli and the ability to think clearly about these emotions and use them as guides for behavior. Health requires optimum coherence or connectedness among the levels, a harmonious functioning that ensures survival.

Trauma interferes with this harmony, causing "unconsciousness." Repression interferes with integration among these three levels and causes a global dislocation of function in both the body and mind spheres. It makes organs oversecrete or undersecrete, warps the physical development, and alters blood vessel function. With repression and neurosis we can feel one way and think another. We may react in ways that are linked to something that happened in the past rather than what is before us in the present. We are reacting to the present through the filter of memories that are stored.

New York Times science editor Daniel Goleman makes the common mistake of confusing recall with memory: "Findings suggest," he writes, "that . . . toddlers acquire the skills for remembering significant episodes in their lives only as they acquire language skills." Quoting scientists, Goleman goes on to note that language is the medium of both memory and retrieval. Until we talk, he says, we cannot remember. The whole notion of preverbal, emotional memory has been overlooked, to say nothing of pre-emotional memory from before birth. We must emphasize that memory is recalled on its own terms, on its own level, and in its own way; it has nothing to do with words per se.

If a child's parents abandon her early in life, the child may not yet be able to describe what has happened in such terms as "they don't love me and don't want to be with me." But the message is still there, as a feeling. Her fragile system can no longer react normally and be itself. It has got to shut down, bury the feeling, in order to get by. Emotional memory can involve a great sadness and emptiness without a specific scene; but here *the feeling is the memory.* In adulthood, it's called depression.

The Mechanisms of Repression

In human evolution there is a wide gap between the development of the first line and the arrival of the thinking cortex. They are literally worlds apart, so a trauma laid down low in the nervous system has a long way to go before it comes to full consciousness. An elaborate system of gates between the levels can slam shut when there is inordinate pain. Their purpose is to keep the upper levels from being overwhelmed by what is going on below, to keep the suffering of early pain from reaching consciousness. These gates maintain coherence of conscious-awareness—the third line. Their purpose is also to dampen hyperreactivity, to hold down the secretion of stress hormones and control the level of blood pressure and heart rate. The chemical agency that mediates gating and can make us unconscious is the inhibitory neurotransmitters, the body's natural opiates. There are more than fifty of them, and they keep the transmission of the pain message from crossing over to other brain circuits; in short, to keep us unconscious.

It has been twenty years since the discovery of many of the neurotransmitter molecules. Researchers reasoned that if the body has so many receptors for painkilling drugs such as morphine, a poppy derivative, we must also produce our own painkillers, otherwise there wouldn't be any reason for the receptors. They also learned that drugs derived from the opium poppy are effective because they mimic something we *do* produce: the endorphins. These repressive painkillers are similar to morphine in their molecular shape.

Some of the endorphins the body manufactures to meet and block highly charged pain are incredibly powerful, hundreds of times stronger than morphine. The fact that the body is able to anesthetize itself from pain explains why a football player can injure himself in the midst of a game but not notice the pain until the game is over.

As I noted, gating (repression) can be provoked in two ways: when the intensity of a single event is overwhelming, as in the pain of being sent to a foster home, or when relatively mild pains summate into information overload. In either case, the feelings are excessive and the repressive neurojuices ensure that they turn into their opposite—no feeling. Thus, if the brain is overly excited, even by electrical stimulation such as in electroshock therapy, the overload causes a shutdown and lack of reaction. This has been clearly shown in experiments on cats, in which electrodes implanted in their brain stems stimulated the production of endorphins. When pain is on the rise, endorphin supplies are temporarily boosted, causing certain nerve cells to become "silent" and fail to react to the barrage of information. We are then dulled to pain.

Gating is like an unconscious conspiracy: The lower levels

won't tell the highest level because they don't want the third line to fall apart. And the cortex is saying, "Don't tell me too much because I can't take it." There are different kinds of neuroinhibitors, with different strengths. When the transmitting neurons or output neurons fail to fire, the higher levels remain ignorant of the message trying to get through from the lower levels. The reactions can be diverted to bodily functions, where the viscera are stirred up by those messages which have failed to reach conscious-awareness. Or, the energy of the message is rerouted to the cortex to produce strange ideas and perceptions. This is one of the meanings of *dislocation of function*. The message no longer travels to its proper destination-connection. It is relocated so that full reactivity will not take place. The central difference is where the gating takes place. The neurotransmitters seem to become more powerful as we descend down the levels of consciousness in the brain. The more highly charged pains on deep levels require the most powerful gating.

The repressive gates are like a system of locks on a river that allow just so much water through at a time. The greater the pain, the more the neurojuices are secreted to shut the gates. Interestingly, we do not develop a tolerance to our own naturally produced opiates, in sharp contrast to the opiates used by addicts, in whom tolerance develops rapidly.

Losing touch with reality means first losing touch with internal reality, which then affects the perception of external reality. Neurosis is the permanent clash between lower-level imprints and cortical inhibition. *The neurojuices affect only the perception of pain by higher levels of conscious-awareness, not the pain itself.* A person can seemingly sit in the ebb and flow of a tropical tide without a care in the world, while unbeknownst to him unusually large amounts of stress hormones are surging through his system, keeping pain down. He soon finds he cannot sit still and relax. There can be a wide discrepancy between how relaxed a person thinks he is and what is revealed by measurement of his physiological stress level.

Endorphins are not the only neuroinhibitors. Serotonin and gamma-aminobutyric acid (GABA) are others. GABA helps the cortex inhibit excitatory messages from the limbic system. When the pain is prolonged, GABA supplies seem to be exhausted, allowing pain to rush toward third-line consciousness. As it approaches the cortex, anxiety is provoked; a warning that danger is on its way. The danger is full reactivity: as imprinted pain comes closer to conscious awareness the vital signs leap to life-threatening levels.

The history of these agents of gating and repression reaches back to the microscopic protozoa, and even to plant life before them. How is it that we have brains that respond to a poppy derivative, unless evolution has favored the use of whatever aided survival through millions of years? Solomon Snyder and others have observed that there is as much opiate binding in primitive fish and the dogfish shark as there is in monkeys and man.

The endorphins are the origin of the unconscious, and in some ways I believe they are the bedrock of evolution and the backbone of civilization. Without repression, I doubt that human life would have come as far as it has. Without gates, I doubt if there could be a thinking cortical apparatus at all. Gates are essential for brain function because each level can cope with less information than the one below it. If our conscious-awareness were presented with all the sensory data and associations constantly pouring upward, it would be overwhelmed. And when third-line repression is faulty, when too much painful information surges upward, concentration is disrupted as well as sleep, attention span, and coherence of thought.

Disconnection from excess pain has been a *sine qua non* for human evolution. For survival we needed a functioning conscious-awareness to steer us around during the day without the organism losing itself in unfinished business. We needed a mental agency that could make us oblivious to suffering inside. The development of the cortex allowed us humans to deceive ourselves and keep the lower levels out of sight and out of mind. Self-deception was an evolutionary necessity, and nothing is quite as infinite as self-deception.

Repression Preserves Consciousness

What is the danger in rising feelings? The answer is impaired consciousness, the development that separates us from all other animal forms. Consciousness involves nothing less than our humanity. It is next to life itself in importance. If we lose it, as in severe Alzheimer's disease, we are vegetables. We no longer recognize our mates, cannot show emotion at the death of loved ones, cannot show joy.

Consciousness provokes and is part of full reactivity. To shield it from exposure to too much pain, repression came into play. When there is pain, we must restrict access to memories residing on lower levels, even at the cost of partial unconsciousness. Almost every defensive maneuver we make—such as drinking or using drugs, talking constantly, shopping compulsively, obsessing about one thing or another, devoting ourselves inordinately to our work—is an attempt to drain away excess energy so that the third-line consciousness can maintain its cohesion, even if it is a neurotic cohesion.

Most tranquilizers ensure that the supplies of neuroinhibitors are adequate to gate pain out of awareness. The widely heralded Prozac serves the almost sole function of seeing to it that one is kept in good supply of serotonin. What is the person calming? Pain. And it is that imprinted pain that exhausts the internally manufactured supplies of repressive chemicals, requiring the person to reach outside herself for more. It is early trauma that chronically depletes serotonin supplies. Monkeys that experience early separation from their parents have been found to have low serotonin levels.

Hypnosis often relies on summoning the mechanisms of repression into action; "hypnotic suggestion" is used to control headache pain, back pain, and excruciating cancer pain, not to mention its use in psychotherapy, all in order to trigger the production of neuroinhibitors. Many strategies used in "behavioral medicine" utilize this "mind-body" link. Biofeedback, progressive relaxation, creative imagery, and the like have been shown to be effective against chronic pain and other ailments. But what has happened to the pain? Take a placebo (a harmless sugar pill), for instance. The patient does not know the pill is a placebo but is told it will keep him from feeling pain during a dental procedure; and it does. Belief becomes stronger than the sensation of a drill touching a nerve. It doesn't mean that the drill doesn't hurt, just that the person doesn't feel it. A mental process (no doubt provoking neuroinhibitor release) nullifies physical pain. Similarly, it can render us unconscious of emotional pain. And that is what neurosis is all about: being dulled to real pain. We stop feeling or feel less. Repression has done its job. I have often thought that anesthetics were one of the greatest inventions ever. But nature had already taken care of that—by inventing anesthetic from within.

The power of ideas to quell pain is also why the ideology of groups like Alcoholics Anonymous are attractive to so many people. Part of the message one receives in AA meetings is: "You are not alone. We will stand by you and help you. There is always going to be help!" This directly counters the repressed feeling of "I'm all alone and there is no one to help!"—a feeling so many of us have been carrying around deep inside since early in life. It is precisely those real feelings that have forced us to resort to alcohol in order to keep them repressed. One goes for help to a twelve-step program, and the first thing that is done is to fill the person with an ideology that runs counter to internal reality. The ideology in turn helps create a good defense and although it is helpful, it is not a cure.

Memories That Form Us

A neglected baby who goes hungry in the bassinet grows up and loses touch with the experience. As an adult she eats voraciously as a symbolic way to keep the early starving feeling away. She goes to a behavioral psychologist, who tries to teach her that it's just a matter of changing her eating habits. Perhaps the new diet will work, but not for long, because the underlying cause of her behavior has not been uncovered.

The fact that repression cuts off communication among the levels of consciousness explains why many people feel miserable and desperate even though their lives look, on the surface, as if they should be satisfying. It also explains why adults can say they feel wonderful when a cauldron of pain is boiling below. When the suffering component of a trauma is shunted away from consciousness, there is a split between the real suffering self and the self that is unaware of it. Thereafter, two separate selves exist in conflict in the same body, putting pressure on the various subsystems and using valuable energy to repress the suffering. Because it has not reached conscious-awareness and been reacted to, the imprint continues to affect the person's physiology and behavior as though it were happening in the present.

The idea of hidden pain is difficult for us to accept for a variety of reasons:

- It doesn't hurt consciously.
- It generally lies so deep and so far in the past that it is largely inaccessible.
- The very nature of repression dictates that the pain cannot be acknowledged.
- The pain usually begins long before we have words, affecting organ systems and physiological reactions that make us neurotic before anyone (including us) can observe us behave. It can be retrieved only on the same level of consciousness on which it occurred and in the same manner in which it was laid down.
- We are too accustomed to thinking about neurosis as behavior, and we are not accustomed to thinking about the fact that organs (such as the brain) react and change according to circumstance, and that the aggregate of those organs is "us."

Unresolved pain can set in motion a chain of events and misunderstood feelings that impact on our personal lives and the lives of those we love. I illustrate this in the next chapter with the stories of Sam, Patricia, and Celia.

6

PERSONALITY AND THE CHAIN OF PAIN

I am going to tell you a story about three different individuals: Sam, the aggressive go-getter; Patricia, the depressive; and Celia, the manic-depressive. They are very different people because they had different kinds of births. Sam, Patricia, and Celia are all neurotic but manifest their neuroses very differently. Let's talk about Sam and Patricia first.

Sam and Patricia: The Sympath and the Parasympath

Sam's mother was frigid. The focus of much of her tension lay in the lower midsection of her body. When she gave birth, her reluctant system finally opened up. Sam struggled many hours to get out, finally succeeding.

Patricia's mother was very repressed, couldn't take much pain, and was heavily anesthetized during the birth process. Patricia struggled for a short time before the anesthesia entered her own body, shutting down many key functions. She couldn't even struggle to get out because the drug given to her mother found its way into her tiny body and effectively immobilized her. She was born blue and had to be slapped into life. Her suppressed respiratory system began to function only with that slap.

Whereas Patricia had to give up all struggle very early and came into this world in a passive mode, Sam came into the world in an active mode, fighting all the way. Sam's fight enabled him to succeed. Patricia's imprint was of ultimate powerlessness, of not having the wherewithal to save her own life. These distinct entries into the world were imprinted into their systems. One became an active, driving, aggressive individual, the other a resigned, introverted, passive one.

The birth process, and particularly the manner in which we are born, is stamped in as a "Cut! Print!" memory in the nervous system, never to leave. This imprint sets the mode for personality, providing a map for how we respond to future events. Moreover, what happens during childhood compounds the problem, because each individual tends to react to new events in terms of the mode of their birth.

In a strict, oppressive parental atmosphere, Patricia succumbed easily and was driven further into herself. She was resigned, seeing no alternative or way out of problems. In the same atmosphere, Sam was rebellious, combative, and disobedient; he clashed constantly with his parents and made their lives intolerable. Sam was never defeated; he was in a mad dash from a hopelessness that he rarely perceived.

Patricia was quiet and reflective. She kept to herself and never volunteered anything. Sam was a hyperactive youngster, rowdy and argumentative, unable to sit still in class. These modes of behavior derive from the autonomic nervous system, which has two branches. Sam became someone dominated by his sympathetic nervous system, a "sympath." Patricia was a "parasympath," dominated by her parasympathetic system.

The *sympathetic system* directs energy-using behaviors such as the fight-or-flight response. It mobilizes us, raises body temperature, and lessens peripheral circulation (conserving blood for the muscles, preparing for fight or flight) so that the face is paler and the hands and feet may be cold. It makes us urinate frequently, sweat nervously, and have a dry mouth and a high voice. By contrast, the *parasympathetic branch* of the nervous system controls the energy-conserving processes of rest, sleep, and repair. It dilates the blood vessels, makes the skin warm, and promotes healing. When we are in a parasympathetic mode, with our musculture more relaxed to save energy, our voice lowers to a slow, mellifluous timbre.

A healthy person has a good balance between the two systems. Ideally, the two work together harmoniously, so that we are more "sympathetic" during the day and more "parasympathetic" during sleep, with a balanced mix of these two tendencies. But traumas that occur before we have seen the light of day can push us in one direction or the other. For Patricia, the parasympath, her imprint put her in the "give up" mode for good. Patricia was always "inside herself," introspective, dreamy, emotionally removed. She had to remove herself from her feeling self because the emotional charge involved in the trauma was more than she could integrate.

Sam is optimistic, Patricia pessimistic, paralleling the outcome of each one's birth struggle. Patricia is forever in the apathetic mode, becoming discouraged and giving up when faced with even the smallest obstacle. "What's the use?" is her attitude, because originally, what was the use? Sam doesn't recognize obstacles, so he is more likely to be successful.

Such dialectical contrasts abound. Determination versus resignation, for example: Sam raged and succeeded, whereas Patricia was quickly overwhelmed and could only go with the flow. Tenacity versus abandonment: Sam learned that effort was life-saving, while Patricia learned tenacity was dangerous. Sam has to finish every project because finishing means life, whereas Patricia has dozens of unfinished tasks because finishing means disaster. She can't quite get herself together to do things; her teachers called it poor motivation. Sam is nothing if not determined; nothing gets in his way. An outgoing fellow, he forges ahead and makes an effort to meet people. Patricia looks inward, having been driven back into herself at the start. Her birth taught her that being outgoing is not safe, so holding back is her leitmotif. She had to be "drawn out" and now you have to "draw her out," a re-creation of her prototype that circumscribes her life.

Patricia is conservative in many ways, Sam is radical. Because beginning to leave the womb had spelled disaster for Patricia, she later made her little cocoon and wanted to stay inside it. Change, therefore, becomes dangerous. She is happy with routine and wants leaders who promise to uphold "traditional values." Sam rebelled against his tyrannical father like he rebelled against his mother in the womb. Rebellion and testing limits are life for him. He manages to account for all this through his revolutionary philosophy, which for him rationalizes the need for rebellion.

Sam is less sensitive than Patricia because he does not take the time to reflect; he is looking to the future. Patricia looks to the past, constantly reacting to a catastrophe that has already happened, but which she imagines lies ahead. In neurosis, the present is seen only through the veil of the past, for the system cannot differentiate past from present.

Because Sam had to learn fast during birth, he learns fast now, so he reacts well in emergencies. Patricia freezes in emergencies. She needs time to react. She is more methodical in her approach, more detailed in her execution of things. Sam sees the big picture, the global perspective. He is not a man for details. He had to act on instinct long before his cortex developed, whose key function it is to inhibit or repress. When impulses rise, Sam plows forth.

Why do the Sams of the world find the Patricias? Why do we fall in love with those who have neuroses that complement ours? It seems as though each of us is looking for the other half of his or her nervous system—the half that would have been, had not trauma interceded.

Patricia is dominated by events and needs Sam to act for her. She needs someone to lead the way and to tell her what to do. Sam needs a passive, give-in type who will put up with his brash ways. He also needs the stability Patricia offers. If Patricia were like Sam, the sparks would fly, and if Sam were like Patricia, both might sink into depression.

But after they marry, Sam is disappointed in Patricia because she never wants to go anywhere, but rather is content to stay home and curl up on the couch. Everything for Patricia is in the energy-conservation mode, as she had to be for her to survive her birth. Sam is driven to move: to get up, run around, find a project. Lying still evokes the threat of dying because passivity meant death originally. But this is not an accessible memory—he just gets very uncomfortable. Patricia is unhappy because Sam can't sit still, is always on the run, and can't take a vacation without thinking about getting back to work. Sam is unhappy that Patricia isn't bubbly like other women. She lost her spark of life long before either of them would imagine; but she is his stabilizing factor, which is what attracted him to her originally.

It is eight o'clock in the morning. Sam wakes up in the active mode, ready for all comers. He bolts out of bed, gets dressed, has his coffee, and is ready for the day. He is a day person, full of energy and ready to go from the moment of waking onward. Patricia is sluggish, almost drugged, slow to come to full consciousness. She languishes in bed until ten o'clock. She can't get herself going. She hasn't slept well, with nightmares of being stuck, suffocating in a cave with no light and no air. She awoke with her heart beating so fast she thought she was going to die—her near-death birth imprint. She has had persistent nightmares all of her life. Sam can't even remember his dreams. He is far from his feelings; she is mired in hers. Patricia is slow. Her slow metabolism, slow physical reactions, and deliberate thought processes make her more careful. She gets less done but does it better. She is a night person, coming into full alertness and activity at night, when Sam is tired and ready for bed.

Sam is impatient when Patricia complains of her depression and despair as she wakes up. He doesn't know, of course, that it's her original birth feeling, the prototypic vague awareness of death. She is certain it will all "turn to shit." Her philosophy unconsciously mirrors what happened: All went well early on,

and then suddenly it all turned bad. Sam never could understand depression.

Re-creating his birth from day to day, Sam manufactures
plenty of pressure to keep him on the run. Lots to do, places to
go, everywhere but in. He is an extrovert with very little fantasy life. Patricia hates Sam's "unreality;" he does not stop to
think because he can't see the negative side of things. Sam
doesn't ask himself too many questions. He acts. Patricia is
constantly mulling over her plight, her life, her choices and
direction. She is not sure what to do because there was nothing to do originally. Sam doesn't like Patricia's pessimism.
Ironically, Sam and Patricia each believe he or she is a realist.
Both see the world through their imprint and think it is reality.
If they could somehow trust each other, they could combine
perceptions and see the total picture.

Patricia has been painting lately, and doing it well. Unknowingly, she has been painting her feelings: gnarled trees envel-
oping people with masks of fear, her nightmare figures,
variations on Edvard Munch's *The Scream*. Sam hasn't got time
for art; there are numbers, not images, in his head: sales figures, projections, and so forth. Patricia knows nothing about
business or money, but Sam excels at it. He is running from
disaster; she sees disaster everywhere.

Sam is ambitious. He is constantly looking toward how to
make things better in the future. Patricia is not a self-starter;
she needs external discipline, but once she's in her groove,
wild horses couldn't budge her. She doesn't want any variety
in her life. Because she had no alternatives at birth, she cannot
see her way out of difficulties. Sam hates discipline. He doesn't
want to be in anyone's hands because when he was, his life
depended on it and he almost lost it. He cannot tolerate rules
and regulations, or a boss over him. He is the quintessential
bull in a china shop.

Sam doesn't like drugs. He needs calming down, however,
as his motor is racing, but if he can arrange his life to rationalize his racing motor, he won't feel the need for tranquilizers.
He thinks he's under all this outside pressure, when he has

just as much inside pressure. He's never happier than when he's under a deadline. But he tends to be too alert and has trouble sleeping. Occasionally he needs something to help him sleep, to turn off that motor that was revved-up permanently at birth. The drugs for Patricia are uppers. Coffee starts the day, alcohol lifts her spirits in the evening. *The drugs each takes, then, are attempts to become normal;* to normalize the system rendered askew at the start of life.

Sam can't stand Patricia's behavior in restaurants. She can never decide what to eat, wanting to know what everyone else plans to order before she makes her choice. When she talks to her analyst about this, he proffers the insight that she feels insecure in her choices. But you have to look deeper for what makes someone like Patricia indecisive. It goes back to the beginning, when she didn't know what move to make. The profound origin of her insecurity was her unconscious fear that any move she did make would have dire consequences. Only by following the lead of others could she learn the "right" move.

Nor is Patricia happy with Sam's brusque, demanding, mannerless ways in a restaurant. Sam runs the show. He chooses the restaurant, the time of dinner, who will be invited, and who won't. He has to have the best table; his feeling that he was never important to his parents drives him to insist on being treated like an important person. Patricia goes along. She needs to be led, and he needs to lead the way.

Sam is not as compassionate as Patricia. She sees more in people. She dreams of a sensitive husband who will recognize her needs. Alas, this is not to be because she "needs" Sam to make up for what she lacks. Thus, Patricia is unhappy. Her needs are contradictory: to be dominated and led, and to have a stable, sensitive partner to draw her out. Sam dominates Patricia but is insensitive and not given to thoughtful discussions. She doesn't like it but accepts it, true to the prototype of passivity.

Sam and Patricia have a sex problem. Because Patricia is deeply repressed, she cannot get excited without shutting off.

She gets aroused to a certain point, then everything goes dead. Sam is unhappy because Patricia just lies there during sex and is not creative; it seems to him that she just tolerates the act. She feels he is not gentle, that he just gets on and off. She wants tenderness and romance. Sam suffers from premature ejaculation; his impulsiveness and lack of control make every kind of arousal an all-out effort for him. He was given little affection as a child and has a hard time loving. Part of the reason is that he was too agitated and wouldn't allow others to hold and caress him. His birth pain and childhood deprivation combine to make him very easily aroused; he has sexualized his pain. Sex therefore becomes a release of tension.

Sam doesn't know why he married her. He has been having affairs, trying to find a mother's love in each one, quite unconsciously. Patricia doesn't care; she just wants to be left alone and not be constantly bothered with demands for sex. Patricia has been thinking about divorce but hasn't the energy to do anything about it. She broods, fantasizing about having an affair. But she doesn't have enough energy to carry it through. Slowly, fantasy is taking over her life. Meanwhile, Sam doesn't reflect long enough about his marriage to consider divorce, because he can never take the time to consider how he really feels.

She doesn't care to see her friends much anymore. It's hard for her to get motivated, and she's a little phobic about leaving the house, since leaving a safe place meant catastrophe before. Sam has been nagging her to tell her psychologist about her phobia, but she doesn't think it is a phobia; she simply doesn't want to go out. Can't he understand that?

Patricia decides to take a class in history. She doesn't do well on the first exam and decides to quit. Sam is furious and says, "You're a quitter. What's the matter with you?" He can't understand her immediate discouragement. He doesn't know that the C on the exam set off the feeling of hopelessness that went all the way back to birth and that she has reacted prototypically by giving up in defeat. Sam is immensely curious and likes to learn, because from the beginning he had to know what was going on in case it could help save his life. Patricia's curiosity has been suppressed; she doesn't want to know because knowing hurt. For her, the massive repression necessary to keep the shattering memory under control is what makes her feel that life is not worth living. It is all so gray and dull and meaningless, she doesn't even want to try anymore. Sam is tired of trying to "breathe life into her," something he often says without knowing what he really means.

In the sympath and parasympath paradigm, the former tends to "act out," while the latter "acts in." Patricia sees struggle is useless, so she gives up too easily. She is chronically depressed and believes all is hopeless. Her energy is funneled internally, turned inward at the organs and the cells, causing symptoms such as her migraine headaches. She may die prematurely of cancer, as the pressure on the cells builds over the years until they become deformed. This is not the case with Sam, who "acts out," trying to get his needs fulfilled. His behavior absorbs his incessant drive. The act-out releases the energy of the feeling. What energy his behavior cannot absorb will militate against organs, and he may suffer from cardiac problems and ulcers and may die prematurely of a heart attack.

Sam and Patricia have a busy day today. Both are going to their doctors, she to her general practitioner for her migraines, he to his cardiologist for his heart palpitations. The cardiologist asks Sam if he has been under stress lately. "No," he says. "You ought to slow down a bit," the doctor advises. "I'll give you a medication to calm you down." But Sam can't slow down. The palpitations are a fragment of the birth memory in which his heart was galvanizing him for the effort.

Patricia's doctor gives her pills that are vasoconstrictors, to counteract the dilation of the blood vessels in her head. The doctor also tells her that coffee will help and that she ought to try two cups in the morning when she gets the headache; she usually drinks five. Coffee is a vasoconstrictor; it drives her away from the despair, giving her the energy she lacks and pushing her away from the imprint of anoxia she suffered at birth.

If there were two words to describe Patricia, they would be *no energy*. That is the imprint; she can't fight and she can't run—she's stuck. The vitamin shots for her chronic fatigue syndrome help somewhat, but her doctor can't see that the fatigue is a memory lived in the present. Vitamins won't cure Patricia because the source of her fatigue is a physiological memory with secondary effects such as increased need for certain vitamins and an immune system weakened by oxygen deprivation at birth. Such secondary effects have to be treated. Patricia needs immune boosters and an immune complex vitamin pack to give her more energy. With his simple vitamin shots, the doctor is only plugging the dike like the little Dutch boy, while the primal force threatens to come pouring out. The doctor cannot see the stress that Patricia is under. He cannot see that birth anoxia has weakened her cells and left them vulnerable to later disease. Her immune system is sluggish because of her global repression. If Patricia doesn't get sick, she will look younger and live longer than Sam, because her pulse, body temperature, and blood pressure tend to be low. But she did get sick. She developed hypothyroidism, caused by an underactive system.

Celia the Cyclic

Patricia has a sister named Celia who has been diagnosed as a manic-depressive. She has periods of euphoric highs followed by monumental lows. She talks a mile a minute, writes reams, sleeps little, and then falls into a funk for days at a time.

Celia's birth was not like Patricia's. It began normally, but then it was discovered that her mother was not dilating properly. First there was a concerted effort, a measured response in which Celia did her best to push her way out. This culminated in a frenzied effort to escape. Then the anesthesia knocked her out and rendered her totally passive. Later, she awakened and began to struggle once more. She tried again and again, almost making it each time and then being blocked from success. This cycle of struggle-defeat-struggle was stamped in. The imprint would later govern Celia's moods and behavior, setting the stage for a psychosis of a particular variety: manic-depression, the lifelong echo of Celia's birth experience. The trauma also altered the set-point of some of her hormones. Later on, a doctor might find a hormone deficiency associated with her manic-depression, and believe that that is the "cause" of her problem. It is an "effect."

Sam is unhappy when Celia comes to visit. When Celia is in a good mood, she's the life of the party, more "up" even than Sam. She is wildly extravagant, buying all kinds of exotic foods for dinner and useless things for the house. Her enthusiasms know no bounds, and she may work eighteen hours a day without fatigue. But this manic phase ends with a brief psychotic break, followed by deep depression. When she is "down," she mopes around with no enthusiasm for anything.

Celia is a manic-depressive *because that sequence of behaviors, mania followed by depletion of energy, brought about her survival.* Her superhuman capacity for work and frantic shopping sprees are really a battle to gain life. Her system "remembers" its first great survival struggle and continues the struggle forever.

Depression follows mania because of an imprint of defeat and utter hopelessness, followed by a last effort that meets success. The system remembers its ultimate failure after a manic struggle. When Celia is depressed, she feels what she felt originally, although she cannot form the concept. In this phase we see the analogue of the original parasympathetic feelings of helplessness and not wanting to live. Then Celia rouses herself in a desperate last bid for life, and the cycle repeats itself.

After a period of normalcy during which she takes on more and more responsibility and works harder and longer, Celia almost imperceptibly shifts into a manic state in which she is all hectic activity. The energy that drives the behavior is *original life-and-death desperation* from the manic phase of the birth struggle. Stores of hidden energy are tapped into as the birth

sequence is run off precisely as it was originally. Eventually
the mania becomes so intense that she is out of control. She
ends up having an argument with her mother, after which she
begins playing the piano, pounding it furiously with her el-
bows and singing at the top of her voice, convinced that the
piano is sending out messages to her mother.

Celia ends up in a mental hospital. She is diagnosed with
acute manic-depressive psychosis and a history of alternating
mania and depression. To ameliorate the high and low energy
levels, both of which interfere with her functioning, the doctors put her on antipsychotic drugs such as lithium carbonate.
But these are palliative, not curative. The doctors are sure her
cyclic personality is genetic, tracing her manic-depressive lin-
eage back to great-great-grandparents. When this pattern repeats itself, and she has to be hospitalized once more, they will
again come to the same diagnosis, because their training does
not take into account the damaging effects of birth trauma,
or the possibility that this past experience is also the key to
healing.

If Celia's manic-depressive pattern is not genetic, then how
can the pattern of profound depression followed by superhuman efforts occurring over and over again in adulthood be explained? Unless one is prepared to believe that millions of
manic-depressives were born with some genetic defect that
makes them go in cycles, one must consider that social events
could cause it. Legions of mental health experts see psychosis
as a sign of pathology when it is simply an attempt to preserve
the integrity of one's personality. Originally, Celia had to be
frantic to save her life, and then she had to give up to save
her life. We have unraveled the mystery of psychosis in primal
therapy, and found that it is explained by the imprint. When
our Celias relive that cyclic trauma, they resolve their manic-
depression. If reliving birth traumas can change personality so
dramatically, it indicates that the original trauma changed and
directed personality as well.

What Is a Good Birth?

If birth trauma is so important in shaping personality, so is a good birth. The ideal birth, as Dr. Frederic Leboyer has demonstrated, involves an invigorating degree of effort by the fetus, crowned with success, followed by nurturing at the breast. This kind of birth means, above all, not giving anesthetic drugs to the mother if it can be avoided. Such a birth creates the expectation that success follows effort, leading later to an optimistic outlook. This birth imprint produces the physiology of optimism. At about nine years old, "Leboyer babies" were found to be well adjusted and usually ambidextrous.

Of course, not every prototype stems from birth. It can take place before or after birth, but always very early in life when basic response tendencies are set. A baby whose birth experience is not traumatic but who is then suddenly removed from his mother and left alone for days in an incubator without touch may have a lifelong terror of being alone. Each situation of aloneness in adulthood triggers off the early prototypic event.

If this sounds like the shoemaker who sees only shoes in the world, consider that personality begins somewhere. Of course, there is the hereditary component, contributing perhaps to a rapid-acting nervous system or a sluggish one. Then there is the nurture received in the womb: Was the mother anorexic, did she smoke, did she drink alcohol during pregnancy? We know these factors significantly affect the development of the fetus.

Does this mean that, after birth, people don't change for the rest of their lives? They do, but not profoundly. They mature, develop minds and intellect, adopt professions and so forth, but the quiet baby is likely to become a reticent adult, and the hyperactive one an aggressive adult. Basic tendencies are circumscribed by the imprint, and that imprint is dictated by the "trauma train." Had Patricia, a compliant, submissive child, been given much love and support and encouraged to be tenacious, then her imprint would have been held at bay but would not have disappeared. Her basic tendency to acquiesce will still be there. Her imprint of not being able to struggle to survive will linger on, and once her cortex is equipped to translate the imprint into logic, it will be conceptualized as helplessness and hopelessness.

The importance of the sympathetic/parasympathetic paradigm is that it provides a biologic basis for understanding personality and our psychophysiological development. It enables us to leave abstraction and metaphor behind, and replace speculation with the precision of verifiable hypotheses. We no longer need to talk about the will to meaning, the Oedipus complex, the id, and other concepts removed from biology; we can talk about personality and biology as a unity. We can discuss the way the nervous system responds to events in childhood, and how those events are translated into physical and psychological ailments. The sympathetic/parasympathetic paradigm links physiology and psychology, giving rise to testable hypotheses and paving the way for psychology to become a science.

Sam, Patricia, and Celia Revisited

Sam, Patricia, and Celia all entered primal therapy. Sam never would have gone to therapy if Patricia hadn't insisted. He went not because he was suffering overtly, but because he was convinced the palpitations were going to kill him. Like Patricia and Celia, he found that there was something he could do to normalize his psychology and physiology.

Sam had complained bitterly about Patricia's sex drive. But after she relived the anoxia in the womb fully, she began to feel more sexual. After allowing herself to react to her terror, she could allow a great deal more excitement without shutting down; she could relax and enjoy it. Meanwhile, her migraines became rare, and the resolution of her depression also resolved her hypothyroidism.

Sam learned that his hypersexuality was early pain eroticized. He was using Patricia to fill a bottomless pit. When he relived his pain, he became less aggressive, and his testosterone level normalized. For him, this meant much less; for Patricia, much more. Sam also learned to identify palpitations as a sign that he's been triggered and is due for a feeling.

Patricia learned that, like all neurotics, she had managed to re-create the past in the present. By reacting first to her imprint of "I can't try, I won't make it, I'm going to die," she was ensuring her failure. Her current situation *became* her old feeling. As a result of feeling this feeling many times over, Patricia gradually changed failure to success by placing the terror and hopelessness in their proper context and no longer displacing it into the present. She could finally separate past from present. This is the key to undoing neurosis: placing the past in the past so that it doesn't drive the present. By doing so, Patricia resolved her migraines, among other positive changes.

When Patricia goes back to school at the age of thirty-five, she won't give up if she gets a C because such a grade can no longer reawaken the old terror and despair. She will never be as tenacious as Sam, who has been practicing tenacity since birth, but she has learned that to persevere is to succeed. Similarly, Sam will never be an artist, for his prototypic early skills were never developed. He can't think in images, and she isn't interested in money or business, but they can get along. She no longer makes him wait because she is now more of a self-starter. He is less dissatisfied and far more patient with her. Their marriage is no longer a playing field for their old feelings.

Their personalities are still basically the same, but they are no longer extremes. Sam can now stay home and relax, while Patricia is less afraid of going out. She doesn't have to have Sam "breathe life into her," and he has found a center and stability he never knew before. Both are more content with themselves.

As for Celia, as a result of feeling, her insight into her own breakdown was that "if my behavior became sufficiently crazy, I would finally get my mother's attention and she would give me what I needed to survive." In a frenzied effort to live, she was desperate for someone to acknowledge her and help her live. Her screams were silent and her pain mute. The argument with her mother was the last straw. Once she had integrated the feeling, her highs and lows vanished without the need for medication.

For Sam, Patricia, and Celia, improving their present lives meant journeying back to confront the traumas of their past. In the next two chapters, I focus on how our own history can serve as a road map to getting well, and how current feeling can be a starting point for unlocking deep, unmet needs.

7

SCANNING YOUR PAST FOR SURVIVAL CLUES

In response to stressful experiences, the body produces high levels of stress hormones. These same hormones play a role in establishing and strengthening the system's memory of these experiences (the imprint). The pain and suffering of the events elicit the manufacture of the natural opiates, which are the agents of repression. Solomon Snyder, as well as researchers Mortimer Mishkin and Tim Appenzeller, writing in *Scientific American*, have determined that endorphins and other neuroinhibitors are manufactured particularly in those areas where pain, both physical and emotional, is processed. (See Figure 1.)

If the structures that process feelings also secrete repressive neurohormones, these structures control access to our emotions. Thus, pain influences not only what we perceive and learn, but also what we repress. Related research supports this perspective. For example, experiments on rat offspring revealed that stress experienced just after birth results in a major elaboration of the rats' pain-receptor system. The traumas changed the structure of the brain by triggering a premature development of pain-mediating cells and causing higher levels of circulating endorphins, which means higher levels of

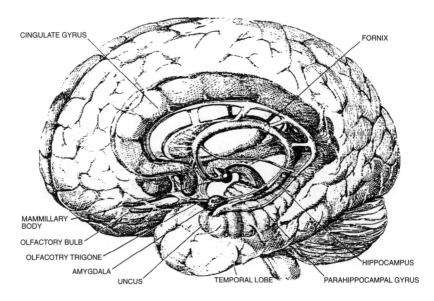

CINGULATE GYRUS

FORNIX

MAMMILLARY BODY

OLFACTORY BULB

OLFACOTRY TRIGONE

AMYGDALA

UNCUS

TEMPORAL LOBE

HIPPOCAMPUS

PARAHIPPOCAMPAL GYRUS

FIGURE 1. Solomon Snyder found limbic structures (shaded) to be loaded with endorphin receptors.

repression. Also, magnetic resonance studies show that psychotics have an excess of dopamine receptors in the emotional centers of the brain. Reasoning in reverse, this increased amount of pain receptors indicates the existence of early trauma. The logical assumption is that their limbic brains have been overwhelmed by early trauma.

As you can see, *once there is pain, we forever react to that pain, changing the way we see the world*. As long as the imprint is there, certain situations in the present will resonate with early trauma. This is why many of us are tense and nervous much of the time. It is why some people find being criticized extremely distressing; even minor reproaches from others echo severe reprimands they had from their parents when they were young. It is why many people feel so devastated when their boyfriend or girlfriend decides to end the relationship. This ''rejection'' resonates with the shattering meaning of a childhood abandonment.

Moreover, the chain of pain explains why we are likely to respond to current stress in much the same way we reacted in the face of the original stress. When faced with a problem or other type of stressful input, the system unknowingly scans for a prototypical response. Some people confront problems immediately and directly. Others try to ignore them, apparently hoping they will go away by themselves. At difficult moments in life, some take action quickly, while others are slow to react. These patterns, part of the chain of pain, reflect how early trauma affects later behavior and how it dictates so much of what happens in our lives and to our health.

Representation and Re-representation

Although we are born with almost all of the neurons we will ever have, the mass of the brain at birth is only about one-fourth that of the adult brain. The brain becomes bigger as the neurons grow in size. The brain is formed in part by its earliest experiences, and survival information is passed upward as it develops, from first-line to third-line level of consciousness (see Chapter Four). Information about what to fear (which means survival) is ultimately represented on the cortical, or third-line, level. Terror in the womb will finally travel to the cortex, where any confining space will resonate with the original terror and make the person afraid. Thus the fear returns, re-represented on different levels. Each level contributes another component: the first line the tightness in the chest (the sensation level); the second line the fear of enclosed spaces (the emotional aspect); and the third line the naming and the rationalization for why it is there (the intellectual level). It is possible to be aware of a phobia but have no idea of its origins. Or it is possible to feel a tightness in the chest and still have no notion of why it occurs. The chain of pain is the name for this representation and re-representation, only in reverse. In therapy one needs to start at the top and eventually, perhaps months later, descend to origins. Once one is locked into a feeling and one lets oneself go deeply into it, one will automatically begin the descent toward ultimate causes.

Representation thus provides a road map for the therapist

and patient. When there is a current *inordinate* reaction, one can be sure that it is a re-representation of something overwhelming early on. It is neurologically impossible for it to be otherwise. Someone who is very uncomfortable or depressed when alone will generally act out, gathering others around so that she won't be alone. The origin may stem from right after birth, when the child was not given enough attention and was left alone for hours. Those hours may have been filled with terror and imprinted as such. It was compounded throughout her childhood by neglect and indifference of parents who made the child feel all the more alone. Being alone as an adult brings on all of the original feelings of abandonment. There is no reason to be fearful and depressed when alone unless it resonates with a feeling of abandonment early in life.

For most of us, our birth is our first life-and-death experience. Our reaction to it—be it a massive struggle crowned with success or a brief struggle curtailed by drugs—will be forever associated with the outcome. Ultimately, we survived, yet later when we are in a threatening situation, we will react in the way that originally kept us alive. Perhaps that is what people really mean when they say their "whole life passed before their eyes" in a near-death experience. Under lethal stress, such as being on the verge of drowning, the brain scans one's history for survival clues. Ultimately, the scanning stops at the prototype: what we did originally in the birth struggle to save our lives, or if not in the birth struggle, then some other early, serious trauma.

Thus, if being paralyzed and immobile helped save one's life early on, when giving a speech before a large group decades later, one again might freeze into immobility. How else to account for it? There is nothing intrinsically devastating about speaking to a group of people. Only our history makes it so, if that history resonates with a devastating memory. That's why I say early trauma continues to affect us forever. Our past is stronger than our present; it is always with us, shaping our perception and behavior.

MARYANNE: "WHAT'S THE USE?"

I think I've been depressed from the start of my life. I was held back because they couldn't find the doctor when I was being born, and I've felt the futility of trying anything ever since. My pulse has been extremely low (around 45) all of my life, and I think that is part of my not having any energy. I found it an effort to walk anywhere, like I'm dragging my body around. I think that everything shut down when I couldn't get out and somehow the exhaustion I felt in the birth struggle has dogged me ever since. I was always withdrawn in school, never had many friends, never felt any great joy in anything, and never had much energy. "What's the use?" was my theme song.

Prototypical imprints can make us feel we are under great danger even if we aren't. Consider a person who gets anxious when he has to wait in an airline terminal with nothing to do. It would never occur to him that what he is feeling is related to his birth. In this kind of person, a current lack of activity causes the brain to scan the body's history, only to find that no movement at the start of life meant death. The reason the scanning takes place and makes the person edgy is that a sudden lack of anything to do produces a malaise, setting in motion the prototypic defense: keeping active. He doesn't know why he is antsy. He is unaware of his real motivation because the real source of his behavior is a hundred million years of evolution away from the experience it describes. No wonder the idea that birth trauma has a lifelong effect seems so alien.

There are two levels of reality operating here. If you measure brain waves, electrophysiology, blood pressure, or stress hormones, you see how powerful the unconscious forces are. At the same time, however, the higher levels of consciousness are unaware of the lower-level struggle. The person may say to himself, "I hate waiting in line." But when you ask the lower levels, through electronic measurements, what is going on, they say, by way of a blood pressure of 200 and a pulse of 110,

"I'll die if I have to wait." And that is why the body is in a frenzy unbeknownst to the person. And, over the long term, ideas cannot effectively combat these impulses. "Talking therapies," which help us "understand" ourselves better, cannot ultimately resolve our problems because of their tremendous physical force.

Here is another example of how the scanning mechanism works. A professor criticizes a student in class. She develops a severe anxiety attack. Her stomach churns. Her hands start sweating and her heart starts pounding. She cannot breathe. The criticism has evoked an old memory. Furthermore, this memory has a meaning on every level of consciousness. Her thinking mind, cut off from the imprint, tells her something about the present: "Try to stay calm . . . It's all too much . . . I'm no good . . . I'll fail in school." This is layered over an unconscious childhood feeling, residing on the second line: "It means my parents don't love me. If they don't love me I'll die!" Perhaps her childhood pain had compounded her birth trauma, which told her, "I'm not going to make it out. I'm going to die." The overall feeling—"I'm not going to make it!"—evokes the death threat. These three levels form the chain of pain, and all three participate in the resulting feeling: the churning of the stomach and inability to breathe (first level), the feeling that "I'm not going to make it" (second level), and the idea that "I'm going to be a failure or I'm no good." (third level).

If you say to this person, "Don't make such a big deal out of that little criticism. It didn't mean anything," it won't really help. Because it did mean something; it meant life or death. Remember, we react *physiologically* to historic imprinted reality rather than to current conditions. Our memories override current input and dictate physiological reactions.

Say someone who has great imprinted stress has a heart attack. If, after the attack, you tell him to "take it easy," it can be like talking to a wall. His body is reacting *logically* to his past and is constantly in the survival mode. The imprint does not know that high blood pressure and a rapid heart rate can kill a person. The person *knows* he should take it easy, but as long as the imprint is nudging him, he cannot. The doctor tells him, "You must take it easy. You'll die if you don't relax!" Meanwhile, his body tells him, "You can never take it easy. You'll die if you do!" The whole system is mobilized against the possibility of death at birth, and this very mobilization is now likely to cause death.

Phobias

Like other anxiety disorders, phobias are an excellent example of how the past plays into the present through the chain of pain. When a phobic enters an elevator, the brain scans its history, discovers a history of suffocation in a cramped space at birth or perhaps in an incubator, and dictates the same frenzied, terrified reaction. The incoming signal sets off the old memory, galvanizing the system. The anxiety attack is a mystery because the source is hidden from cortical view. The phobia is the exact response to the original event and is logical in its context—a memory that makes the past present. It is now *memory* that the person is reacting to.

The feeling of impending doom sometimes arises, paradoxically, when one starts to feel happy. Say, for example, that you're having the perfect dinner with the perfect companion, good music, and cozy ambiance. All of a sudden you sense a vague uneasiness, a sense that your happiness can't last and something terrible is going to happen. When good feelings reach a certain level, their very intensity may trigger other feelings, good or bad, including the memory of trauma. The person develops a sense of dread and is certain that something will intervene and turn happy feelings into misery. It can happen just after sex, after the birth of a child, after a wedding, after one meets a new wonderful person, or after one has been given some award or been told some wonderful news.

That is why the system, in its perfection, conspires to repress excess emotion when there are intense, old memories lying about. That is why it allows just so much sexual excitement and no more; why it shuts off feeling at the maximum intensity. A certain level of sexual excitement will trigger the birth trauma, and sex then becomes the vehicle for the discharge of that early pain. We can observe one's sex life and retrospectively understand what the birth was like. It has to do with the level of excitement. The body doesn't differentiate between sex, a car crash, and a football game. At a certain level of intensity there is an automatic release of the early trauma, which then runs off from beginning to end.

Many neurotics automatically sit on all their feelings, to prevent the original bad feelings from surfacing. Better not be exuberant if one doesn't want to fall apart. It is all done automatically by the body. In Chapter Five we saw it in Patricia in her low-energy, self-protective mode, and in Celia in her manic phases. Ontogeny—one's personal development—seems to be the continuous recapitulation of the primal imprint. Contrary to what Freud thought, you don't have to study dreams as the "royal road to the unconscious." If your moods are cyclic, look to your birth for their origins.

Migraine: A Manifestation of the Prototype?

Patricia, the parasympath discussed in Chapter Four, had chronic migraines. Her doctor prescribed vasoconstrictors in order to reverse the migraine process. According to conventional wisdom, migraine headaches are the direct result of contraction and dilation of blood vessels in the head. Furthermore, headache experts say that serotonin depletion is an underlying cause of migraine. Among the other factors that may "trigger" migraines are stress, alcohol, sex, the food additive monosodium glutamate (MSG), nitrites, hypoglycemia, bright lights, and loud noises. Some continue to attribute migraine to "psychosomatic" factors. Headache experts conclude that because up to seventy percent of all migraine patients have a parent who also has migraines, this condition is often genetically based.

One may imagine that a psychological event such as a fight

with one's spouse sets off the physical reaction of a migraine, but in my opinion, the origin is not the marital disagreement, and it is not just a "psychological problem" or a genetic one. The "psyche" came long after the "somatic" component, another way of saying there was matter before "mind." Migraines are in the body, not the mind.

Migraine in adulthood is often a response to the lingering memory of anoxia, and it is set off by the scanning mechanism. Current stress triggers the brain to seek out how to defend itself. It looks directly to the prototype. In the case of asphyxiation at birth, this may mean getting by on little oxygen and may have involved vasoconstriction to conserve oxygen, which in turn is what happens in the early stages of migraine. In the first phase of migraine the internal blood vessels of the head respond to hypoxia (lessened oxygen supply) by constricting and decreasing oxygen delivery to the cells. At a critical point, when even that response becomes inadequate, massive vasodilation takes place, and with that comes the migraine. The vasoconstriction followed by massive vasodilation is the survival mechanism. Something in the present triggers the early pain, and the head responds at age thirty as though it were being born and suffering from a lack of oxygen. *Migraine is part of survival.*

JOANNA: CAUGHT IN A CYCLE

Lately, when I wake up, I have what I call an "angry headache" within five minutes. It is located in my left temple, eye, neck, and shoulder. It is a similar pain to the migraines that I get on my right side, but a bit less intense. The first thoughts that enter my mind are: "Here we go again, fighting through another day."

I have slowly begun to feel (after sixteen months of therapy) an early feeling that I believe rules my life and is the basis of my neurosis. It is a feeling of constantly having to fight for my life, that I have to fight all the time to stay alive. It is a present-day reality for me to have to fight in my everyday life just to stay on my own two feet. My "natural" (I should say neurotic) inclination is to just give up and not fight. The cycle goes: fight, get nowhere, give up, want to die, not want to die, decide not to die, and fight again, get nowhere, and so forth. It has constantly been that way for me.

The more I take care of myself in the present, the more I feel this feeling. Taking care of myself makes me feel how hard my aloneness is, and how there is no one to help. Getting my life together means starting to really live in the present and to feel the feeling of fighting to live as an old feeling.

The farthest I go back is to the age of one (except for a slight birth feeling I've had, which I will speak of later). I am lying in the crib just waiting for my mother. I wait and wait and wait, but she never comes. And I want her so badly. After waiting for a while, I start to choke and gag, breathing heavily, and I feel like I am going to die if she doesn't come for me. I feel so empty. I need my mother. I need to be taken care of. I feel this feeling in bits and pieces at various times. Often it is when a migraine is starting. Other times it is after I have an orgasm. The stronger the orgasm, the stronger the feeling. It seems as if pleasure brings instant pain. I often find myself holding back from fully enjoying the orgasm because of the pain it so often brings.

I still don't think my life is in good enough shape to feel the utter pain of this feeling. The migraine pain is pushing on me most of the time, telling me my pain is there. So the stage I am at now is just being very angry at having had it so hard my whole life. I am angrier ever since I went on vacation to the Caribbean and had three wonderful days where I didn't have to fight. I just lived. And I realized what I missed out on my whole life. I think that once I get past this tremendous outrage, I will go deeper into the feeling on the way to resolving it.

Below the feeling of fighting to live is another feeling that I have experienced only slightly. I have gone back to the feeling of being stuck when I am being born. I have to fight my way out of the birth canal. Finally, my head is out, but the rest of me won't come out. This feeling is such an analogy to my life: My head is out, but the rest of me is inactive. My body doesn't feel connected. I so often live in my head, and I only recently started to feel my body as part of me.

Back to the birth feeling: I feel stuck and my neck hurts. It hurts even as I write about this. It feels as if someone is pulling on my neck and it's very painful. My head is swaying from side to side and my voice lets out small wails of fear. Again, I am fighting for my life. I even have to be born on my own. My mother does not help me out. That has been a constant all my life from the very beginning—no help, fight on my own.

If one suppresses migraine with drugs, the stage may still be set for later disease due to the memory of anoxia in the cells. It is not that migraine leads to cancer, or that high blood pressure ends up as cancer (which it sometimes does), but that the same imprint may cause both. How do we know all this? If it were not true, we would not have had such success at the Primal Center treating migraine among a diverse patient population. When patient after patient comes in with migraine or high blood pressure and relives birth anoxia, the symptom is either attenuated or disappears.

Incidentally, one of the important treatments for migraine and cluster headaches is oxygen. The primal treatment for that same affliction is to *feel the lack of oxygen*. Therein lies the important difference between treating the symptom and treating the cause. Oxygen therapy helps; *feeling its lack cures*. Feeling the lack lifts repression, liberates oxygen stores, and makes the migraine response sequence unnecessary.

8

Neurotic Behavior: The Acting-Out of Repressed Feelings

A patient of mine had lost her mother at an early age. She never had a chance to "say good-bye." This loss left a deep wound. Throughout her life, she would linger on the telephone for long periods of time because she didn't know how to say good-bye. She also stayed in a bad marriage for the same reason.

Many people who have been abandoned early in life, for brief but crucial periods, such as being put in an incubator after birth, or for longer periods, such as being put in a foster home, may not like to be alone. Unconscious feelings color their entire adult life, driving them to do whatever is necessary to have company. Such a person, for example, won't happily choose to be a writer who spends all day working alone. He prefers to work with others. Instead of relaxing with a book at home, he goes out all the time to be with friends. Each time a companion leaves, he's likely to feel anxious, though he doesn't know why.

A mother slaps her young child often. The physical hurt is not great; that alone would not become primal pain. But the meaning behind the slap might become the pain. What the child senses the parent really means is "I don't like you!" This meaning is too much to bear and is shut out. Thereafter, the child struggles to be liked through her behavior. She might get involved in a long series of relationships or become promiscuous. Her pain might conjure up mystical beliefs, and she might devote herself to God, seeking fulfillment in the embrace of a loving deity.

As we have seen in previous chapters, neurosis is not always evident. Something as subtle as talking on the phone at length, unable to hang up and say good-bye, doesn't seem obviously neurotic but is often driven by pain. When trauma threatens a person's fragile system, he often adopts behaviors designed to shield himself from the truth. The person begins to act out in an attempt to fulfill unmet needs symbolically. *It is the way we behave to deny the truth of our feelings.* Act-outs are always symbolic because they are an attempt in the present to fulfill old childhood needs. An act-out is a voluntary action and is different from an act-in, which is an automatic action. The energy of old needs and trauma move against organ systems, causing asthma, ulcers, migraine, and colitis. The need to act out carries over into adult life, and when one digs deep one always finds the old feelings inside the act-out.

If we could not act out, we would be faced with the primal feeling and agonizing pain. Act-outs are part of the defense system. They can be as simple as a person who talks incessantly to get attention, because as a child her parents never listened to her. Or, it can be more complex; for instance, a person is chronically busy and keeps her schedule crammed with plenty of appointments. This may be a childhood feeling from being in a violent home: "If I don't move I'll feel totally helpless and die." Someone who felt powerless at home might strive relentlessly for power over others later in life. In another example, a mother ignores a child's complaints of incest by the father because to acknowledge them would mean abandonment by the husband. The mother herself may have been left alone at an early age. It is also true that mothers who have denied their incest in their own childhood will not be able to

face that of their children. Therefore, someone who was abandoned as a child might be the type of adult who clings to a
mate she really doesn't love even if it means damaging her
child.

Every neurotic is by definition a child—not a real child, but
someone with a child's needs. For the neurotic, life is a stand-
in for one's childhood, an interminable series of behaviors
driven by needs for love, affection, attention, acceptance, se-
curity, a sense of belonging and of being important, and so on.
Acting helpless at age thirty or forty and getting someone to
take care of you is a good example. So is acting as if you
needed no one to take care of you, pretending that you are
wholly self-sufficient and without needs.

A twenty-five-year-old primal therapy patient of mine had a
recurring pattern in her relationships with men. After a series
of fights with a boyfriend, they were breaking up. Two months
earlier he had moved in with her and started paying the rent
and most of her bills. He was considerate and kind, often
bringing her breakfast in bed before he left for work. He fixed
her car and took her dirty clothes to the cleaners. She became
aggressive with him, finding fault and picking fights. Finally,
he couldn't take it anymore and decided to leave. This is the
third time this has happened in her life. It is an example of an
act-out repeated over and over again, seemingly beyond her
control.

In a therapy session she began recounting how anxious and
irritated she felt when her boyfriend brought her breakfast in
bed. Slowly she slipped into the feeling underlying her uneasiness when treated so solicitously. It took her back to her
mother, early on, when she needed her mother to take care of
her. Her mother did so, but only reluctantly. For example, her
mother helped her with her homework but was irritable and
impatient. The little girl soon learned not to ask for help. Asking for help meant risking anger and rejection and not getting
taken care of.

It was a double bind: Needing to be taken care of led to the
anxiety over not being taken care of, followed by rejection of

the need and flight from it. The child unconsciously concluded that it would be better to take care of herself than to risk having care and then losing it. And it was superimposed on the present in a lifelong pattern of behavior.

On several occasions she had quickly fallen in love with someone who she thought might take care of her. But once the person *did* take care of her, she would become irritated, because her past experience told her that the attention would not last and she knew she could not handle the pain of being rejected again. Indeed, she *expected* the rejection and ended up causing just that.

Unlike her mother, her latest boyfriend did not mind taking care of her. But she saw the present through the filter of her unconscious need. In her mind, he was just like her mother. She would become angry at him even when he helped her screw the cap off the marmalade jar. She was not aware of why she would have this reaction. She could only pinpoint a vague anxiety. She ended up picking fights with him and managed to make him aggressive and resentful. She then thought it proved her point. She could now say that, like her mother, he really didn't want to help her. She made it inevitable that he would eventually reject her.

Why did she want to run the minute she started to feel taken care of? Because being taken care of meant the fear of being a burden and being rejected. The men in her life were symbols of a real context. She acted out the past over and over again with them. This is the unconscious self-fulfilling prophecy that symbolic acting-out achieves over and over.

Because she couldn't feel her past or know that her behavior was an outgrowth of it, she focused her feelings on the present. Her feelings were real, but the context was wrong. This is the essence of symbolic acting-out. The past is inaccessible and is therefore filtered to the present, where one creates the past again. She didn't even have to think about transferring mother feelings onto her boyfriend. In therapy, my patient got to the underlying feeling, which was: "If they take care of me for long, I will be a burden and they will resent me and then they will leave me!" So, because of her conflicting needs, she ruined relationships with good people. In therapy the feeling became conscious. Now that she has felt and integrated what was below her pattern of acting-out, she does not have to act it out anymore in the present.

Another patient of mine would never fix anything in his house, no matter how simple. He needed to be helpless until his father (or a substitute figure in the present) came to help him. Acting as though he could do things meant unconsciously that he no longer needed anyone to guide and help him. Since he *did* need these things, *still* needed them because he had never gotten them in childhood, he was forced to act out being helpless.

Early on in his life, he wanted to turn to his father, but he sensed that his father was never going to be any help. On the contrary, asking for help meant possible rejection by his father for being weak and helpless. His father was a self-made man, and he expected the same from his son. He would not tolerate a "useless" child or a needy "weakling." It was important that the child do things on his own, whether he knew how to do them or not. The child was stuck: He needed help but was scared to ask for it. The father's act-out to be tough and independent and totally intolerant of anyone's weakness, his child's or his own, had the result of subordinating his child's needs, with lifelong negative consequences.

This kind of subtle, unconscious communication happens in the first years of one's life. One does not have to be deliberately taught. Children are sensing machines. They pick up on the most nuanced of clues. They can't articulate it, but they act on those clues, nevertheless. They "know" that they cannot confide in their parents, know that they cannot talk about their fears and failures, know that they cannot cry because it won't be tolerated.

The old feeling is always contained in and expressed by the act-out. In this person's case, every time his wife asked him to light the pilot light in the oven and he claimed he didn't know how, he was saying, "Help me. Guide me. Teach me!" Had he acted independently, it would have been tantamount to losing all hope. It would have meant never getting the help from his father that he so desperately needed. Although he did not know it, he was engaged in a struggle, employing a subtle survival technique. He was fighting to fulfill his needs, fighting for his life.

The Act-Out as Survival

If we want to know why people can't get along, why relationships are destroyed, why people can't find love, why they can't hold onto jobs, maintain their pursuit of particular goals, or make sensible decisions, we must look to the act-out, and beyond the act-out to unfulfilled needs. Those needs cannot be ignored. How many neurotics get anxious when relationships become intense and then begin to reject the partner? They are so afraid of experiencing the earlier rejection as a child that they try to control events and people to ensure it won't happen again.

During a session one patient of mine had the sudden impulse to leave the room. It gave her a sense of relief to get out. This in itself was an act-out, a reflexive way to avoid repressed feeling. And it fit the pattern of her act-outs throughout her life: not wanting to stay at home as a child, running away time and again beginning at age eight, moving from place to place as an adult. Eventually, she relived being in her crib and seeing her mother clipping the sheets over her so that she could not move. She felt all tied up.

With this and more catastrophic feelings going back to her birth (being alone in the dark, not being able to breathe, struggling, choking, panicking, being near death, unable to move but needing to move to avoid death), she had the insight that she had been needing to "get out" all the time, "running away all my life around the world, like a comet, never staying anywhere really, so I wouldn't have to feel that nobody loved me at home or anywhere else in this world." For example, she kept packing her bags whenever a lover or friend "asserted control" over her, and she left men when she felt afraid that they would leave her. These flights from people were impulsive because she had not been able to control them. After acknowledging and integrating the feeling that she had to get away (in her infancy and childhood), she no longer felt that she had to get away (as an adult in the present). That is the dialectic.

One person I knew produced a computer printout of all of his daily phone calls. Listening to the answering machine was not enough. He needed to "see" the list to feel reassured. It showed that he was wanted. The real feeling: "I'm not wanted." A list of thirty calls meant he was wanted. The list was part of his symbolic acting-out. Each and every day he produced a symbol to cover the real feeling, because each and every day the feeling was there lurking just beneath the surface.

A woman I saw in primal therapy had the repetitive pattern of finding men who could not love her. They just wanted sex, which replicated her early life with her father, who never loved her but sexually abused her for years. The feeling was, "I'm just useful for their needs. I have no other value. I'm not lovable for myself." It was only what she could give men that made her feel somewhat acceptable. Her behavior was extremely seductive. The kind of men who fell for her only wanted one thing because that was the message she delivered. Then she was surprised when they did not love her. Her act-out involved the hope that someone would finally love her and not just use and abuse her. Hope is buried at the bottom of most act-outs. The unconscious feeling drove her to re-create the old situation in the present because the past situation, in the brain, was ever-present. If she acted seductively and got her needs fulfilled in the present, she didn't have to feel the past deprivation. She was never aware, until well into therapy, that she had been sexually abused as a child.

The act-outs do not have to be blatant. Doing nothing all day is an example. The feeling: "Why do I have to go out to people (my mother)? Why can't they come to me, draw me out, hug me, be interested and concerned?"

Another way people act out is by being useful to everyone. The only way she got approval from her depressed mother was to do things for her: to make herself useful. It carried on into adulthood. She knew that if she was useful she was wanted. When she was invited to a friend's home for dinner, it was she who became the hostess, clearing the table, washing the dishes, and so forth. The real feeling was that she was useless and therefore not worthy of love. The act-out kept the real feeling away.

Although overachievement isn't always an example of acting out, consider an individual who has always energetically pursued and obtained what he has wanted: a good job, a lot of money, a family, a nice house, leisure time. Suddenly he feels let down, depressed. Hopelessness sets in. Having achieved everything, what else is there to "get"? There is nothing more to struggle for. But the underlying need to "get" remains. What he has gotten in the present is not exactly what he needed as a child. So he feels disappointed, and that disappointment may not be conscious. The person simply sets his sights on other lofty goals: more money, more success, bigger deals, more freedom. This keeps the struggle alive.

On the verge of making things go right, a person does something to make it go wrong. This is sometimes known as self-destructive behavior. It may have begun at birth, when things suddenly went terribly wrong—a tumor blocked the way out, or there was a delay because the doctor did not arrive on time. In adult life the person re-creates the early trauma in exactly the same way, allowing things to go fine for a while and then doing something to ruin everything. It enables the person to avoid the depression and hopelessness and reaffirms the realization that things going fine now will not resolve what went wrong back then.

This type of behavior is often acted out in relationships. We all know people who get married for many reasons, but two years down the road they discover who their partner really is and they don't like him or her. They put so many of their hopes onto the other person that they never saw him or her for who they were. They were acting out. Who suffers most? The children they have, who are victims of their neurosis. People without deep pain know with whom they are getting involved. If they have no overarching past to project onto the present, they stand a better chance at a decent and enduring marriage and successful parenting.

It's no news to anyone that most problems in relationships stem from the act-outs of unfulfilled needs. A loved child is not driven to act out. Fulfillment in childhood allows us to have mature, adult needs and relationships. As adults we can give and receive love without using the partner as a symbol for getting the "old" love. We don't need constant reassurance that the partner loves us. We don't have to "possess" the partner as a means of having someone (a mother) all to ourselves. But serious problems arise in a relationship due to the carryover of unmet needs from childhood. Couples may seek counseling, but almost everything they do to make things better is battling against the need to act out.

Remember, the act-out is based on hard-wired, inviolable, must-be-fulfilled-for-survival need. A spouse who is unhappy about her partner's passivity may demand that he "take action," but her wishes will be up against his personality prototype. Telling one's mate to "Stop acting helpless!" is unlikely to lead to the desired results when the person needs desperately to be helped (as a child does). It won't do much good to say "Stop your rages!" when there is a cauldron of anger bubbling just below the surface. You can no more stop the act-out than stop the need.

One of my patients actually plotted to kill his next-door neighbor over a property dispute. He bought a gun and decided to kill the neighbor and then himself. In the primal he got to the bottom of his motivation: He felt that he had to kill himself because once the other man was dead, there was no hope left. The neighbor was a stand-in for his tyrannical father. He always wanted to kill him as well, but once his father was gone there would be no one to take care of him, no hope left.

Converting Unmet Needs Into "Needs for"

When our basic needs are not fulfilled early in life, they later become transformed into the "needs for"—the need for help, for stability, safety, money, success, power, drugs, drink, and so on. And we spend much of our time pursuing them. But it is never just a "need for" drink, for example. It is the need for love that drives us to soothe our discomfort as best we can. Our "need for" riches and fame may be a symbolic need for the real one that was never fulfilled: the need for attention and to feel important when we were children.

Unless you address the real illness, rather than the "need for," the problem cannot be cured. Perhaps you help get someone off drugs for a time. This is all to the good, but it is not healing. The person will never feel completely at ease. As long as her early memories and feelings remain repressed and unconscious, they will drive her into other symbolic act-outs, like the "need for" drugs.

The function of the act-out is to be well, to finally have one's early needs fulfilled. This may bring the level of pain down for a while and bring a little relief. But it is only temporary. Only history holds the resolution. Primal pain can be diverted, rechanneled, or suppressed, but it cannot be erased by advice, insight, will, twelve-step ideology, or psychotropic medication. Once it is imprinted in the system, a mountain of willpower can be put into service to hold the need in check, but it is a vain enterprise. The only way the primal pain and the act-out it generates can be eradicated is through experiencing the memory of the trauma, to make it conscious.

At the beginning of this chapter I discussed the patient whose mother had died when she was very young, who had never been able to say good-bye. Ever since her mother's death, not having been able to integrate the feeling, she had unconsciously been driven by the hope that her mother would come back. Feeling the pain of losing her mother, with its agony and finality, meant finally saying "good-bye." It meant putting the feeling in context. Only this allowed the healing to take place and put an end to the act-outs.

KITTY: STARVING FOR ATTENTION

I'm anorexic. For the past seven years I've systematically starved myself. My rationalization for almost never eating was that I wanted to be thin. I wanted to look consumptive, with jutting hipbones and hollow cheeks. I envied people who were so ill they had to be fed intravenously. Boy, you could lose weight that way! I was never fat, but I was never thin enough. More than that, I always wanted to be empty. I got crazy when I felt full. All I know was that my feeling full was certainly more than just an anxiety about getting fat. It was something profoundly systematic. If I ate too much I became lightheaded, dizzy, and irritable, with pains in the back of my neck. This translated itself into an urgent need to vomit. Vomiting brought a sense of relief.

I hated this obsession with food because it meant that I was always thinking about what I was not eating. I never understood the reason for this bizarre reversal of body responses. Why was I always so driven to stay empty? I'm beginning to understand it now.

Most people who are deprived of food or love early in life somehow remain in touch with that deprivation. They seek out some kind of fulfillment. They try to get love somehow, somewhere. But others are deprived beyond their capacity to integrate. They and their bodies simply shut down. They disconnect from their own needs very early because the pain is just too much to face. These people, myself included, avoid warmth later because it reminds them of what they didn't get. They don't want anything that might upset the apple cart. They think they are fine the way they are.

The same is true of eating. I avoided it because feeling full reminded me of how empty I felt. As long as I stayed empty, I didn't have to feel it. I began to eat a bit of food in therapy. How odd and how obvious: food as a cure for someone who is starving herself. I began to feel a great pain with this food. I woke up at night with a terrible back pain as though the small of my back had a crank in it that was tightening my legs and spine. It became difficult to breathe. I didn't know what was wrong. All I knew was I felt empty. I also felt that I didn't know what was going on.

I suddenly had an image of myself as a baby lying in the crib, eyes wide open, all stiff and tense. I knew I wasn't supposed to cry and bother my mother. I wasn't supposed to cry or hurt or need. Rather than risk the sight of her angry eyes, I clenched my whole body and bore it in silence.

Time seemed to go on forever in my feeling, minute by minute of pure pain, of waiting for her to check up on me.

All of my life I waited quietly for her to glance at me, to see that I was suffering. I remember standing at her bedroom door after a horrendous nightmare, looking at her sleeping and trying to mouth the word "mama." I would tiptoe back down the hall to my room and spend the night paralyzed with fear. Still, I thought, *Maybe she will come.*

I was never able to ask directly for what I wanted. I was yelled at and called a nuisance if I cried. It became easier to withstand it internally. Although my body was registering stress, my mind simply quit paying attention to the need messages. After enough denial of its needs, my body no longer bothered to communicate them. It was like an endless shock. Stiffness became my mode of survival.

Feeling full was like a huge lie and it drove me crazy. I didn't know it, but my body did. Starving was my way of keeping pain at bay. If you don't get any warmth in your life, you don't have to feel what you've missed. You just stay in your igloo. If I stayed thin, there was always the slim chance that my mother would notice I was dying and take care of me.

SUSANNAH: RUNNING ON EMPTY

I can't remember a time in my childhood when I was happy and carefree and open to the world. In classrooms and with other children, I was withdrawn to the point of virtual muteness. I could not initiate interactions of any kind. So many events in my childhood made me into a quiet, downcast waif.

It all began with a long birth (twenty-eight-hour labor) in which I could do nothing to get things going. After that ordeal I was at last born to a mother who was completely unavailable to me physically; nothing I could do could make her come and hold and soothe me. To me, depression equals no mother. My "blues" are beginning to lift now that I feel precisely that I need Mother and Mother is not there. My mother couldn't be there for me no matter how much I needed her.

My mother loved pregnancy. To her it represented complete incorporation of another individual, absolute possession and control. Perhaps it was the only time in her life that she felt she had someone. Naturally, she didn't want to let me out of her. She only relented when the doctor finally told her he was going to do a cesarean. *Whoosh!* I was born a half hour after he told her that.

I can only imagine that I was born horrified and desperate for consolation. Instead, I was separated from my mother and brought to her to be fed every four hours. These "feedings" were no doubt more torturous for me because there was no milk, yet my mother chose to masquerade as a nursing mother for the benefit of the hospital staff for three or four days. Appearances were always very important to her. She needed people to think she was the model mother. It was all an act, smile and pose for the cameras, for the audience. I was just a narcissistic object for my mother. There you have the recipe for depression: not one chance in the world to get anything for myself; sheer futility.

Photographs of me as a child show a very worried, serious countenance. I never believed my parents were there for me, because they were not. Legend has it that my father left the hospital, came home, and watered the lawn in a stupor because of my unfortunate gender. My father was an absent and peripheral figure. Even my "transitional object," a stuffed animal—a dog I named Bowie—was taken away by both parents. I learned very early that I had no right to need anyone or anything.

As a little girl, knowing that my mother was completely unavailable, I tried to get something from my father. I adored and worshipped him, even though he teased and ridiculed me from the beginning. At least he came near me to teach me something about the world. But he was always laughing at my expense. I remember sitting in my playpen at an age when I couldn't do much more than sit up. He came into the room, dumped several books over my head, and said, "Here. Read." Then he turned on his heels and walked away. It was devastating.

I could never go to my father for love. He was cold and unaffectionate. He would lift me up mechanically to put me into the car, and my heart would swell with the hope of getting something from his touch. It never happened. I remember trying desperately to perform some task for my father, such as tying my shoelaces or telling time, but I could never get it right the first time around as expected, and he would get angry and walk away in disgust. Intimacy or mere proximity still makes me frantic. I feel that I must do what I cannot do; that I have to do something even when there's nothing to do. Nothing I could do could make my parents love me.

After six years of misery, with my parents at each other's throats on a daily basis, my father delivered the final blow by leaving home without saying good-bye. His departure did me in completely. I no longer had someone to strive for. And I was never allowed to express my need and my loss due to my mother's unending bitterness and inability to allow me to be. I felt responsible for my father's leave-taking. At six years old, it was all over for me. I could never be loved. And yet I still had to try to get love, much as I had to try to get born. Depression feels like hopelessness seeping through all of my body.

My history turned me into a person who is comfortable only when alone. The presence of another person sends me into a frenzy. The contact brings up all of my old needs in a torrent as well as all of the hurts and wounds that took place in the years since. When I was a child, I once shut the cats out of my room rather than allow them to sleep with me. I came to live with the refusal of love. I could no longer get comfort from any living creature because I never got the nurturing I so desperately needed. Even today, at thirty-one, I am unable to fall asleep with someone by my side.

The amount of pain I experienced trying to be born was enormous. My whole body became enlisted in repressing the pain of that crisis. I began therapy with drop-dead vital signs that indicated the extent of the repression at work: a pulse of forty and blood pressure so low that, after commenting on my "athlete's heart," nurses always asked me if I had fainting spells. My body is depressed because I'm stuck in my imprint of running on empty at all times. The more tired I become, the harder it is for me to slow down because during my birth, as labor stretched on past a day, I was increasingly tired and had less and less energy for the hard task of being born. Exhaustion signals to me that I must keep going, that I must work harder still.

I was not tended to when I was sick, even when I was in a delirium from pneumonia, even when I was lying on the floor with two bones broken in my leg. My mother could not be mobilized to help me out. And I was a helpless witness to my mother's transient psychotic episodes in which she would stomp around the house yelling like a deranged lunatic, or stumble about with her menstrual blood streaming onto the floor, screaming, "Look at it! Look at it!" My mother was so invasive in her posturing and her overwhelming neediness that there was no room left for me to exist as a person. All I could do from the beginning of time was just to lay still and take it in. And that has defined depression as it has functioned for me in my life. Hopelessness. Uselessness.

All my life I've been unable to rest and take it easy. Insomnia has plagued me my whole life. No amount of sleeping pills, wine, or antidepressants can knock me out when I'm in that enervated state. The groggier I become, the more fervently I resist resting, which is, I suppose, equivalent to experiencing myself failing to make it at birth. On the rare occasions when I do get a good night's sleep, I wind up feeling anxious because the increased energy plunges me back into the start of the birth process, the phase before I got stuck. It is clear that being tired (down, depressed) literally is my way of existing.

Now that I am in a loving relationship, so much of the pain from the past is surfacing. One recent insight I had is that I am always trying to get love. Every word, every gesture, everything I do is about trying to get love. I do not and cannot know how to feel loved; I only know how to grope for it. Actually being loved only brings up the pain of never having been loved at all. In my feelings, I go searching for the light, for the good stuff, for the happy ending. It is nowhere to be found, and all I can do is feel its absence. I have had the insight that I feel there is no place for me in the world because I had no place on my mother's body, no place with her.

I am a true believer in this therapy. Feeling really makes me come alive. My eyes become bright, my smile undeniable, my voice full and rich. I used to be shut down completely, a near zombie stumbling about, running on empty, with not the vaguest idea of how to take care of myself because no one had ever taken care of me. I used to worry and agonize and berate myself constantly. I've felt enough of my pain to the point where I can actually experience anticipation; in other words, I can look forward to upcoming events rather than dreading each moment of my existence. I still have a tendency to struggle to be all things to all people, but when I stop and feel the underlying futility—that my parents wanted no part of me as I was—my lifelong depression quite literally evaporates.

9

LEAKY GATES: WHEN REPRESSION FAILS

A child is distressed and unhappy. He conveys this to his mother by complaining about something. She points out to him that "it's a beautiful day" and tells him to stop complaining. Perhaps she reminds him how good his life is compared to how it would be if he were crippled or if he were a starving child in Africa. If he is told these things often enough and sees that if he stops complaining, his mother treats him more kindly, the child learns not to complain or even let his face reveal that he's suffering inside. He shuts down, aided by his gating system. Eventually, what he thinks has little or no relation to what he feels deep down.

When someone has experienced trauma early in life, such as being ignored continuously by his parents, or even abandoned, normally there is an external manifestation of this feeling: the facial grimace, the gesture of supplication, the agonized cry. There is also an internal manifestation, the wound of "Mommy doesn't love me." Together, they form a complete reaction to the event. But if the pain is too great, something strange happens: It turns into no pain. There is an amount of pain above which agony *decreases*, an intolerable level that sets repression in motion. Reactivity diminishes and pain abates.

The feeling goes into storage. There is no longer a grimace, or a cry for help. There may even be a happy, bubbly air. The person is in agony but doesn't know it. The lower levels "know" but they're not telling. Any aspect of feeling can be locked away by repression. The facial expression, the affect, the idea of it—all can be disconnected from the feeling itself.

As discussed in Chapter Four, gating, mediated by our internally produced opiates, ordinarily stops you from sensing what's going on inside your body so that you don't suffer. Therefore, repression actually functions to protect the cortex from having access to primal pain. But for many, repression doesn't work. They have what I call *leaky gates*, when repressive mechanisms can't handle the pain inside of them. The result may be anxiety or hyperactivity, anorexia or bulimia, compulsions and obsessions, phobias, sleeping problems, nightmares, paranoia, psychosis, or even suicide. All of these are the mind's way to "rationalize" the pain in the present and to keep the individual from being overwhelmed by his past. Leaky gates often require reinforcement in the form of drugs or alcohol.

Repression may not be sufficient to completely hold down pain for a variety of reasons. For one, imprinted pain uses up painkilling chemicals. For another, early trauma may damage the system's ability to produce inhibitory neurotransmitters. James W. Prescott, formerly of the National Institute of Child Health and Human Development, has stated emphatically that sensory deprivation during the brain's formative period harms the endorphin system. In Hooper and Teresi's book *The Three-Pound Universe*, Prescott says that deprivation stunts the branching of the brain cell dendrites and reduces the normal two-way traffic of emotions between the cerebellum and forebrain. Other traumas are likely to have the same effect.

Markku Linnoila of the National Institutes of Health found very low levels of the neurotransmitter serotonin in the spinal fluid of murderers and others incarcerated for violent crimes. As reported in the *Los Angeles Times*, overwhelming evidence from Linnoila's research shows that those with low levels of serotonin have less capacity for inhibition, and that those with the least amounts are impulsive and violent. The results of this study led researchers to look for the gene for violence, but they overlooked the possibility of reduced serotonin output due to early trauma.

From my observations, the reason for impulsiveness in low-serotonin individuals is that, due to early damage, the cortex never developed its full inhibitory potential. It seems that early trauma may play a role in diminishing the output of the serotonin system (there are numerous inhibitory neurohormones) so that we cannot produce enough thereafter. The result is a leaking of repressed feelings that begin to move toward conscious awareness. (Consciousness means the fluid interaction of all three levels.)

In a study carried out at Yale and the University of Texas, researchers manipulated the diets of their human subjects in order to lower the concentration of serotonin. They found that in most cases this "caused" increased aggressive behavior. They also found that autistic individuals who had lowered serotonin had more aggressive symptoms, while increased serotonin levels produced fewer symptoms. Why? Because early trauma that lowers serotonin levels is likely associated with the development of autism. Many experts believe that in addition to any possible organic brain damage resulting from birth difficulties, the trauma itself might impair serotonin output and account for increased violence, among other manifestations.

The leaking of pain through the system's repressive mechanisms is really no different than government leaks: Information seeps out in obtuse code, and unless we decode the information, we will be governed by it. That is why exhortation, pleadings, education, and lectures don't necessarily stop impulsive individuals from committing crimes and often do not make someone who was abandoned as a child feel less rejected in adulthood. The best help we can offer is to resolve the early trauma so that the cortex can finally succeed in its task of inhibition.

The various levels of consciousness have different capacities for integrating pain. In our therapy we see that first-line pains, due to their life-and-death nature, have an enormous charge value that severely taxes the system's integrative and repressive capabilities. If the first line has a capacity of fifty, for example, but first-line pains amount to seventy, then the gating system is overwhelmed and can be permanently impaired. Consequently, first-line pain will have prevented the orderly development and integration of the individual's personality. Later, when the cortex is more operative, leaky gating is more likely to produce aberrations in thinking and psychosocial functioning. When repression fails, the ascending pain can speed up brain activity enormously and threaten the functioning of one's intellect. We may experience this as an "antsy" feeling, with diminished ability to focus or concentrate.

Imprints of early trauma are permanent, constantly threatening to overtax one's repressive capabilities. If repression can "hold," the person may simply become "dead and dull, or depressed." If repression falters, the person suffers. In both cases the suffering is intact. The difference lies only in how effective gating is.

Interestingly, observations of a number of psychogenic epileptics indicate that they have suffered from early anoxia. In an epileptic attack, a current stressor triggers an upwelling of pain with a random massive discharge of neural energy. The repressive gates cannot contain the imprinted energy pushing upward toward consciousness, and the result is an inundation and a total blotting-out of consciousness. As a survival strategy, the victim is rendered unconscious. The individual defends against consciousness with unconsciousness. Similarly, some faint in shock after they witness a catastrophic event. Seizures happen when repression has been too effective for too long. Instead of a single impulsive act, there is an amorphous general release.

BILLY: BREAKING THE SURFACE

In the beginning there was only the womb, the garden of Eden, the cosmos. The golden womb of succor and nurture. It was my golden age, a paradise I never forgot. Then the womb contracted and I couldn't breathe and I later had migraines.

What happened to my mother? She said once that her water broke at home. Another time she said that she stayed in another room contracting so as "not to wake up your father." She held back from going to the hospital and I was born forty-five minutes later. They gave her a shot of Demerol. Whatever happened, it was totally inappropriate.

I'm almost certain I suffered a concussion in the birth canal. At first everything was so smooth and rhythmic, then *wham!* the womb went rigid and slapped my head. The birth scene was, I think, my prototypic seizure. It was, like the first stages of death, a result of helpless anoxia.

As a child I got the message that I wasn't to call for help, complain, or show any signs of imperfection. When my mother was screaming in my face, virtually any response could be dangerous. When I banged my elbow and couldn't call out at age seven, I had a seizure. After being asked whether my brothers and I should go to an orphanage, I seized on a regular basis. The hundreds of seizures I've had in my life were just unconscious attempts to react fully to the initial deathly horror of my being oxygen-starved at birth. Merciful unconscious saved me from knowing something that was too much to know and feel.

Over the past few weeks I have repeatedly felt myself regaining consciousness, halfway out of the birth canal, beginning to breathe. In my feeling everything seemed to be violence and discord. I slurped air in great hiccups. I wriggled to free my arms and head, but mostly I just lay and gulped air. My cries came out sporadically as whoops and wails. The electric buzzing (what I believe was my first seizure) happened with my birth. As I sucked air, my body tingled (the same tingling I get with my seizures) and then coalesced into agony and sensations of suffocation and concussion.

I've slept poorly all my life. My nightmares were full of those same early sensations of suffocation (dreams of drowning and of huge waves keeping me from breathing), and I see how those early sensations were always trying to get out and be free.

The theme of my life has been "no air." That's what I said about my schoolteachers and parents; they gave me no air. In my early feelings I was pawing the air, begging my mother to let me go out on the front porch. I wanted her to sit with me on the porch, to take in the sun, the fresh air.

My headaches went away with my feelings of birth and the lack of oxygen. I think I had no way to discharge the accumulated poisons.

Now in my feeling I'm alive at last. A lifetime spent in agony has come to an end. I want to live, to breathe, to see beauty free from the dark morass I've inhabited all of these years. I am seizure-free. It has now been nineteen years. I still primal, irregularly. I kind of tend to avoid it now since there is never any time, but I try to do it once every couple of months. My concerns have shifted more to rearing my own child.

Anxiety and Panic Attacks

Some say we're living in an age of anxiety and that the widespread existence of anxiety is due to pressures coming from the world around us: crime, danger, job problems, economic insecurity, pollution, and so on. It is true our society lives in an age of anxiety, but it is also an age of pain.

Memories that challenge the repressive system tend to intrude into awareness and make the person uncomfortable. For example, many of us sometimes wake up in the morning feeling depressed, without enthusiasm for the coming day, with a stab of apprehension, emptiness, or loneliness. Typically, the cause is a mystery to us. But it may be that, emerging from the lower levels of consciousness of sleep, we are close to our pain that resides on the second line. In effect, we wake up in a beginning primal, only we don't know it. We drink coffee, have a cigarette, get busy, or take tranquilizers to keep the feeling away. If we knew we were in the grip of unconsciously based feelings and could lie back and let them take over, those morning assaults would eventually cease for all time.

This is also true of anxiety. When our suffering threatens to become specific and burst into conscious-awareness, it is experienced as fear of a memory that is as yet unknown, and is both a fragment of our reaction to the original trauma (visceral terror and panic) and a harbinger of pain on the rise. *Anxiety is a reaction to suffering:* butterflies in the stomach, shortness of breath, perhaps a feeling of impending doom. Anxiety is a diffuse warning system, alerting the organism to immense suffering that is rising toward consciousness.

In its dual role, anxiety is also a fragment of our reaction to the original trauma, a warning that something in the present is resonating with a past imprinted memory. The rapid heart-beat is part of the old memory. It is, therefore, a survival mechanism that makes us vigilant in order to diminish the suffering and keep the third line intact. With its implicit sense of urgency, anxiety is a mandate for action: "I've got to do something, anything, to end this suffering, now!" Anxiety is saying that it's time to have a few drinks, drug yourself, book a ticket to go somewhere, think good thoughts, adopt mysticism, or do whatever you have to do to keep pain out of consciousness.

There are some who constantly complain about their work: "There's no space for me. The pressure's too much. I'm suffocating in this job." This may all be true, but it may also reflect an early imprint where the person was indeed strangling and being crushed at birth. Only a primal will tell us. Remember, it is the job of the neocortex to translate the lower-level imprinted energy pushing at consciousness into something manageable. When the third line has to deal with a massive and dangerous overload of information—such as the memory of oxygen deprivation—it has no alternative but to rationalize the feeling. Thus the person believes his job is strangling him. Gating has blocked the context of the early trauma but is insufficient to keep the suffering from conscious-awareness.

Most of us would be hard-pressed to make the connection between an event forty-five years in the past and negative attitudes toward work in the present. The same imprint can be triggered with a spouse who "leaves me no space," blowing the "trapped" reaction out of proportion to the marital problem itself. Such a person may want a divorce because of sensations and feelings from decades ago.

If the gates are under continuous assault, there may sometimes be panic attacks. Panic is a sign of the first line of consciousness about to burst through to conscious-awareness and signals a sudden break in the defense system. A person who had an original birth imprint of "I've got to get out to save my life" has an engraved desperation. As it mounts toward conscious-awareness, only the panic aspect, the physiologic frenzy, becomes evident. It feels like a sudden terror, and it is. The terror is low-lying energy that has suddenly found its voice.

Panic attacks are traceable and treatable. As soon as there's a lull, a lack of movement or lack of progress, there may be panic. Thus, one keeps traveling all the time, perhaps finding an occupation that keeps one on the move. Such a person may suffer when she cannot travel. But with no access to the past, she must focus that suffering on the present: "I get agitated when I'm home for too long." The real feeling from the birth trauma may be: "I'm terrified when I'm helpless and cannot move!" Because the past is ever-present, because it takes a cortex to be aware of time, it seems like disaster is forever just over the horizon.

JULIE: A WANDERER

When I was in Los Angeles, I couldn't wait to get out. I was feeling overwhelmed by my work and my personal life. All I could think about was getting away on a trip. But when I finally went, I kept having the feeling that I had to get out of where I was, just as I had felt in Los Angeles. At first, there would be a sense of relief when I arrived somewhere because I had, in fact, acted out the feeling and got away. But after I had been there for a very short time, the feeling would come up again, and all I could think about was wanting to get away. So I would go on to the next place and after a short time, the feeling would come up again, and I would want to move on. The feeling is the one I had at birth, which is, *"I have got to get out of here!"* It's a terribly compelling feeling that drives me. I just want to go from place to place to get away from that bad feeling.

It's the same with any kind of routine job; that's why I have always avoided anything that was routine. There is no movement in routine. For me, no movement has always been the danger. The thing is, when you run away from something, it is always there when you get back. The more I move, the more the feeling moves with me. I am sure that if I had gone on being driven, I would have collapsed from a heart attack as a young woman.

The pressure is really a physical sensation. I am probably unconscious in some respects, but I am sure aware of the pressure. It is like you are driven in your body; that's why I can never sit still. I always have to be doing something. I'm getting up, doing this, doing that, always moving. I guess moving meant life for me; it meant survival.

What's awful about my situation is that I can't stand peace. Peace gets to be like routine. There is so much turbulence inside me that I have to get out and drive somewhere in order to get peace. The only peace I seem to know is in movement, so I can never relax and just rest.

Although researchers at Harvard University's School of Public Health recently reported that anxiety is becoming one of the strongest risk factors for sudden death by cardiac arrest, they do not speculate as to the cause of that anxiety. Recent research has found that men who complain of chronic anxiety are six times more likely than those who are free of it to suffer from sudden cardiac death. Anxiety is most definitely physiological; the heart pumps in a frenzied flight. But from what? Pain. Eventually, the constant stress may trigger coronary vessel spasm and a heart attack. The proof? When patient after patient feels his or her early pain (which is the ultimate stressor), the anxiety disappears. And indeed, the beginning phase of most primals is an anxiety attack, including radical rises in body temperature, blood pressure, and heart rate.

Drugs that help gating will usually reduce the frenzy of the heart. It is not that the frenzy is no longer there. What has happened is that *the reactivity to the imprint has been blocked—a very important difference.* Most tranquilizers ensure that the supply of serotonin and endorphins is adequate. This is what Prozac does. So much has been written lately about the magical powers of such drugs, but in almost no case do they actually change personality. What they do is aid repression in order to keep pain out of consciousness. Drugs like Prozac temporarily achieve what a prefrontal lobotomy does in a permanent way: The former blocks feelings on lower levels and prevents them from turning into overt suffering, while a lobotomy physically severs the lower feeling centers from the evaluative higher areas. The pain is still there, it just doesn't bother the individual anymore. Some drugs prescribed by psychiatrists today work on certain catecholamines (a class of neurotransmitters) and galvanize the system, giving us more energy and a greater ability to withstand stress.

When a person has leaky gates and is flooded with pain, concentration becomes difficult, associated with the inability to focus on a single subject. This is because the individual cannot repress the diverse impulses from a variety of early traumas impinging on his consciousness. The person does not feel the impinging impulses for what they are. All he knows is that he cannot concentrate because of the "noise" in his head. Such individuals are notoriously poor sleepers. Going to sleep requires progressive repression of levels of consciousness, beginning with the third-line cortex, traversing down to the dream level or second line, and finally progressing to deep sleep on the first line. Repression is deficient if the gates are damaged. It may take constant repressive-type sleeping pills to help put the brain to sleep. This may be called an "addiction," but it is only to make up for a real deficit in internally produced repressors caused by early traumas. Note that tranquilizers work on *lower* centers to block obsessions in *higher* centers.

Individuals who lacked oxygen at birth often have difficulty later in life in planning as well as sticking to plans. Lacking self-discipline, they find it highly difficult to study systematically, find and hold on to a job, and maintain relationships, because they have no coherent third line to tell them about the far-reaching consequences of their acts. They need great freedom and "room to breathe." They act out until they are restrained in one way or another by external forces. For example, if they talk too much, someone else will have to stop them because they have lost their internal boundaries. Such people need interruptions from steady work, such as constant phone calls. If such distractions don't exist, they will create them. They need exactly what happened to them originally: detours from their goal.

All of the above—poor concentration, great distractibility, erratic conduct, and attention deficit disorders—are third-line dysfunctions and should not be classified as separate problems. It happens to most leaky gaters, who cannot shut out the accumulated pains of a lifetime that are moving toward conscious-awareness at all times. Unfortunately, before they get there, gating steps in and blocks consciousness.

When repression is iron-clad, when there are relatively few outlets for feelings and all of the energy is bottled up inside, the pressure builds, and blood pressure mounts and may become life-endangering. This unrelieved pressure, which may have caused chronic colds or asthma during childhood, may eventually lead to chronic health problems in adulthood, not the least of which may be some form of cancer.

DANNY: ANOXIA, ANXIETY, AND ASTHMA

It is not true that a person who is fearful is necessarily lacking in courage. To the contrary, and in my case, I think it's fair to say that I have been a courageous person. Yet, for most of my life, I have been plagued by crippling anxiety. In what appears to be a paradox, I seem to be calmest when there is external crisis. It's as if the unsettling conditions on the outside match, in valence, my internal alarm, creating a balance or subjective experience of calm.

In my experience both as a patient in psychotherapy and as a school psychologist, I have encountered few if any persons who experience anxiety exactly as I do. Yet I am sure that the following description will not be unfamiliar to anxiety sufferers. My anxiety presents itself in social situations where there is time for anticipation and where some level of performance is required. In such situations I have all the symptoms of a sympathetic nervous system crisis—You know, the old "fight or flight" syndrome. Subjectively, I feel my body cold and shivering. Coherence in thought processes dissipates as my conscious brain races in a vain effort to hold the line against a tide of upsurging pain. I am shaky, my legs fail me, there is nothing to support me. Clearly, the pain surging is coming from a time and place before motor development was mature. No deep breath, no attempt at muscular relaxation, and no thoughts, beliefs, or ideas can contain such pain.

Long before I became familiar with primal theory, I was curious about the similarity in subjective sensations of a panic attack and an asthma attack. Now, it is clear to me that three of the conditions that I have had in my life, namely, asthma, low back problems, and panic, have more than a coincidental relationship. Their common thread is their origin, which I now believe to be one of oxygen deprivation at or around the time of birth. This belief is based on my experience as a student at Dr. Janov's Primal Center and is also inferred from Dr. John Sarno's discussion of oxygen deprivation in his book *Healing Back Pain*.

I am one who functions mostly on intellect and wit. Yet it is fragile, constantly under siege. Reinforcements in the form of medication, namely early pain blockers, are necessary to stem the tide. On those occasions when I have been able to feel deeply, it is because the first line has been sufficiently quelled. Suddenly and without effort, the second line in the form of a wave of sadness becomes accessible. Unfortunately, these occasions are few and far between. The more typical sensation is that even if I start to cry, the ever-present first line swallows the second line, allowing only surface access to feelings, that is, shallow crying.

Obsessions and Compulsions

Sometimes unknown messages surging up from below produce compulsive ideas and obsessive acts. Obsessions represent the clash between rising feelings held in storage on lower levels and cortical forces pushing them back. The recurring fearful thought, *Did I lock the door downstairs?* drives an obsession to try the locks twenty times a day. Fear has driven through the faulty gates to the prefrontal cortex, where obsessive ideas are organized. The specific content—"I don't feel safe!"—still lies below. The obsession is a third-line act-out of a first- and second-line feeling, a cortical attempt to try to feel safe after being made to feel unsafe throughout one's childhood. One doesn't even know that one feels profoundly unsafe, yet it is that very feeling that moves the cortex to decide to try the locks over and over. That is why obsessions and compulsions are easily treated in our therapy; we simply allow the unsafe feelings to rise to consciousness. Then compulsions are no longer pressed into service to hide them.

SYLVIA: THE CHAOS WITHIN

I have always lived by lists. I have a general one for use day by day, and another one for weekends. Despite this seeming organization, I am a messy person. I never feel "caught up" or that I have it all together. My purse is jam-packed with "essentials," which I almost never need but can't let go of. Because I never was taken care of as a kid, my father left us and Mom went to work, I never developed a trust in myself. I don't trust myself to remember and I'm terrified to make a mistake, so I compile list after list. Lists reassure me.

I am upset if someone comes early or unexpectedly. It disturbs my routine. I don't easily adapt to change. I need warning. I need to feel in control of every situation. My preset ideas take precedence over my feelings. I need to have a certain regimentation and will stick to something no matter what the inconvenience or discomfort. I hate and love rules. I detest unstructured social situations where I might meet strangers and don't know what to say. I fear that I can't gauge how I or they will react, and then I feel stuck as I was originally at birth, and later in my crazy home.

My constant worry is not being able to take care of things properly. It is part of the helplessness I felt as a child. In school I worried all of the time—about losing my books, umbrella, keys, and so on. I needed my mother to help me and make me feel secure, but she was away at work.

When my teacher told me something nice, I felt desperate, like I couldn't hold on to his words. So I wrote them down and kept them in my purse. For weeks I had to take the paper out and look at it and feel good. It was like getting a shot of love each time. Obviously, I was holding back feeling so bad about myself. I see now how many of my hundreds of rituals are designed to keep those bad feelings and my anxiety away. I never had anyone at home to reassure me. My rituals, at least, serve that function.

When I'm alone my mind works overtime, going over my latest schemes to make life better. It's a way of life. If someone hurts my feelings I obsess about it constantly; what I should have said or done, what I'm going to say. I go over and over the shortcomings of my boss, which is identical to what I did with my mother.

The clearest example of this revolves around romance and sex. If I develop a crush on someone, I spend my waking hours thinking about him, working out hundreds of fantasies of how we will be together (gazes, hugs, kisses, romance, and sex). I now see how these fantasies are spun out of a longing in my body to be held and loved. It's half pleasure, half pain. It goes to the longing I had for my mother when I was little. As my needs come up I get more and more obsessive in my thoughts. I flirt outrageously during these times. I literally feel like an animal in heat.

I needed love from my mother with every cell in my body; as early as the crib I could feel it. And no one ever came to soothe me. I have to set up situations now where I can re-create the feeling of longing I had for my mother, so I obsess about men. Now my need has become erotic. The more I feel my early need, the less I obsess erotically about men in my life.

I see how chaotic I feel inside. Trying to make some order outside reassures me. Part of me feels so out of control that I have to control everything. I feel like if I don't try to keep it all together I'm going to fly apart. My birth and my home life were pure chaos. I needed stability and routine; so I make it everywhere I go.

The reason tranquilizers work on obsessions is that they quell the pain from below, thereby putting less pressure on the cortex. Without the pressure from below, the cortex no longer has to manufacture obsessions and worries. When the prefrontal cortex is overwhelmed or damaged, feelings cannot be put down so easily. Then shapeless fears, obsessions, and compulsions take form automatically. Fear can find new worries each and every minute. The person is afraid of her history and imagines it is in the future. It is about a catastrophe *which has already happened.*

In a book titled *Over and Over Again*, Fugen Neziroglu and J. A. Yaryura-Tobias discuss obsessive-compulsive disorders (OCDs). After discussing all of the concomitants of the disorder, such as doubt, perfectionism, and so on, they assert the following: "OCD is not curable." They also state that it is a "nonsensical" symptom, and one must learn to let go of control in order to conquer it.

The problem here is the same no matter what book discusses what symptoms: taking the symptom as the disorder while not seeing the dialectic—that symptoms are an attempt to establish an important homeostasis, not something to be overcome with this method or that. Obsessions are not to be "overcome." They are part of the psychic economy. They have an important function as part of the defense mechanism. It is not a matter of learning to give up control. It is a matter of keeping that control until one has experienced the terror that requires such control for mental stability. The person who is terrified must keep that terror away. One way to do that is to disperse it into various fears, doubts, and apprehensions that are called obsessions. These are attempts to make the terror manageable.

Neziroglu and Yaryura-Tobias go on to say that the "person is not the illness. They have an illness." I disagree. The person is the illness. It is in her physiology, in her brain and blood cells. They treat it as if the illness is something apart from the person, which cannot be the case. It is embedded inside the human being. The symptoms are not "nonsensical." Once we understand what lies below, we see that the obsessions and compulsions make perfect sense. We should know that no symptom exists gratuitously. It is the counterpart of something else. The problem in psychology has been to take the symptom as something viable and treat it as if it has no roots, particularly no biological roots.

The authors discuss the symptoms as "intrusions." And that is what they are: intrusions of low-level imprints into conscious-awareness. The person now becomes aware of the intrusion instead of what is intruding. One little step more and he would get it right. It is not thoughts that are intruding; it is feelings, which then drive thoughts in an attempt to master the feeling.

KAL: LETTING GO OF FEAR

I was born in England. Throughout my life I have had strange things happen to me. When I was young I used to lie in my bed and feel like the room seemed to be closing in on me and was going to crush me. I was always obsessed with compulsive thoughts and strange dreams, I always thought I had cancer or some kind of disease and thought that something just wasn't right inside. My mum is an alcoholic and my father finds it so hard to show any kind of love or warmth whatsoever. He even had (has) trouble calling me by my name. Instead of saying "Kal" he would say "Oi, you!" But I grew up thinking that all this was totally normal and that this is how families are—crazed, drunken, angry people. I suffered many long nights of being scared to death in my bed when arguments would break out between my parents and all hell would break loose. I felt they could come in at any moment and kill me. I struggled on and on. I found drink at age fourteen and drugs at age fifteen. After a couple of years of smoking dope, doing speed, and drinking heavily, I was sixteen and at a cousin's house when I mixed some dope into a drink. I had never done this before and had heard that you get really high. My cousin and I both had a hash coffee. I put a little too much in and about thirty minutes later began feeling terror, a kind of terror I had never felt before. I fell to the floor and felt myself choking and being compressed. I was conscious of it all. My body became numb and I lost total function of my arms and legs, too. All I could do was twitch uncontrollably on the bed. Two hours later I began to come back. But since that day I had sensations shooting through my body on a regular basis and was always in fear that I was going to suddenly choke to death. Little did I know then that what I had was a birth experience, only a very messed-up one due to the drugs trashing my gating system.

When I started my therapy I still believed deep inside that I was going through something that nobody would understand. Then one night I awoke in total fear. I let myself go into the fear, and then—*bang*—all I could see was a bright light, a light that hurt so much I could barely see. It was a horrible sensation. My body was shaking like a jackhammer. I had just been born. I felt a hand grab my legs and turn me upside down above the floor. I was swinging helplessly in the air in total terror. Then a hand struck me on my back and I felt a sharp, burning pain. For the next two weeks I felt totally human and real. I was not anxious and had no terror seeping through. I was alive, something I had not been for many, many years.

I phoned my mum up and asked her, "Why did you let them hang me upside down and hit my back?" which she incidentally had never, ever told me about. She was totally shocked and I think I scared her with how much I knew, telling her how my back had been hurting for years and had required treatment. After my birth experience, the pain went away totally and my back and whole body seemed to sit comfortably in place. What damaged my back was the big slap I received straight after birth.

I would like to mention another major insight I had. When I was very young I used to be terrified of "the hand." I used to think a hand was going to make its way into my bed and grab me. I used to tuck myself tightly in my bed to keep the so-called hand out. Well, now I know where it comes from. I was in a feeling and suddenly I started wrapping the covers around my body tightly. I felt cold and scared and then it came to me. My granddad was trying to touch me under the covers. I don't believe he raped me, but his hand felt around, seeking me out.

I now no longer feel like I am going crazy. I am a much more caring person. I still have a long way to go, but I am making very good progress and I know I will have to feel my birth and other feelings probably for the rest of my life, but it's worth it.

In her mystery novel *Original Sin*, author P. D. James gives an example of how a terrifying birth can give rise to fears that deceptively appear to arise out of present circumstances but are really echoes of the past:

It never occurred to the adults that she found the foot tunnel terrifying, and she would have died rather than tell them. She had known from early childhood that her father admired courage above all virtues. She would walk between them, holding their hands in a simulation of childhood meekness, trying not to grasp their fingers too hard, keeping her eyes down so they couldn't see they were tightly closed, smelling the distinctive tunnel smell, hearing the echo of their feet and picturing above them that great weight of slopping water, terrifying in its power, which one morning would break the tunnel roof and begin to seep through, at first in heavy drops as the tiles cracked and then, suddenly, in a thundering wave, black and evil-smelling, sweeping them off their feet, swirling and rising, until there was nothing between their fighting bodies and screaming mouths but a few inches of space and air. And then not even that.

There is only one key biologic defense against pain: repression.
When repression is faulty, secondary defenses come into play.
Drugs, drinking, smoking, constant talking, constant movement, overeating, obsessions, compulsions, and phobias are all
secondary defenses. They take up the slack, absorbing and discharging the escaping energy. One may become constantly
sexual, for example, because repression alone is inadequate.
One may masturbate several times a day to relieve the pressure. This rising tension and need for relief is what underlies
addiction to painkilling drugs. If one is surrounded by drugs
during one's youth, drugs may be the track taken. If one grows
up in an atmosphere where fat babies are considered healthy,
then overeating may be the symptom. Whether the pain results in obsessions, phobias, substance abuse, or gorging on
food, these are signs of inadequate gating and different cul-
tural upbringing, not separate diseases.

Attention Deficit Disorder

Attention deficit disorder (ADD) is an ailment common in children, characterized by distractibility, impulsiveness, and hyperactivity. Children with ADD have a hard time sitting still
and have problems learning. The name *attention deficit disorder*
describes the person's behavior but does nothing to explain the
cause. Scientists are not sure what causes it, but they do know
that a stimulant called Ritalin helps.

The symptoms of attention deficit disorder indicate faulty
inhibition. Ritalin activates brain structures that ultimately
work on the cortex to aid inhibition resulting in slower movement, less hyperactivity, and focused attention. Ritalin also inhibits the suffering system that ordinarily causes thought
disruptions and distractibility.

ADD, like many other syndromes, may be the result of anoxic damage during birth or other severe early trauma. This
damage produces faulty gating, causing all of the primal power
sequestered below to erupt into consciousness. The person
cannot stay with something for very long because there is too

much pain pushing from below scattering thoughts. Again, it is rarely felt as pain. It is simply agitation. The child or adult simply cannot inhibit because early trauma disrupted inhibitory functions of the cortex. When we reduce pain levels in our patients, obsessions subside. The cortex is no longer required to hold back feelings. Years ago, both epilepsy and hyperactivity in children were treated with Ritalin and other activating drugs. Such drugs "normalize" the brain by increasing prefrontal activity. I recall a therapist who came to work in our training program. Early on, he says he found that the minute there was a lull in the session he was conducting, "*Bang!* There was an eruption and the old pain kicked in and set me off on a hypervigilant state again." To slow down was to be in danger of death from the original imprint at birth. His system combated this by being hyperalert against the danger. The result was poor therapy as he pushed the patient too soon, not allowing her time to feel what was coming up.

DARYL: THE QUEST FOR RELIEF

I was born in Los Angeles in 1950. My mother was English and met my father during World War II while he was stationed in England. He was born and raised in New York.

My mother is a stone cold lady who cannot stand to see anyone enjoy themselves. She is obsessed with herself and only feels good when others are suffering. My father was absent. He was never around and to this day he forgets my name. Neither of them showed any warmth toward me, let alone toward each other. I was never touched, played with, or showed any kind of attention.

When I was young I could not keep still. I loved running around. I couldn't concentrate very well unless something was really stimulating or I was active. I loved to watch TV. It could hold my attention. And my mother hated to see me enjoy myself so she would not let me play. She would force me to sit in corners and literally not move.

I grew up thinking that this was totally normal behavior on my parents' part, that there was something terribly wrong with me and that anything I wanted or needed was a defect in me. I was constantly told that I was a lazy, good-for-nothing son-of-a-bitch who wouldn't amount to anything. I felt so bad that I had impulses to cuddle up to my mother or to ask her for any attention. When I did, she would literally push me away. I felt there was something wrong with me for even thinking or feeling that I wanted her touch.

I suffered terrible loneliness. I was terminally hyperactive. Everything I did met with anger and punishment. So I started to close myself off from the hurt and the anguish and I started to hate them. I started to steal from them and I took the thing they prized most: money. I became agitated, got into fights in school, and became disruptive in the classroom.

At the age of seven, I was clinically diagnosed with having hyperactivity disorder. The school psychologist said I was emotionally disturbed.

I was expelled from junior high school at the age of twelve for being disruptive and was sent to boarding school. They tied me up with rope and put me into solitary confinement.

My mother told me I was a paranoid schizophrenic and my father thought nothing of chasing me with a fireplace poker and ramming it into my back. I ended up hating them and everything they stood for. The trouble was, the more I hated them, the lonelier I felt. I stopped all contact with my parents and still do not have any contact with them to this day.

I started taking any drug I could get my hands on: pot, downers, LSD, opium, and uppers. I thought I was finally going to get some relief. What I really needed was attention. One night, after ingesting LSD with a girlfriend, I was lying with her and I started to feel myself sinking into the pit of my stomach. I found myself just crying terribly and I could not stop. A picture of my mother's face appeared in my mind's eye and I wept for what seemed like hours. All this hurt and anguish I had buried had come back up. It was terrifying and yet I felt a relief afterward I had not known before. Little did I know that I had just experienced something akin to a primal.

About two years later I picked up a book called *The Primal Scream*. I read it and knew right then and there what I had partially experienced, and what I needed to do was to go for primal therapy.

When I began therapy, I was scared shitless but I was determined to do everything I could to make it work. I had failed at everything I had tried. Conventional therapy didn't work, I had been kicked out of junior high school, relationships had always ended in disaster, and work situations always ended in disaster with me either being fired or quitting.

I pushed myself to feel. The trouble was, the more I pushed, the more pressure I put on myself, the more frenzied I became, the less I could feel. I knew that if I could start to cry, I could relieve myself of some of this internal pressure that I constantly was under. But whenever I could cry, it would come up and leave so quickly.

I found a therapist at the Primal Center who showed genuine warmth toward me. I have always been hypervigilant to people who patronize or pretend to be warm and I didn't know what to make of it. I think I even tried to test it by pushing her away. But as I began to trust that she would not use my feelings against me, my hypervigilance began to let down. I began to allow her to get closer in the sense that I started to be able to express some of the fears and shame I felt about myself. As I started to do this I could feel myself resisting every step closer I came to feeling. With every step closer, there seemed to be some other shameful thing I had to say, and finally the dam burst and I was in agony on the floor, crying like a two-year-old, in the memory of what was happening to me. I was now back in the corner at the age of five, crying for my mommy to pay attention to me and feeling her response of utter hate that I was even moving a muscle. The words that I had so desperately looked for in past sessions and that never came now just came by themselves. "I'm sorry. . . . I'm sorry you hurt me. . . . I'm sorry I hurt. . . . I'm sorry I need you, because you hurt me!"

I found myself banging my head against the wall of the therapy room, and actually feeling a sense of relief. I found out much later that during labor I kept banging my head against my mother's cervix over and over. They had to pull me out with forceps, and in the process the doctor had crushed my skull and broken blood vessels all around my eyes and I was born with a bloody head. I would never have even known to ask about this if I hadn't had the feeling.

Primal therapy is not about pain. Pain is what has always been there. Primal therapy is really about *relief*. The relief I feel after a primal is why I go through the suffering component of feeling. It makes it possible to go out and be with people, to be able to let in warmth and to be able to give attention to others. It is about being able to sleep at night without tossing and turning.

Attention deficit hyperactivity disorder is a perfect name for the particular symptoms I suffer from. Having received no attention from my parents, I was forced to distract myself in any way I could so as not to have to face the awful truth that I was hated and not wanted, that I was a burden. The only outlet I had available to me was the only outlet I had available during my birth. Weakness and helplessness set in during my struggle to be born, because my mother would not dilate. I was getting nowhere and losing the battle to be born, losing available oxygen in my struggle to be born. I know this for a fact, through the birth primals I have had to feel and through outside sources who have verified what happened during my birth.

Through the years I have tried various means to relieve the internal pressure inside myself. Exercise, drugs, sex, bad relationships, you name it, but to no avail. The only way I can relieve it is when I am in the feeling and it is connected to the memory of the event itself. Afterward, that awful uncomfortable drive is no longer pressing and only the memory of what happened is left. The memory doesn't have force anymore. It is just what it is, a memory, no more, no less. The driven part of it has been felt for what it is; my need for attention that never came, the need for love that never was there, the need to breathe and move, and finally those same needs on a level before there were any words to describe them.

What Is Crazy?

Someone who is neurotic may worry now and then and may feel depressed from time to time but generally is thought of as functioning more or less "normally" in the world. Her problems are typically chalked up not to her individual history but to current factors in her environment and relationships. If she goes for treatment, her symptoms are taken at face value, and treated with drugs, "talking therapies," stress-reduction techniques, and so on. What generates them is usually ignored.

PSYCHOSIS AS FAULTY NEUROSIS

When neurosis fails, psychosis may result. Psychosis is what happens when the repressive gates leak constantly. To be psychotic is to appear to be "out of touch with reality" or "crazy." Psychotics have bizarre ideas and exhibit unusual behavior because there is too much reality inside. It is a desperate last-ditch effort to keep overwhelming pain repressed. Consider two so-called psychotic delusions from two different patients of mine:

"I caused the war. They're killing each other because of me." "What war?" I ask. She answers, *"the* war."

"There is a lady in England who is sending messages through the television to cut off my breasts."

Both are psychotic statements. Neither one is merely a distortion of reality; both are total fabrications. When pain is near, many people adopt a socially sanctioned unreal belief: "I am saved. God is watching over me." Sometimes it's a more idiosyncratic belief; one sees himself as the latest reincarnation of Jesus Christ or finds that he can communicate with aliens from outer space. The more bizarre the idea, the greater the valence of unintegrated pain from childhood.

The degree of unreality is generally commensurate with the force of imprinted reality impinging on conscious-awareness. Usually a major disaster or a series of losses compounds early trauma. By conventional standards, the two patients who vocalized the delusions I mentioned above are "crazy." They might be said to have "lost touch with reality." Their thinking has "gone wrong." But thoughts don't "go wrong." Thoughts follow the lead of feelings and biologic distortions at all levels of consciousness.

So what is being "crazy"? "Crazy" is a dislocation of function. It is a quantum leap beyond being merely neurotic. It's the difference between thinking someone who offers to help you is insinuating that you're helpless and thinking that you're the cause of a war somewhere.

One usually "goes crazy" because the only alternative is to feel the catastrophic trauma surging toward the third line. Psychosis is the last waystation, the court of last resort before the naked pain makes it through to consciousness. Since we have seen what reactivity to even moderate pain means, we know that full reactivity to the kind of pain residing in psychotics can be life-threatening. It no doubt was life-threatening when it occurred, and for that reason was shut down. Later on it is consciousness-threatening. The cortex is pressed into service to ward off total consciousness. In this sense, psychosis is often a defense against death, an alternative to death. The system seems to say: "Better crazy than dead!"

We are captives of our cellular biology, not its masters. You can't talk a psychotic out of his delusional ideas. Trying to get a psychotic to "face reality" is a contradiction in terms. He's crazy because he can't face it. He's crazy because reality is nudging him all of the time.

One can be "crazy," as well, on the first line or second line. One can walk down the street talking to oneself, making odd gestures over and over again (second line), or one can be totally immobile, as in catatonia (first line). This person has gone crazy without the aid of ideas, has withdrawn from the world and lives inside herself completely. It all depends on the previous personality structure. A withdrawn, nonverbal parasympath may become totally immobile during a psychotic break. Years ago I played in a band at the Brentwood Neuropsychiatric Hospital called the Psychopathic Syncopators. One of the members (all patients) had what was called waxy flexibility. One could turn his arms in an upright position and they would stay there as though made of wax. This was a first-line parasympath psychosis. He was mostly nonverbal, but he could play music. Another second-line psychosis patient would go into a false rage every fifteen minutes, start to pound the walls, scream out, and then stop himself. He had no specific delusions or hallucinations; it was emotions out of control. You don't need ideas to be crazy.

Being "crazy" on the third line can involve notions such as that of the woman who believed messages were being broadcast over the TV to lop off her breasts. Sometimes the current pain is so great that ideas cannot absorb it. Say the person has lost a job, lost his spouse, gone broke, and had his home seized by the bank. These shattering current blows, combined with old pain, are too much for the third line, and a serious act-out occurs. His emotions burst through, uncontrolled, and he runs amuck on a killing spree, or just starts shouting at everyone on the street.

There are as many ways to go crazy as there are people, just as there are many ways to be neurotic. The way one goes crazy is largely determined by the prototype, the initially imprinted survival response against overwhelming trauma. If one tends to "implode" under stress, the psychosis will be more of the schizoid-withdrawn type. The emotion is flat, there is no "contact," no direct eye gaze, and hardly any words expressed. The sense is that the person is not there: Nobody's home. If one acts furiously to ward off pain, the psychosis will likely be of the manic variety: hyperactivity, behavior out of control, with explosiveness and volatility.

OUT OF THE PAST

Normally, we think of crazy as a state in which the past is totally the present, and there is no differentiation of past from present. Take the first delusion I mentioned earlier: "I caused the war. They're killing each other because of me." After many months of feeling in primal therapy, this patient finally felt the terrible feeling from which this idea originated: "I was the cause of the breakup of my parents when I was six years of age." Her mother had told her so immediately following a violent argument between her parents. Her father stormed out for good, and her life changed radically. She was always made to feel it was her fault. Not only did she lose her father, but a six-year-old was made to feel that she was the cause. On top of that her mother began to drink, neglected the child, and was often violent. The child became disturbed, was thrown out of school, began to drink and take drugs early on, and finally became delusional.

She had caused the war between her parents, and that was a catastrophic feeling. Later, the early context was lost and it became a delusion: "I caused the war." The past became the present with not enough third line to step back and say, "That's crazy." She thought her ideation was real because she had no idea that there was a past that fed the present. She was considered crazy. Her ideation was real, just out of context. Once she put it in context, she was no longer psychotic; she was in terrible pain. Having felt that pain, she knew where the origin of her ideas lay.

My other patient, the one who perceived that someone in Europe was sending a message through the television to cut off her breasts, actually took action against "the evil forces" that were sending these messages. She hung icons around her neck, which she never took off even while showering. She explained that she "had to check the icons all of the time to make sure they were there." Why did she need them? To ward off the evil forces. "If I wasn't protected, my breasts would be taken away." After numerous primals over a period of many months, the feelings this patient finally had were: "I feel unloved. I must be ugly to be so rejected. If my breasts are cut off I will have to feel how I feel . . . ugly, with no hope of love." She explained that there was a power outside of her (which was really the power of her feelings inside of her) that could make her feel ugly and unloved. The real power was her parents who rejected her and made her feel, therefore, ugly.

What did her delusional ideas mean? Her third line was busy trying to find a hook, a rationale, a behavior that could save her from the hopelessness. She created beliefs that helped her. There were times when she knew that her beliefs and behavior were "crazy." She was merely obsessional; she could still distinguish between sense and nonsense. But then her obsession turned into psychosis, and she became convinced of the reality of her beliefs. And the only way to make her "not crazy" was for her to relive how ugly and unloved she really felt.

"THOUGHT DISORDER" OR "THOUGHTS IN DISORDER"?

When one becomes paranoid and psychotic, there is a leap into a different kind of ideation that is "crazy" on the face of it. One patient told me that General Manuel Noriega was somehow using the television to direct thoughts at him. There is a transition from simple suspiciousness, "I don't think this guy likes me," to paranoia, as in "People on the street are laughing behind my back." It is a matter of how well the gates work (and the level of pain) as to whether one is obsessional or psychotic. In paranoia the ideas are bizarre because the third-line mind has to "stretch" to make feelings rational that have no intrinsic rationality. The feelings a young child has when sent away from home for no apparent reason, or due to severe anesthetic asphyxiation at birth, never had a concept to wrap around them. Suffocation during birth is not a rational experience that can be explained away; it can only be experienced for what it is. But since the person has no idea that there is trauma, she has no option but to try to make the experience rational: "They want to strangle me. So-and-so is suffocating me." The rationale is, of course, going to be strange, because the experience occurred before the ability to be logical.

Obviously, when someone is convinced that people are out to get him—the window cleaner, the janitor, the mailman, an anonymous person he passes on the street—the danger isn't specifically occurring in the present. The damage had been done in the past. Those whom he imagines are trying to hurt him now are merely symbols of those who hurt him back then. "Someone's out to get me" may mean that he was constantly hurt as a child for no reason and he now imagines it is in the present. Father coming home drunk and beating up the children has no logic. But those experiences linger and, with enough additional pain, can later turn into "They are trying to hurt me." It is logical to expect hurt when you have been hurt all of your early life.

You're in trouble when you are unable to reflect on your thoughts. It means that the totality of your thinking processes is the captive of buried feelings, and that there is no independence of thought apart from them. You are not aware that your idea that Martians follow you wherever you go is crazy. You're convinced it is true, and you constantly do things in order to elude them. Freud described this condition as not having enough ego left.

The patient who perceived the messages from Europe was able to judge that her ideation was crazy only at times when the pain was better repressed. She knew, during her neurotic-obsessional phase, that if she didn't keep her compulsions, the delusions would enter and plague her. She explained: "The delusions were sitting behind the obsessions, like the obsessions were holding back the delusions." The whole obsessive apparatus kept her from knowing that it was past pain she was dealing with. That is the function of unreal beliefs: They absorb the pain so that it remains unconscious.

A patient told one of our therapists that the latter wore a black dress that day because she knew doom was coming and it was her way of informing the patient that a catastrophe was on the way. The catastrophe *was* on the way; it was the patient's feelings of total doom derived from being sent to a foster home at age five. Another patient believed that the therapist moved a pillow into the corner to send him (the patient) a message that he was hopeless. "It was a trick to get me to quit therapy," he explained. The variety of unreal beliefs is endless.

When one's thought process is not attenuated by any notion of reality, it is generally known as a thought disorder. Many psychoses fall under this rubric. But they are never just thought disorders. Inside the delusions one finds the real driving feelings, just as inside a convoluted dream story lies the real feelings that brought it into existence. We don't attribute bad dreams to an "image disorder." Images accommodate the feelings. "Being crazy" is not just "mental" illness. It is a total state, a disease, with mental or ideational manifestations. The ideas are not the disease. They are what the person does with the imprint. *There is no such thing as a thought disorder, but there are thoughts in disorder when feelings are pressing to scramble them.* And the drugs used to treat psychosis don't just work on thought processes. The drugs work on lower centers and thereby help repression along.

The problem in psychosis is that the defense system has been shattered. It is no accident that, in primal therapy, seriously troubled patients invariably relive birth in the first three weeks of therapy. The pain is right on top. Usually, tranquilizers are called for to help the patient repress until some of the pain is out of the way. *Drugs are not the treatment here; they are used so that treatment can happen.*

Hallucinogenic drugs like LSD can shatter defenses and lead to psychosis. What sometimes happens months after an LSD trip is that the person develops what I call a benign psychosis. He becomes mystical, may become a believer in UFOs or "channeling" or a Hindu deity. For the most part he can conduct his life and manage to appear rational. He simply has irrational ideas that surge forth from time to time. These pockets of insanity are relief valves designed to keep him "sane," a benign psychosis to maintain sanity. The hallucinogens that give one instantaneous, profound access are the most dangerous because their effects last a lifetime, particularly among those who have had more than fifteen or twenty LSD trips. A person who takes too many hallucinogens becomes a poor sleeper, cannot focus or concentrate, is fidgety and flighty. Why? Because the drug has caused leaky gates and a deficient serotonin system.

We must not neglect incest, particularly in women, which sets psychosis in motion. The birth trauma plus incest for a woman is almost a sure prescription for later psychosis. One of my patients saw violent and dangerous eyes everywhere: on mannequins in store windows, peering at her from other cars, and so on. Years later, during a reliving of incest, it turned out that those eyes where her father's, hovering over her at night as she lay there, terrified out of her mind.

There is some controversy as to whether psychosis, along with attention deficit disorder, manic-depression, and cancer, is genetic. It may well be that there is a genetic factor in these and other afflictions. But it takes an interaction with the environment, traumas from the time of conception, to make genetic possibilities manifest. The reason that psychosis has been laid so often to genetically determined biochemical factors is that the field of psychology has overlooked birth and prebirth events: nine months of trauma undergone by a nervous system that is fragile and vulnerable and has not as yet developed defenses that diminish the impact of the pain.

Our success in helping psychotics heal in our therapy is another indication of the power of feelings. When traumatic feelings are unfelt, they can transform one's neurosis into psychosis. Feeling them can transform one from psychotic to merely neurotic. Eliminating the pain reduces the psychosis and neurosis systematically.

Sleep and Dreams

The brain doesn't change into something else when we sleep. Every night in sleep, we revisit our ancient history in reverse order, visiting levels of consciousness we ordinarily avoid during the daytime. When we fall asleep, the third line is repressed, so that we begin to exist on lower levels. Or, conversely, in order to begin to sleep we must first begin to repress third-line consciousness. We slip then into dream sleep (second-line), then deep sleep (first-line), moving ever farther away from consciousness. We travel back in time to our beginnings, the dawn of the species, the first-line, instinctual, salamander brain. We journey back in a kind of coma with only our vital functions operating. Coming back up from deep sleep, we follow our evolutionary development, traveling back up through dream levels to third-line consciousness and wakefulness.

Why do we dream? Because like all else in human life, our thoughts and behavior must serve a survival function. Not surprisingly, one of the agents producing sleep is serotonin. This neurotransmitter suppresses levels of consciousness and helps us become unconscious; the same happens with pain. The hot new drugs for sleep are melatonin enhancers, which also increase serotonin levels. Dreams encapsulate lower-level rising pain. Dreams disguise and attenuate the force of the pain, winding a story around it so that we can go on sleeping, healing, and repairing.

When one's dreams can no longer hold back the primal tide, one has nightmares—the psychosis of sleep. Very low-lying imprints move upward and press against the imaging (second-line) and thought (third-line) levels. The story is insufficient to hold back the frenzy and panic, and it bursts forth. "I'm being crushed and suffocated by a large black hand; I'm being squeezed to death by a monster with a death mask." Nightmares have that bizarre quality that characterizes waking psychosis, with its "crazy" ideas.

The story of a nightmare is usually not particularly complex. Instead, it's a direct offshoot of an early sensation: "I'm strangling . . . I can't breathe . . . I'm dying." "Someone is after me . . . they're going to catch me . . . they want to kill me." The former echoes a memory of oxygen deprivation. As for the latter, that "someone" might have been a parent. Time and time again I have seen in nightmares how direct and uncomplicated the ideation is.

In both nightmares and waking psychosis, the pain mounts directly and has too great a force to permit the second and third lines to form a complicated symbolic story. "They are sending messages through the TV to kill me" is a simple, direct, and obvious symbol of a very real feeling inside. In reality, your feelings are after you, and if you feel them you might die. The ideation for the feeling that "I might die" becomes "They are after me and want to kill me." The ideation is just one step removed from reality. In our nightmares we are into something so primitive, so devastating, it seems to come from another planet. That is why we are often at a loss to understand them.

Our deepest sleep happens to be the level where first-line life-and-death traumas lie. In deep sleep, long, deep brain waves help ensure repression on that level. We wake up from our nightmares because the system won't run the risk of our demons rising up out of the slime to bedevil us. We wake up into conscious-awareness out of a nightmare in order to *remain* unconscious; this is the distinction between consciousness and awareness. We can be quite aware and quite unconscious. The cortex is now in service. We are now aware of external reality so as not to know inner reality. Isn't that true of so many intellectuals? They develop an awareness of so much in order to know nothing of themselves.

PAULO: CONQUERING NIGHT TERROR

When I was twelve, my brother told me I had been screaming, yelling, and physically acting out my dreams for some time. This is when debilitating sleep problems began to interfere with my life. Unlike some people who have the same recurring dream, my dreams were always created anew with new story lines, new characters, and new contents.

What I had was not a consistent image but a consistent set of feelings that I experienced as many as five times in one night. I always felt fear, terror, impending doom, imminent death, and a need to flee. In my night terrors, I am usually in a life-and-death situation: venomous snakes crawling in my bed or hanging over me, ready to strike me in the face; broken shards of glass falling down upon me; a huge blade like the one in *The Pit and the Pendulum* racing down to slice me across my belly. Sometimes I just have fear of something that can hurt me and make my life full of misery, such as rats in my bed, or mice, squirrels, or a vicious dog about to attack me. Like a compressed metal coil stressed passed its limit, I would spring out of bed to get away from the thing I feared. In night terrors, my body is physically involved in the dream: I spring out of bed or I run across the room. One night I dove headlong across the floor to go under a strand of barbed wire keeping me in a concentration camp while prison guards were trying to spray me with machine-gun fire. Strangely, I've rarely gotten hurt during a night terror, even when it is totally dark. I seem to have enough knowledge and memory of my surroundings to jump over or run between real objects in my environment in an accurate, safe, but unconscious way. But with the "concentration camp" night terror, I ended up with painful carpet burns on several parts of my body.

I did not enter Primal Therapy to get rid of my night terrors. I entered Primal Therapy to deal with the repressed feelings that caused them and all the other problems in my life. I am not completely through the process, but I can clearly see my steady progress and the healing path I am on.

My night terrors have evolved. Up until about six months before coming here, I always physically fled from the things I feared in my dreams. In the six months after my therapy intake interview, while I was waiting for my three-week intensive to begin, my dream-time responses to the things I feared in my dreams began to change. Instead of running or fleeing from the imagined things I feared, I began to face them in such ways as literally rolling up the "snake" or "rat" in the blankets to contain and immobilize it. I would then turn on the light and go back to check it out. It usually took me a few moments to come to consciousness enough to realize that I was having another night terror and that there was nothing there.

Animals and objects were eventually replaced by vague impressions of individual people who intended to harm me in some way. My responses to these "people" were to sit up in bed and face them head on, to sit or stand ready to defend myself against him or her, or to physically lash out at him or her as if he or she were really there. On several occasions I yelled into the vague darkness, "Who in the hell are you?!"

Somewhere and at some time in my life I unconsciously found that dream sleep was a painkiller for me. Now, unless I have a responsible need to get up earlier, I get up when my sleep turns into "dream" sleep. This is hard for me to explain, but it is one of the most significant connections I made in my therapy. Whenever I "crash" or sleep a long time, there is a segment of my sleep where I dream and dream and dream. I have never taken drugs, but I can understand the addiction and attraction some people have to drugs from my experiences of "dreamy" sleep.

When I am in dreamy sleep, I have no desire to get up. I want to stay in that dreamy state forever. I am especially held by dreamy sleep when my waking life is more painful than I want to feel. I have almost lost jobs over it because I have had so little will while I am in dreamy sleep. While in dreamy sleep, I had the feeling and attitude of "I don't care," because I felt so good and removed from both the old and present stresses in my life. At times I wouldn't get up to go to work on time, I wouldn't call in to say that I would be late (because I didn't want to wake up or risk waking up), and I sometimes never went in to work at all. Such an act-out can really screw up one's life. This was a form of passive suicide; I just didn't care if my life ended as long as I felt good going out in the process. During primal therapy, I became conscious for the first time while coming out of dreamy sleep. I realized that my dreamy sleep was a narcotic for me, and for the first time in my life I felt a real sense of involvement, choice, and control in my processes of sleep, feeling, and repression. Prior to that day I felt no control over the underlying processes going on inside of me that were making me manic-depressive with regard to sleep. I was fragmented and the fragments that made up "me" were all disconnected from each other. I did not work as a unit. The morning I became conscious that dreamy sleep was a drug for me, I became connected. For the first time, I saw real hope of finally correcting my sleep disorders. At that moment I was on a newly created threshold: I could make a decision about where I went from there. It was the first time I had real choice and a sense that my life was totally up to me.

Depression

After studying the literature, the only conclusion I can come to is that no one is sure what depression is. Is it a reaction to circumstance, a state of being, a disease, a neurosis or psychosis? Is it a syndrome, a collection of little symptoms, or one entity? Most agree that how the person feels is crucial. The DSM-IV lists the following symptoms: consistent depressed mood, marked loss of interest and pleasure, sleep disturbance, loss of energy, guilt, poor concentration, and suicidal thoughts. But almost any category of neurosis can include some of these. How long do you have to have suicidal thoughts to be classified as depressed?

One can see the circular reasoning involved. If one feels depressed and thinks about suicide, then one is depressed. If one is depressed, one is depressed. Generally, most suicide attempts involve depression. Even if there is a precipitating event—the loss of a spouse, for example—the basic depressive tendency, the self-destructive aspect, must already be in place. In *Depression: An Integrative Approach*, Herbst and Paykiel report that 15 percent of depressives ultimately die of suicide. The authors claim that the incidence of suicide is different from that of depression. Fifty percent of suicide attempts, they claim, have some depressive symptoms.

Then there are the famous "unipolar and bipolar depressions:" those who are only depressed, and those who are agitated and manic alternating with depression. Some claim these are two separate diseases. There used to be a category called "endogenous depression," a depression that arises from inside for unknown reasons. It has been replaced with "melancholia." I'm not sure what progress that is supposed to represent. "Neurotic depression" has been removed from the DSM-IV. Unfortunately, "neurotic depression" has not been removed from the sufferer's physiology. And depression does mean "neurosis" in my view, since it indicates a major degree of repression and dislocation of function.

It has been found that an early loss of a mother, between ages eleven and seventeen, is associated with later depression. Thus, pain now enters the equation, although in looking over volumes of the literature one rarely sees the word *pain* in discussions of depression. Emotional support is paramount in avoiding serious, suicidal depression, yet the depressives have a difficult time keeping others around. They tend to be ultraneedy, down, and dependent, and want to live through others. Research has found that those who develop a "new concept" or the idea of a fresh start are those most able to get over depression.

Many neurotics have high stress hormone levels. The difference for the depressive is that there is no place for the stress to go, no outlet for release. Other, acting-out neurotics can find avenues to release the tension. The depressive can't do that. Their repression is global, due both to massive trauma early on and to a suppressive home environment that allowed few outlets for behavior. Parents of depressives tend to be strict disciplinarians with no back-talk allowed and no misbehavior to go unpunished. One parent or the other is removed emotionally from the children so that they have no place to go with their feelings. The prototype is reinforced and repression increased in these kinds of home situations.

Not so surprisingly, those who take downers tend to exacerbate their depressions, while those who take uppers find relief from them. Those who take drugs, such as dopamine, which kills pain but also works on the excitatory system, find some relief from depression. The global repression is somewhat lifted and energy is supplied to help them get out of bed and get going. We might recommend such drugs early in therapy when a patient is below the primal zone and cannot feel at all.

We bring the pain level down a bit to allow some access to feeling until the person can feel on her own. Otherwise, there is a constant trying in therapy with little success and a feeling of further hopelessness. Research has shown that those who took precursors to serotonin (the inhibitory neurotransmitters) found some relief from depression. Though it may seem paradoxical, more repression through drugs can lift the burden from the system of having to do it all on its own and helps the person find some relief. The body is "maxed out" in staving off the pain. Adding repressors eases the load the body is carrying so the person can relax.

Many of the newer tranquilizers such as Paxil, Prozac, and Zoloft also contain some dopamine enhancers, so what one gets is painkillers with something to soup up the system, giving the person more energy. Dopamine is largely sensitive to stress and acts to galvanize the system. The key sensation in depression is repression. That is because repression is failing slightly and global repression is moving up toward conscious-awareness. The person "feels" the repression, the heavy, labored sensation, the difficulty to breathe deeply or even move one's arms, and calls that depression. To help suppress is the role of most of the new antidepressants. What sometimes also helps is a drug to quell some of the agitation. The antianxiety drugs help here. When there is less repression, the person feels less depression.

Depression is a result of the repression of many feelings and traumas early on. "Sad" is a feeling. Depression is a result of feelings being "numbed out." It is a normal response to events in life such as great loss. Depression is when a person cannot feel sad, cannot cry out his misery, cannot express himself fully. After a time depression sets in. This fits in with the fact that depression is a highly agitated state, even though the person may feel no agitation; rather he feels immobile and paralyzed. There is agitation by many unexpressed feelings which are reverberating below conscious-awareness. Why is there no outlet? For two reasons: The first is that during the original trauma, perhaps around birth or earlier, there were no alternate behavioral avenues and the lack of alternatives was stamped in. Second, childhood was not conducive to expression of feelings. Those who have had "no alternatives" stamped in will react with submission to a repressive household, thereby enhancing the repression.

In a study by Keith Hawton reported in *Depression: An Integrative Approach,* he states: "Among people who kill themselves or attempted suicide, approximately two-thirds have visited doctors . . . within the month beforehand." It seems that they were looking for help. The question is, How do you help a depressive? Their symptoms are usually vague; they are aware that something is wrong but don't know what. They are just uncomfortable. Of those who do finally kill themselves, more than half have a history of previous attempts. The recent breakup of a relationship is paramount in the prediction of a suicide attempt. What Hawton reports is that "the prediction of suicide [depends on] the degree of hopelessness experienced by a patient." It is more important than the severity of the depression. In my view, the degree of hopelessness *is* the degree of severity of the depression. If there is no possibility of change, then suicide is a high risk. If the person believes things can get better, then he is less of a risk. Too often, the degree of hopelessness pervades everything so that even when there is hope the person sees only hopelessness. About fifteen percent of individuals who have attempted suicide will repeat the attempt within one year. The greatest danger of succeeding is within three months of the first attempt.

The tendency toward depression can begin at birth. The feelings during a birth trauma—hopelessness, futility, lack of energy, and lethargy—are the very feelings associated with the earlier trauma, which then become the prototype. Those are the suicide risks. The sympath will never give up, or if he does it is only after every effort has been made. The parasympath can only begin to make feeble efforts before futility sets in. It is the sympath, incidentally, who will take the more violent way out, such as a gun to the head. One patient whose head was crushed at birth always imagined jumping out of a window and bashing his head on the pavement.

According to Willem Nolen and colleagues in their book *Refractory Depression*, the evidence in the general literature seems to be that the treatment outcome for depressives is not terribly good. An eleven-year follow-up study in Canada "produced comparably poor outcome." If patients are followed up with drug treatment such as Prozac, the results are better but not marvelous. Electroshock therapy is being used again. It has been found that depressives taking only antianxiety drugs do badly, by and large. That is because the agitation aspect has been dealt with but not the repression. For that one needs the drugs that enhance repression, particularly those that block the re-uptake of serotonin, thereby increasing the amount of inhibitory brain chemicals in circulation. What all this means is that the stress levels are raising repression to the breaking point. We see it on our brain maps and in our electrophysiology studies. Ultimately, what we do is reduce the pain level and that feels good because less repression is required and the system itself becomes adequate to the task. What Nolen et al. have found is that "after five years, 75 percent of chronic (depressed) patients had remitted." Three-quarters, then, returned to depression. Not a good batting average.

In the manic-depressives, those who alternate agitated, hyperactive states with depression, the standard treatment for years has been lithium—a salt. Lithium helps repression by slowing or blocking the transmission of nerve impulses, particularly the pain impulses. The advantage of lithium is that it takes very small doses of it to produce the desired effect. In primal therapy we seem to block the firing of nerve impulses dealing with pain simply because the pain is no longer there. The brains of our patients show less amplitude, less total neurons firing, and a slower firing rate. Lithium has been well studied and yet its exact physiologic mechanisms still are not fully understood. It is known that it alters the sodium pump of the cell so that transmission of messages is changed or blocked. In many cases lithium enhances synaptic transmission and speeds the message along. The calcium and potassium of the cell are also affected by lithium, again altering the transmission of neural messages and often preventing the rapid transmission of the pain message so that suffering is no longer felt. Lithium seems to help balance all of these chemicals within and outside of the cell, an imbalance I believe to be essentially caused by early trauma.

Other studies find that lithium changes oscillations in catecholamine receptor sensitivity. Here, it is hypothesized that termination of manic states is associated with a progressive decrease in receptor sensitivity. One is biochemically less revved up. There are endless biochemical explanations for this, but I think that ultimately it is not a biochemical affliction; rather, the biochemistry follows the psychophysiology, which follows the imprinted trauma. For example, it has been found that lithium will increase the binding affinity of opiate binding in other places. A number of authors believe that lithium stabilizes the catecholamine receptor oscillations and thereby stabilizes mood. What it seems to do is help balance the trauma that has been thrown off balance. There may be a genetic imbalance as well. My observations of the reversal of this affliction in our therapy makes me doubt such a hypothesis, however.

There have been all manner of scare stories in the press about the side effects of many of the new antidepressants. We have never seen a deleterious effect. I believe the answer is as follows: Some of these drugs can offer better access to feeling. Those who do not know about feelings have no alternative but to act out. There are reports ranging from suicide, alcoholic binges, and even murder. It is not the drug doing that but the fact that the person cannot handle the feelings he now has access to. The minute our patients feel a bit of relief from drugs and drop into the primal-feeling zone, they are able to primal away the pain and feel much better afterward. They have an alternative. Not to know about feelings is to be rendered a victim of them.

One patient of mine reported having suicidal feelings while

on Prozac. Before taking the drug, he felt numb and blank. With the drug, he had access to his early imprints, including a specific feeling of hopelessness, which in turn made him suicidal. When he *felt* the hopelessness in primal therapy, instead of suffering from it, the suicidal feelings subsided. With no ability to feel, suicide is a real danger because suicide offers hope, the way out of the feeling of hopelessness, even when the person is unaware of the feelings he is wallowing in.

It is no accident that many depressives have sleep problems. The amount of underlying agitation, the fact that first-line, very early traumas are approaching conscious-awareness, means that the cortex is galvanized for defense. The result is an overactive prefrontal cortex working to keep early pains at bay, resulting in tremendous nervousness and feelings of anxiety. Meanwhile, all this lower-level input is gobbling up serotonin supplies, so the person needs something that will quell lower-level pain and boost serotonin supplies at the same time. When that is successful, the person is less depressed and can sleep. We accomplish that by lowering pain levels permanently so that less and less repression is called for as time goes on. We lower pain levels by taking small bits of giant pains and bringing them to consciousness for connection. When we do that, we change the configuration of brainwave patterns. Thus the drugs someone needed previously are no longer necessary. Patient after patient has reported on the lesser need for drugs as therapy progresses. The pain is now out of the system; only the memory shorn of the force remains. Because the pain is gone, the repressive system can rest and does not have to be constantly hiding it in the unconscious. Once the great pain of the prototype—the near-death experience around birth—has been relived many, many times, the preoccupation with death as solution is also gone. Our biochemical research shows that once these birth pains are relived there are significant changes in many hormones. The person has much more energy and can now function. Something as seemingly benign as hypothyroidism can normalize after therapy so that the person no longer feels dragged down by life. And, incidentally, the fact of early trauma may be involved in lowering thyroid output, permanently playing a part in later depression, as well. Traumas in the first months of life in the womb may imprint a "hypo" or "down" state where some of the hormones such as thyroxine will have a lower set-point. This could be more likely to happen if the mother is on constant tranquilizers and sleeping pills while pregnant.

The danger of suicide is when the pain is rising. As long as repression is totally effective, the person is zeroed out and repressed but is not suicidal. There is not enough energy for it. An event in life, a loss of a mate or close friend, can precipitate a crisis by challenging repression and upsetting the delicate balance of defense. Danger lurks when agitation begins, when everything seems bleak and futile. Agitation means, by and large, that the imprint is on the way to conscious-awareness. When it arrives and cannot be felt for what it is, the person is in danger of acting out the feeling in a self-destructive way.

I close this chapter with two case study discussions. In their respective battles with depression and bulimia, Harry and Denise describe how primal therapy helped them open the door to their past traumas, confront them, and learn to live again.

HARRY: THE MEANING OF BEING ALIVE

I was born after a long, sedated labor. Things went wrong from the word *go*. According to my mother, she had been to the doctor for a ninth-month checkup, and on the way out she fell onto her stomach and her water broke, initiating labor. Under normal circumstances the baby sends the signal that initiates labor, that says it's time to start. I didn't have that.

They immediately sedated her into twilight sleep—half awake, half asleep—for the delivery. The experience (without words or concepts to understand the sensations) is of everything suddenly going like a bat out of hell, with the world and me running along together. Then the world disappears, and I am alone. The labor stops. False labor, the doctor says, and sends her home.

Now I am struggling inside to move, to go without the help I need to go forward and getting nowhere. I begin to go numb, piece by piece. I am losing the sense of myself. My mother couldn't feel that I was still moving to get out. The fetal heartbeat had slowed almost immediately after the contractions stopped, so there was no discernible fetal stress. She was just too numb to feel me, too stupefied by the drugs to care.

After twenty or so hours of this, the drug begins to wear off. My mother wakes up and labor begins in earnest this time. But I'm not there. The world is returned to me but I am lost and dying and too far away to help. Then it happens. The species imprint takes over again and I begin to make a Herculean effort to get out. But it isn't enough. I've gone too far. I do the only thing I can: I pass into unconsciousness.

The renewed labor is short and the contractions come fast with no time between. I am coming out and as the head begins to crown, the doctor reaches in with forceps and grabs me around the top of my head and pulls, twisting the tiny head almost completely around. As soon as the pressure is off my lungs, I begin to breathe. I breathe but there is no cry. The doctor cuts the cord, triggering an even harder breathing response. There's not enough air to breathe, there's not enough to cry, not enough to struggle. The doctor turns me upside down, grabbing my ankles too hard, and slaps my bottom. I scream and, gratified, he puts me down, wraps me up, and shows me to my mother. Then I'm shuffled off to the nursery.

I am alone. As I begin to come out of the drugs and feel myself again, my body begins to shake. I feel enclosed and once again I'm fighting for my life. I breathe as hard and as fast as I can. If I stop I'll die; that's all my body can say to me.

I have never been a self-starter. My infancy was relegated to survival and survival meant not re-creating the disaster of my birth. I didn't ever want to go a step too far again; that had been reinforced a hundred times over, reliving the flight from anoxia and death. "Do what you have to do and save the effort for when there's no choice left" became my watchwords of life.

I was a good baby because of that. I never cried, never complained. I had finally repressed the memory of my birth but not the abject terror that was the reaction to danger. That was reinforced by a father who was jealous of his sons because I took Mommy away. If I cried for my mommy, he was as likely to come as she was and he would "give us something to cry about." When Mommy came, it was the two of us together the way it should be; if he came, I was alone. When she returned to work and my father became our sole caretaker at night, I stopped asking. I had to struggle alone with no one to help me and lived in a constant state of panic. Mom would get ready for work while I watched from a distance, sucking in the "sense" of her—Ivory soap and glycerin and rosewater and scented talc, rayon, cotton and chiffon, lipstick and hair spray. I held on to the touch and smell and sight of her so I wouldn't feel how alone I was when she wasn't there.

My brothers and I struggled for attention where there was little to be found. We fought and yelled constantly. It seemed that we were vying for crumbs of affection from our increasingly distant parents. I spoke with a stutter, so even asking for anything became a monumental chore and I gave up easily. I needed to be listened to but couldn't say what I wanted to say and no one took the time to let me say what I meant. I was the loser in a very real sense in the family. Someone was always bigger, faster, stronger. I began to imitate the other members of my family as camouflage, a trait that let me get close sometimes but meant losing my self in pleasing them. My oldest brother was an artist, so I copied his drawings rather than doing my own; another brother was into sports, so I copied him. I could move if someone else was there for me. My life became a waltz where I followed and others led. Around my parents I tried to be what they wanted but I could never succeed. I felt that if I could somehow be what they needed me to be, they would love me and then my mother would stay home and my father would stop hating me for wanting. I became the good boy, always willing to help, always pleasant.

The older I got, the more I felt that I was on my own. At thirteen my parents separated. Until this point I had worked hard outside of the home to begin to build a life. I was a small, skinny, gawky kid who lived in a state of quasi-terror, afraid to speak because I always said the wrong thing, physically backward because I was unable to sustain the energy needed to excel at anything. Yet I had slowly begun to make friends and move in the world. We had lived in the same house for eight years, had the same neighbors, the same schools. I was growing up and I was beginning to feel like I had something that was mine, albeit outside the family. The world was stable even if my family wasn't. Suddenly that world was taken away from me when my parents split.

My brothers and I moved in with my mom and my particular brand of panic set in. I couldn't think, couldn't move, couldn't feel anything except terror and despair. I felt like I was drowning and the world was getting farther and farther away. I couldn't concentrate on schoolwork and was always off balance. There was no one to reach out to. After about six months my mother told us she couldn't take care of us anymore. We'd have to go live with our father. It was like hearing a death sentence. I remember two apartments and a house that we lived in over the next year and a half, but little else. My mother had always been the brake on my father's rages and violence against us. Without her he was without control. My brothers and I lived in constant fear for our lives. I could be invisible most of the time but it seemed that one of us was always being beaten or yelled at or punished.

I became suicidal. I would crawl out onto the roof of our house and on my belly stare over the edge at the cars on old Route 40 below, seeing myself smashing against their front bumpers. I was terrified at the thought but couldn't face going back and being with my father again. I felt as if the world was mean and crazy and death was all I had to look forward to. I stayed out there until my older brother came and told me to get back inside before I got in trouble. As I crawled back through the window, I felt that I had died. I said nothing, showed nothing, felt nothing.

Eventually we went back to live with my mother. We tried to tell her what happened to us, but all she could talk about was herself and what Dad had done to her and how hurt *she* was. Even after my older brother fell to the floor in a primal with his hands over his head, crying, ''Don't hurt me anymore, Daddy!'' she still didn't get it. I didn't even try. She said she loved us, loved me, but the words weren't enough. I was unreachable, anyway. I was in limbo. The world went on without me.

After I moved out on my own at eighteen, the patterns of my birth and childhood repeated themselves over and over. Relationships began and ended because I couldn't express my feelings unless pushed too far and then I'd explode and push my lovers away. I never let *their* caring in because I couldn't let myself believe it existed for me. Jobs were dead-end. I'd start fine, falter after a while, then give up and eventually walk away.

I read *The Primal Scream* in 1970 but didn't enter therapy until 1984, when someone offered to give me therapy at my oldest brother's behest. Over the next few years I continued therapy, gaining back my feelings, some sense of self, and a basic understanding of how the process worked. What was missing was the connection between what was happening in my life and the memory of my birth, a birth I had yet to feel.

Again, at someone else's behest, I entered the Primal Center in Venice, California, when it opened in 1988. The first two years I continued my old patterns and stayed withdrawn. Then, I began to take my feelings back in my life and make them mine again. I did it by feeling, piece by piece, how my life had been taken from me.

The turning point in my therapy was when I went against my imprint. We were at a mini-retreat. I kept thinking about an article in Dr. Janov's book, *The New Primal Scream*, in which a woman described someone standing naked in front of another group. The image stayed with me until I became obsessed with it. During group that night I stood and talked about how I felt I'd been hiding all along, not showing my real self, not showing who I was or what I could do. I then said that I knew only one way to show how weak I really felt. I slowly stripped until I was naked. Holding my arms out, I then turned to face everyone, saying, "This is all I am. This is me." I was baring my soul, my weakness for everyone to see. I couldn't hide and didn't want to. This was the supreme effort. I cried with everything my body had and tried vainly to cover myself. I felt I'd gone too far and nothing would come of it and I'd have to crawl away and die alone. France Janov said softly, "Put a blanket over him," and someone did and I could finally let go.

Depression saved my life. If I had never been able to shut off at birth, I'd have either been stillborn or died of crib death within days of getting out. If I hadn't cut myself off from the world, I'd have been driven insane by the insanity around me at home. If I hadn't given up so easily, the drugs or alcohol would still have me. What I did was give up my life in order to survive. The price of survival was surrender.

In feeling, I'm taking back my life and returning the past to the past, where it belongs. I'm like a baby who's discovered after crawling that he has, however tentatively, the power to walk. Parts of me that were never used are now mine in a way I only imagined before. I like doing, feeling, being, as scary as it sometimes is, as hard as it is sometimes to *be* me. I know now what it means to be alive.

DENISE: THE ENEMY WITHIN

I started becoming bulimic when I left home to attend college in another town. I was on my own and feeling miserable. One day, I started to eat very quickly whatever was there. I felt ashamed that I was stuffing myself with food. Then I made myself throw up by putting two fingers down my throat. I felt a bit of relief, and *I knew I was going to do it again.* That day I found my way to push down my pain.

Unfortunately, it didn't work that well after a while. I had to eat more and throw up more, and the relief was getting shorter and shorter. At the end, I sometimes had three crises per day. I hated doing it, but I couldn't quit. I realized I couldn't keep on going like that. I needed help. I started primal therapy in July of 1993. I was twenty-nine and had been bulimic for eleven years. I haven't had a crisis since.

I think the tension I tried to get rid of by eating and throwing up went away when I started to feel my pain. The only difference between feeling and bulimia is that there is a real resolution in feeling. Now, when I feel the same tension coming up, instead of eating I lay down and feel whatever is there. I no longer have to fight the pain and try to repress it. *I feel it.*

After having birth primals, I can relate my birth to my bulimia. There are two different parts in my birth that I can relate to the two parts of my bulimia: struggling during birth and stuffing myself, and giving up during birth and throwing up.

When I got stuck in the birth canal, I went into a frenzy, fighting for my life. That's where the rage I feel sometimes comes from. When I stuffed myself with food during a crisis, I did it with the same frenzy. What happened in my birth after the frenzy was the inability to get air. I couldn't breathe and my body would go into convulsions. Sometimes in primals, I feel I want to throw up at that point. I seem to have re-created the airlessness of my birth through the throwing up of my bulimia. That's why I always think that having a crisis without throwing up doesn't make sense—something would be missing. Whenever I put two of my fingers deep down in my throat, I couldn't breathe, and my body would go into convulsions and throw up all the food I had in my stomach, and then I could breathe again.

Another thing strikes me: the feeling that comes from the birth sensations is, "I'm so alone and nobody is there for me." I wouldn't have a crisis if I were not on my own. Again, in the present I re-created the loneliness at birth.

When I was under a lot of stress, I think I started to react according to my imprint, and bulimia is a way to re-create my birth and therefore get close to my imprint. Why did I "choose" bulimia? It seems to match my birth perfectly. In bulimia, the physical body is involved, and that brings me closer to the physical sensations of birth.

Bulimia calmed me down and left me exhausted afterward. It felt like the storm was over, and I was left with a burning throat. But it really hurt me physically. I got weaker and weaker because I was losing minerals when I was throwing up; therefore, I would get sick more easily.

When I had my first birth primal, I made some connections with my bulimia. The energy I put forth as I pushed through the birth canal was the same kind of energy I would feel when I had a crisis, that is, something that I can't stop that is driving me so strongly. After a few years of primal therapy, I had a session that helped me to understand more about my old act-out. In the session, I was feeling fear and disgust for somebody in the present. The fear and disgust turned into physical motions of throwing up. The sensations I felt then were the same ones I was re-creating with my bulimia. It made me realize *it wouldn't have made sense to me to eat without throwing up. I had to throw up.* After feeling in my session, I felt very peaceful and relaxed. In that session, I felt the need to let my body go and let the sensations, the tears, the disgust, and the fear happen.

10

HOW THE CELLS GO CRAZY

Neurosis begins in the cells. In a sense, we are simply a collection of colonies of cells: immune cells, nerve cells, muscle cells, cells that store memories, cells that receive messages about pain and other sensations, cells that are involved in controlling the body's vital functions. All these cells work together in remarkable harmony. But when early trauma intervenes, biochemical changes are produced at the cellular level. Neurosis replaces harmony with disharmony. This imbalance is found in both the physical and psychological spheres and implies permanent dysfunction on both levels.

How the cells "go crazy" will give us a better idea of how an individual, as an agglomeration of cells, becomes neurotic or psychotic or even develops cancer. In this chapter I outline a paradigm for how early trauma affects the cells, and how such cellular dislocation is analogous to neurosis, underlying severe types of "mental" and physical illness.

The Immune System: Where Mind Meets Body

In an experiment, UCLA researcher John Liebeskind injected rats with cells of tumor tissue, then subjected them to foot shocks. The rats became helpless and hopeless. After a time, they developed tumors that eventually became malignant. Evidently, through lowered immune function, their helplessness was translated into cancer. Other research with lab animals shows the same connection. There are some cancers that are highly related to immune system function. For example, the incidence of cancer is unusually high among older people who have recently lost a spouse. Those hospitalized for depression have impaired immune function. Studies show that people who are lonely are more prone to disease than those who are not. Those in poor marriages experience immune suppression; research has even revealed that during and after an argument, the immune system may not function as well as it did prior to the dispute.

When you are in bad shape psychologically, you are susceptible to illness—not just stress-related symptoms, but significant alterations in cellular functioning. The fact that primal therapy has helped alleviate and heal sicknesses from epilepsy to asthma suggests that many of these illnesses, which are often assumed to be associated with adulthood stress, may be the end result of a long chain of pain reaching back to the beginning of the individual's life.

When a person loses a spouse, feels desperately lonely, and soon thereafter dies of cancer, the loneliness that counts is not from simply being left alone as an adult. Rather, it may tap into the alienation one felt and continues to feel from being abandoned early in life by one's parent. Early pain—be it in the so-called emotional trauma, such as a lack of love in childhood, or so-called physical trauma, such as being blocked at birth—can make children feel as helpless and hopeless and vulnerable to disease as Liebeskind's rats. The deep repression of that terrible feeling can play a role in later cancer.

It is in the immune cells where psyche (mind) meets soma (body). Psychological pain acts directly on immune cells, which manufacture painkilling substances all on their own. It is where "psychologic" events such as criticism and neglect find their somatic home in altered immune cell function, alterations that ultimately produce disease.

In a review of many studies, it was found that the condition of defeat and despair is associated with higher stress hormone output and lowered immune function. Another study showed that stress to a pregnant mother will lower the immune strength of her offspring. This has been corroborated in experiments with animals. Pain in the mother can make the offspring susceptible to serious illness. A mother who smokes, for example, predisposes her fetus to be vulnerable to oxygen lack, which will exacerbate the effects of any anoxia during the birth process. It is no wonder, then, that some children are born with allergies and asthma. What appear to be genetic effects may indeed be due to the chemical interaction between baby and mother.

Say a pregnant mother is left by her husband without money or anyone to turn to. She will be under great stress. There will be a massive outpouring of stress hormones that affect the fetus. It is no longer normal and must alter its functioning to adapt to the new circumstances. Because the fetus does not yet have well-established, "normal" set-points for many of its physiological functions such as blood pressure and hormone output, deviated set-points may be set in place. The young, vulnerable system has been recast into a new physiological system, a neurotic one. Some hormones may be in short supply while others are oversecreted. This may include later alterations in sex hormone output (perhaps leading to homosexuality) and thyroid function. The biochemical changes that occur when there is pain and repression in the womb may cause developing organs to be slightly abnormal. The baby may be born with eczema or severe allergies.

Again, one may look to heredity when social influences in the womb are to blame. The abnormalities may only become manifest as life goes on and other traumas occur. People who suffer from chronic fatigue syndrome, for example, have been found to have abnormal interleukin II output, a function that may have been upset during the birth trauma and remained that way. Furthermore, if the mother is under considerable stress, the secretion of stress hormones may interrupt fetal functioning so that the baby is delivered prematurely. Similarly, the immune system may be weakened even before birth, so that prebirth experiences can predispose one to a range of later illnesses.

Because the system always reacts first to history, then to current reality, an imprint at the beginning of life can have lifelong effects on one's physiology. That is why a fight with one's friend at age thirty can set off an asthma attack or migraine, reactions that had their origins very early on.

In the immune system, there are different kinds of cells with different functions. Some detect foreign elements such as dust, virus, or pollen. Others direct powerful cells, known as natural killer cells (NK), to "gobble up" prospective cancer cells. In addition, immune cells react to and deal with "emotional" pain with the output of the same painkillers the brain produces against trauma. Our research in conjunction with Saint Bartholomew's Hospital, London, indicates that primal therapy enhances natural killer cell output. The immune system perceives, registers, and codes information, including psychological hurts. It tries to deal with these hurts by the secretion of opiates that serve to suppress the pain but which, by attaching to immune cell receptors, may eventually make them less effective and weaken the immune system. The point is that it isn't the brain that necessarily sends the message to the immune cell to react to hurt; the immune cell can do that all on its own. Psychologic hurt, therefore, is translated into immune cell alterations directly, and that may then be translated over time into catastrophic disease, whether arthritis or multiple sclerosis.

One of the functions of the immune system is to establish who the self is, and in so doing to detect the "foreignness" of something. When functioning properly, immune cells identify and wipe out unwanted intruders. A vaccine generates long-term memory in the immune system for those who, for example, never had a specific infection before. Some cells in the immune system ingest bacteria and release toxins in return. But trauma and repression transform the organism. It is no longer itself; it has been thrown out of its natural equilibrium. In a sense, it is confused; it doesn't know who it is anymore. When "we" don't know what to do, there must be a corresponding cellular reaction somewhere. Immune cells, for example, may no longer recognize their enemies and not really know what to do with them. That heightens the person's vulnerability to disease. There are fewer natural killer cells and other immune cells ready for the fray, and those that remain do not seem to have the potency they should.

It is largely long-term, imprinted stress that weakens immune function. Stress can galvanize the system into action, but constant vigilance seems to fatigue the system. When it is fatigued, one has a greater likelihood of immune impairment, leading not only to tumor development but also to larger and rapidly developing tumors.

Oxygen Deprivation at Birth and Cancer

During a difficult birth in which the fetus is deprived of sufficient oxygen (for example, the cord is wrapped around the neck or partially crushed, or tumors are blocking the exit), it is not "business as usual." The organism is about to die from lack of oxygen. The system must adjust; massive repression and unconsciousness are called for. Just when vital functions are finding the set-points for their homeostasis, just as the hormones are establishing their normal secretion patterns, these functions must be altered in the service of survival. The cells must adapt to this oxygen-diminished milieu. Eventually, they may begin to regress down the evolutionary scale towards the original prototype of all life: *anaerobiosis, or low-oxygen respi-*

ration. By doing so, they may be moving toward a malignant state and be on the road to cancer.

The reason the cells may be harking back to origins is because under stress, we return to the prototype for guidance. There is frenzy in the newborn no matter what kind of trauma threatens oxygen supply. Frenzy diminishes oxygen reserves, exacerbating the problem. At a certain point it can lead to immediate unconsciousness, depending on how severe the trauma is, rendering one unaware of threat and danger.

Asphyxia is a disturbance that interferes with the respiratory system due to a lack of oxygen. There may be excessive amounts of lactic acid in trauma such as this. The newborn can hardly breathe—exactly what we see every day in our therapy when patients relive traumatic birth. Many babies have to be resuscitated at birth. The result of this lack of oxygen, apart from producing learning disorders and psychological aberrations, is slight lesions in the brain that often go undetected. They may play a part in later clumsiness and lack of overall coordination, poor eyesight, digestive disorders, and inept eye-hand coordination.

Generally speaking, how we develop as individuals reflects the development of mankind. The first microorganisms were anaerobic (able to function without oxygen), but evolution favored aerobic respiration since it produces ten times the energy of anaerobiosis. Under stress or adversity, humans regress back to the prototype. All cells, when under attack, whether by pollution, a bad diet, bacteria, or childhood pain, may be in danger of reverting to historical forms. For example, lung cells must adapt to the assault of diminished oxygen caused by heavy smoking; the link between smoking and lung cancer is well known. Trauma can produce a lifelong effect in the molecules within cells. It may change the expression of the DNA—the molecules that determine heredity—in the cell, which dictates how that cell will behave, or even alter the DNA itself. Once the expression of this genetic template is changed, the

kinds of proteins manufactured will also change, with consequences for cellular homeostasis and for the entire organism. I
believe that the repressed memory of anoxia *causes* anoxia, in
that the imprint of anoxia may cause lifetime low-oxygen levels, perhaps leading to DNA damage and cancer.

In response to oxygen deprivation at birth, the trauma creates an anoxic imprint. The anoxic imprint may, among other
things, produce a tendency later on for shallow breathing. This
prototypic tendency originally enabled the survival of cells in a
low-oxygen milieu. The imprinted memory of anoxia constantly sends the message that there's not enough oxygen, and
the cells must operate at less than optimum oxygen levels. The
alteration in cells over time is what puts the organism in danger. The cells don't know that the anoxia is "back then," because that memory is an ever-present reality in those cells.
That reality tells the cell to alter its use of oxygen. These cells
are stuck in a time warp, if you will, being truthful to their
history. Interestingly, the inhibitory neurotransmitter serotonin is the precursor of melatonin, a powerfully protective anti-
oxidant, but serotonin is likely to be in short supply where
there is anoxia.

Cancer cells are characterized by their high sodium content,
while normal cells contain much potassium and little sodium.
My hypothesis is that the equilibrium or homeostasis between
these elements may be altered by anoxic birth trauma because
low-oxygen conditions limit energy production in the cell, lessening the rate at which the ion pump can remove sodium from
the cell. Should low-oxygen conditions prevail too long, a vulnerability to serious disease is set in motion. It may take decades of such deformation before the cell breaks down and
cancer or some other disease results. In his book *The Metabolism
of Tumors*, Otto Warburg recounts a study in which he found
that malignant tissue, having deviated metabolically, no longer
responds to the growth restraint signals of surrounding normal tissue. One might say the malignant tissue has "gone
crazy."

We can readily measure the altered cellular sodium content associated with malignancy. It is easy to assume that excess sodium "causes" cancer, but we must look deeper to what really altered the sodium exchange. Only in a primal can we observe the anoxia below it. By uncovering the anoxic imprint, we locate what may be the true cause of catastrophic illness.

Repression cannot eliminate pain. It only puts us out of conscious contact with it so we don't feel the misery, but the damage goes on. If a patient develops cancer, we don't call her crazy, yet cancer can be thought of as the psychosis of the body. The cells have overspilled their boundaries and have gone into disarray, or become "crazy." *The same chronic repression welded to chronic pain that can make someone "crazy" can possibly result in cancer.*

By contrast, active suffering may be a good antidote for cancer and other severe physical illness; if repression is faulty, the cells must absorb less pain. As I reported in my book *The New Primal Scream*, experimental evidence suggests that if the endorphins are rendered ineffective in animals, cancer incidence is lessened, but the animals' overt suffering is likely to be increased.

It is not just pain that makes us sick; it is pain plus repression. It seems likely that all manner of symptoms could be reversed by administering an endorphin antagonist such as naloxone, a drug that reduces repression by taking over the endorphin receptor sites. Time and again in animal experiments, when animals are put in pain and given naloxone to prevent their repressing it, they show fewer symptoms than those animals who are allowed to repress. The truth is that what we don't know *does* hurt us. All things being equal, the more you suffer consciously, the longer you will live—maybe not comfortably, but long.

In January 1995 the U.S. government gave approval for the use of naloxone in alcoholic patients, with the rationale that the drug has morphinelike effects. Alcohol itself has to be the most widely used painkiller of all time, and it's obvious why:

It aids repression. Weak repression through drugs may help one avoid cancer, but mental illness may take its place.

Primal Trauma and "Mental Illness"

A number of studies have revealed or suggested that traumatic experience can make both the cells and the person "go crazy." At a recent meeting of the Society for Neuroscience in New Orleans, Stefan Bracha, an Arkansas neurologist, reported that he had found something common in a number of schizophrenics. He studied twenty-four sets of twins. One twin in each set was schizophrenic. Bracha found that the schizophrenic twins had deformities of the hands. Their thumbs and index fingers were shorter in relationship to the overall size of the hand, and were shorter than those of their healthy twin. Bracha concluded that the cause may have been a trauma during the second trimester of gestation, when the hand is forming and brain development is critical. Among possible causes he considered were viruses and *oxygen deprivation*. The altered thumb served as a marker dating the trauma.

Autopsies on schizophrenics have revealed that cells in the hippocampal region of the limbic system (where emotions are organized) are in disarray, some rotated from their usual position. Doctors Joyce Kovelman and Arnold Scheibel of the UCLA Brain Research Institute believe that the upside-down neurons are probably in place before birth and "may distort messages going to other parts of the brain." Among the schizophrenics and psychotics, the arrangement of the brain cells seems literally to have gone crazy!

It is likely that these brain distortions create an exaggerated vulnerability to later mental illness. When the pressures of life overwhelm the feeble emotional centers of the brain, the neocortex is wildly overloaded and can cause a disintegration process. A child with intact hippocampal structures may survive birth and childhood traumas relatively unscathed, while a child with rotated hippocampal cells due to trauma in the womb may succumb.

A study carried out by psychiatrist Nancy C. Andreasen and her colleagues at the University of Iowa Hospitals and Clinics, reported in *Science News* in 1994, compared the brain size of healthy men with that of men diagnosed with schizophrenia. Magnetic resonance brain scans showed that the average healthy brain was larger than the average schizophrenic brain. Further comparisons revealed that the thalamus of the average schizophrenic male was substantially smaller than that of an average normal male, and also revealed differences in the strength of signals from the thalamus to the cortex. The researchers noted other abnormalities in the right hemisphere of schizophrenic brains—the side where most feeling is organized. Andreasen noted that impairment in the circuitry running through the thalamus, which *perhaps occurs before or shortly after birth*, may underlie schizophrenia. Such changes could be the result of trauma occurring before or during birth.

Another study, reported in 1986 in *Science News*, found an excess of interferon, a disease-fighting substance released by infected cells, in the blood of schizophrenics. Their systems were reacting as though they were infected by a virus. That is why some doctors believe a virus may be responsible for schizophrenia and other psychotic "thought disorders." What I see is that the whole system mobilizes against pain, and *the immune system treats threatening feelings as if they were a viral threat*. In psychosis the body does not distinguish between a feeling and a virus, and it uses every weapon it can when feelings threaten. These studies reinforce my belief that early physical factors underlie so-called adult "mental" problems; soma and psyche cannot be separated.

A case in point. For a brief time I treated a severe psychotic. Unfortunately, we had no inpatient facilities, which her full-time treatment required. Because this patient could not function in everyday life, we had to refer her to a mental hospital. There she was heavily tranquilized for over a year, at the end of which she developed cancer, and within months she died. She died of psychosis of the body. She died because early in her life she was sent to foster homes and was abused, molested, and neglected. She died of primal pain—the real disease.

11

DRUGS, DRINK, AND BELIEF SYSTEMS: BECOMING ADDICTED TO OUR NEEDS

Why do people crave alcohol and drugs? Because they want to feel better. Some do so because they suffer overtly and want to stop the suffering, at least temporarily. Others feel vaguely uneasy, stressed, agitated, and they want to feel more at ease. Still others—probably the majority of cases—simply like the feeling drugs and drink give them.

Alcoholism has been called a sickness. There are those who claim that it is either a genetic disorder, due to lack of an enzyme, or a hormone disorder. Having reversed many cases of alcoholism in primal therapy, I believe it is primarily a symptom of an illness involving early neglect and a lack of care, touch, and concern.

Those heavily into alcohol and drugs, both legal and illegal, often have had bad births or other first-line traumas compounded with later deprivation. Very early trauma affects serotonin and endorphin systems. What they are trying to achieve with their use of drugs is to feel "normal" again, to normalize what was thrown out of kilter by early pain. It seems logical: One is in pain and one takes painkillers to feel better. Most street drugs are like endorphins in that they are good first-line blockers.

Recent brain research at the Primal Center demonstrated the resting brain activity of one of our patients, who was addicted to drugs. His brain was racing at almost three times the speed of a normal individual. This indicates that lower-level pains are intruding into consciousness, creating a sense of constant pressure and making the patient feel perpetually ill at ease. His lower-level repressive mechanisms were faulty, and the cortex was almost alone in its battle against the primal imprints stemming from early trauma and a loveless childhood. He took drugs in order to keep the lower-level pains gated, so that he could feel comfortable and ease the sensation of being "out of whack."

Deprived Need and the "Need For"

No one craves painkillers unless there is a reason, and people who use drugs do so because they need to fill a more basic, hard-wired, unfulfilled need.

When someone takes drugs for a *current pain,* they dampen *primal pain.* For example, if a doctor prescribes medication for back pain, as long as the patient is taking painkillers for the back pain, he is not considered addicted. But sometimes when the back trouble or acute anxiety is over, the person still craves drugs. Why? Because he is still in pain. If there weren't that historic pain, there would be no need for painkillers. Only now it's a pain that neither patient, doctor, nor anyone else is aware of. And because the pain cannot be seen, he's now called "an addict." But the drugs are not the illness; drugs are a symptom of the real illness.

DEENA: DRUGS AND HOPE

When I was thirteen, there was a small section in our health book in school warning us against drug use. I was enticed. I knew then that given the opportunity I would use drugs.

At fourteen and fifteen I started hanging around with street kids even though I was a good student with plans for college. I also started drinking with them and acting out a lot of rebellious antisocial behavior. I loved the excitement and danger. I started smoking marijuana at sixteen and experimented with Dexedrine, barbiturates, and heroin throughout the rest of high school. I was arrested twice on drug-related charges by the time I was eighteen. Luckily, charges were dropped both times.

The drugs and the lifestyle were related for me. I needed to escape from my home and parents. They fought constantly; there was nothing for me there. I could identify better with the kids on the street than the white-bread kids in the honors classes. The rebellion and drug use made me feel different and special. It was a way of getting attention. I had been a good girl up until then, and it never got me anywhere. Also, I had always been very shy. The drugs and alcohol took away my shyness and gave me a sense of belonging, something I never got from my family. With drugs there was always the hope of feeling different, feeling better, maybe feeling good if I was lucky.

I somehow survived and went to a state college twenty miles away. The students were pretty straight. I was bored and scared and shy again. A friend sent me some LSD. It was frightening, but I was curious about the altered perception. Unable to relate to the people around me, I suffered through the rest of the trip alone in my room. My mind was racing; I was terrified and thought it would never wear off. I had some difficulty with school after this. I finally found other people who were doing drugs, other artists, and became friends with them.

After that I fell apart. My family split up, my boyfriend joined the Navy to avoid the Vietnam draft, and I ended up in Boston, at loose ends and alone. I became totally alienated and part of the drug subculture. My life revolved around getting drugs. I discovered mainlining with a needle. I loved it. It was erotic and satisfying. The rush as the drugs entered my system was electric, pure ecstasy. I would shoot up crystal meth and sometimes heroin. I had a lot of headaches and started showing symptoms of anxiety.

After college I went through a stage of using alcohol and barbiturates together. As I went through these different periods I would take on a different personality. Anything not to be myself. My self was a little girl who was scared and alone. I was a sort of Sally Bowles from the *Berlin Stories* living a decadent life. I could go out and do all the adventurous things that the scared, shy me was afraid to do. I stopped when I realized I might die from it. I went through a period of taking prescription Valium and Darvon for the anxiety and headaches. I stopped cold turkey when I realized I was becoming addicted.

My last fling with drugs was at age thirty. I spent a winter in Key West, Florida. I would do cocaine and Quaaludes. They were the drugs that made me feel the best. I stopped when I returned north. I wanted to grow up but didn't know how to. This is one of the things that eventually brought me to therapy.

In therapy almost every feeling goes back to feeling scared and alone. I think I was left alone a lot as a baby. I never learned to connect and feel comfortable with other people. My mother was tense, anxious, and angry.

As the feelings of alienation and fear arise, I can let myself really feel them for the first time. I don't have to look for drugs and decadent friends in order to bind and rationalize the overwhelming emotions and sensations. I also see that the people I was drawn to only made me feel more scared and alone. Most important of all, the drugs represented hope. Each time there was the hope that I would feel better for a while. Now, as I finally let myself feel the hopelessness, I can get off the roller-coaster ride. I can be vulnerable and real and finally grow from the scared and lonely little girl that my mother despised into an adult with a life in the present reality.

One girl I treated came to primal therapy from a halfway house. From the age of fifteen, she had drunk heavily in order to get away from her "empty" feeling. She also became promiscuous, and her parents couldn't control her. The feeling she had was: "When a man is in me I feel full and not alone." It was about interpersonal connection. The hard liquor and the sex both gave her the same warmth. Her primal feelings were of being alone and alienated from human (parental) contact. Her parents couldn't control her because she was being controlled by a need for human contact and warmth, which was much more powerful. If they had fulfilled her need for warmth and closeness, they wouldn't have had to worry about controlling her.

Perhaps someone develops a drinking habit during a time of marital strife. She feels so tense and troubled that she has a few drinks each evening to "relax." Her husband has been doing it for years with his drinks to "unwind" after work and has wine with dinner and brandy after dinner. Both of them think it's because of what's going on in their life, the conflicts over money, problems with the kids, the poor communication between the two of them, maybe their desire to find more "fulfillment" from life or simply a way to relax. These are certainly stressful problems, but what drives their drinking habit is that their current stress resonates with imprinted pain from their pasts.

The same is true for those who become addicted to hard drugs. The "need for" drugs is just a symbol of something deeper. Part of the problem with hard drug addiction is social: the crime and chaos the addicts create. Because their main concern is to kill the pain, they will do anything, including lie, cheat, and steal, to medicate themselves. One can never rely on an addict to tell the truth, but they don't lie because of the drugs. They lie to avoid pain. In habitual users who quit, as the drug wears off, the pain often returns with twice the force. In this cycle, they need more and more drugs to stay comfortable. The returning pain causes withdrawal symptoms that are so painful that addicts are driven to extraordinary lengths to obtain more.

Even if an addict manages to get off drugs, the misery still lies inside. Perhaps he will smoke three packs of cigarettes a day, drink cup after cup of coffee, and take "legal" tranquilizers, which will accomplish the same thing, only with less effectiveness. Although an addict may be better off for the moment, he or she is in constant danger of returning to addiction. A drug problem will subside only if the need is felt *in context* of the original pain.

A rock star stated that he had overcome his addiction to alcohol and drugs. He added, however, that "the dragon always lives inside you. And it's a disease that will never go away." This is fundamental in thinking about the problem, and it is intrinsic to the philosophy of twelve-step programs such as Alcoholics Anonymous as well as most substance abuse treatment centers. These programs see that their methods do not "cure" anyone. Alcoholism or any other addiction is incurable. The best you can hope for is to temporarily arrest drinking or drug use.

Support groups are the route millions take in place of drugs. People with "addictive personalities" meet regularly with others like them and develop an ideology that reiterates that you are helpless before the addiction, that there is a higher power which will watch over you and protect you, that you are not alone with your suffering. These ideas "work," as long as you get ongoing infusions of them, because they directly counter the real feelings of being alone. These groups offer defenses against an imprinted reality that means: "I'm all alone. No one cares about me. I'll never get any support or encouragement. There is no higher power (parents) to help out."

It is fine to get support from others. Obviously, the alcoholic or addict is constantly in danger of reverting to his habit, and the support helps him resist it. But if he goes to a group to confess his addiction, to shed a few tears and then to be applauded as honest and wonderful, how is he ever going to feel what's real?

DORIS: THE LEGACY OF ABUSE

From the age of nine months to six and a half, I lived in foster homes. In the second half of this period I was terrorized by daily beatings, humiliation, and deprivation of many basic physical needs, including sleep, intake of liquids, and access to the bathroom. During the last and worst period I was sexually abused by the foster father, while his wife's behavior was not only deliberately, but even worse, unpredictably sadistic. I learned to hide my pain, to not show hurt or fear, which only provoked further violence.

When I returned to live with my mother and stepfather, the repressed terror at first manifested itself in waking nightmares (monsters under the bed and so on). Two years later, when my half-brother was born, I became terrified of my stepfather, whose behavior was increasingly severe and at times sadistic. My mother did not protect me, was of no support, gave no comfort. As a teenager, my relation with my stepfather did not improve. During this period I acted out "living dangerously" in different ways (daredevil exploits). I also had recurrent terrifying nightmares whose main themes were life-and-death situations, being taken by surprise, feeling the indifference of the entire world.

Throughout my childhood I was unconsciously driven close to death in order to try and get love. From being a four-year-old swallowing candy wrappers in order to die (but in reality to have my mommy come) to taking ether as a fifteen-year-old and depriving myself of food, I re-enacted the same scenario. I attempted suicide and nearly died. Shortly after this attempt, unable to cope with the pressures at home, I left my home and family.

I first took drugs as an eighteen-year-old in London in 1969. Later I found myself living in the Paris "counterculture," characterized by extremist politics, rock 'n' roll, sexual permissiveness, experiments in "mind expansion" through drugs, and a challenging of all "establishment" values. My inner conflicts and aspirations were intimately reflected in the mood and circumstances of the times.

My initial impulse toward drugs was due to their forbidden status; my desire to establish my personal identity required behavior radically different from, and unacceptable to, my parents, those "in authority." At the same time, this was one means of creating a bond with those of my own age. I used marijuana and hashish over a period of two years, at a rate of between one and five joints a day, only with friends at first, then later on by myself. The first time I ever smoked I got violently sick. I felt my stomach being turned inside out. The violence of my body reaction scared me. I lay down and looked at my boyfriend and started hallucinating; his face was slowly transforming itself into that of a furry monster with a wild and dangerous look about it.

Why, in the face of such disturbing effects, did I continue taking drugs? The reason requires me to backtrack several years. One of my strongest fantasies in my middle teens was wanting to become crazy. I truly saw it as a future goal. Drugs could perhaps make me crazy and therefore loved. So I continued. As I fell more deeply under the drug influence, a subtle change took place. At first I indulged in the pretense of being "crazy" by letting my imagination create "crazy" visions that I could stop at will; I was experimenting and making the world believe I was crazy. But soon I started losing control. One day, lying on my bed, I looked down on the floor and saw myself lying there in a pool of blood. I totally freaked out because I did not know if the "me" was the one on the bed or the one bleeding to death on the floor.

A further effect of the drugs was psychotic episodes. I became terrified by pieces of broken glass, forks, knives, scissors, any pointed object, investing them with a life of their own and a power and desire to harm me. I also felt that my hands had a will of their own and would grab a knife and kill me. I became terrified of going to sleep, convinced that while "I" was unconscious and unprotected, my body would take over, get up, and kill me.

I went with friends to Amsterdam to enjoy the legal freedom to use drugs. One night one of us brought provisions from a stranger and before I knew it, instead of smoking hashish, I found myself under the influence of something very different. Within seconds I felt a violent blow to my stomach, and my heart felt like it was going to explode. I spent the longest night of my life curled up on a bed or walking around in a state of frenzied agitation, praying for my heart not to burst, for my body to recover control, for this nightmarish experience to stop. After the effect of the drug wore off, I vowed never, ever to take drugs again. This time the fear of the drug had become the most powerful force. The actual confrontation with fear of death had wiped out the attraction of the fantasies of danger and the "razor's edge."

Within twenty-four hours of stopping drugs I experienced the first of what I call my panic attacks. It terrified me, but initially I thought I was simply suffering from withdrawal symptoms. As months and years went by, the panic felt more like an endless reliving of the Amsterdam episode.

For years before I entered primal therapy, the panic attacks continued intermittently; their frequency, intensity, and timing uncontrollable, their origin a total mystery. Since entering therapy at age twenty-seven, I have relived many traumatic episodes in my early life and connected them to the patterns of my neurosis.

After I left home as a teenager I created an entire life of danger: parentless, homeless, penniless, etc. My defense system was shattered. My instinct in taking drugs to break the barriers of my inhibitions (around sexual contact and emotional closeness) had the unforeseen consequence of leaving me open to the "old" terror. Drugs had destroyed my gating system, which in my case had never been properly developed. By changing the body chemistry, allowing messages to pass through channels previously closed, the memory of the childhood terror was pushed suddenly close to consciousness. To try and maintain defenses against the pain, the brain created scary scenes that expressed the terror in symbolic form.

The feeling of being split seems like a last-ditch defense, to stop the memory imprinted in the brain and body from reaching consciousness. The impression of being two persons corresponds to the real self trying to remember, while the neurotic self, sensing danger, tries to repress and keep control of the situation.

This disconnection between the body and the mind produces the panic attacks. I have identified the panic attacks as the perfect defense against "old" terror. Primal therapy has given me a way to heal.

Treatment of drug addiction or alcoholism is an important first step, but it is only the beginning of the therapy, not the end. The downfall of Alcoholics Anonymous is that addicts merely replace one symptom with another: going to AA instead of drinking. Although twelve-step programs are less destructive than drinking, below the surface there is still racking pain, and that means a possibility of drinking again. That is why these groups say, "Once an alcoholic, always one."

This is not to say that an addict can be allowed to run loose when under therapy, particularly our therapy, since drinking or drugs are defenses against unleashed pain. Recovering addicts need halfway houses and support until the initial period of therapy is over. That period differs with each individual, depending on the load of pain underneath.

When treating addicts, it's important to monitor certain physiological measurements such as brainwave frequency, heart rate, body temperature, and stress hormone levels in blood and saliva. All these indicate the level of feelings, their strength, and how well the repression is working. We recently saw a patient who was coming off fifty tablets of Valium—a total of 250 milligrams—a day. When he first came in, the amplitude of his alpha waves was over 1,000 microvolts, indicating a tremendous amount of pain and repression. This isn't to suggest that Valium wasn't keeping the pain down; his brain was in fact working desperately to do it. As he resolved his old feelings, his amplitude dropped by two-thirds into the normal region. Less pressure pushed at his consciousness. He was no longer addicted, and it was reflected in various physiologic measures.

The more feelings patients can access, the fewer tranquilizing drugs they need. In the *Journal of Primal Therapy,* Dr. Michael Holden noted that primal patients require *more local anesthesia* because they have diminished repression. Conversely, their brains need *less general anesthesia* because they have less activated brains which need less quieting. Before therapy there is so much activation that drugs would slow the brain only slightly. After therapy the brain no longer has to be on alert all the time. Similarly, those who could "hold their liquor" before therapy may get drunk quite easily afterward, and those who could drink coffee with dinner may no longer be able to. When someone has fewer defenses, what is ingested affects consciousness far more easily.

Being Addicted to Ideas

We had a patient who was an alcoholic. She had given up drinking and become fanatically mystical. She had studied the twelve steps to higher consciousness and used a mantra to keep the demons away. She embraced every mystical path available in order to remain unreal. She was still addicted, but now she was addicted to ideas. Mysticism was her survival mechanism, a device to keep the pain down to manageable proportions and out of consciousness. It protected her from the pain related to being abandoned by her mother right after her birth. What was wrong with her wasn't the mystical ideas or the mantras. Like drinking, they were just the act-outs. She didn't need to be disabused of her beliefs; she needed to deal with her inner reality.

Remember, a crime had been committed against the humanity of this person. Her life had been threatened, but the original threat was now buried. The secret code that contained the details of the crime was hidden. We needed to decipher the code and follow the trail wherever it led. We didn't want to cover up the crime. She had already tried that with a fifth of whiskey a day. Her need for a loving mother became the need for a drink that made her feel warm inside. The alcohol was available and warming, unlike her mother, who was unavailable and cold. Her switch from alcohol to mysticism was her mind's way of continuing the cover-up, of protecting her from dealing with reality too quickly, which could have been shattering for her. We helped her by encouraging her to face and re-experience her early abandonment.

If the system cannot blunt the energy of the pain, the pain begins to rise toward conscious awareness and the person begins to suffer. This is why belief systems are often adopted by those who leave drugs and alcohol behind. It is no coincidence that so many people who are "born again" are ex-alcoholics. God, guru, or ideology takes the place of the drugs or alcohol. The fervor of the belief system is as strong as the addiction, since it serves the same purpose: to supply painkilling chemicals in the brain. The addict doesn't get over his addiction; he just trades one for another. Instead of getting his drugs from outside, he gets them from inside.

A belief system arises automatically out of overwhelming unmet need, or pain. It is designed to protect the integrity of consciousness, which is at risk of being shattered. To this end, it reassures and comforts. The belief system seems suddenly credible to the beholder. He's convinced that God is watching over him, or that by meditating he can put an end to his sorrow, or that in a past life he was one of Robin Hood's cronies. It doesn't matter that he is a college professor, or that his beliefs seem to contradict the level of his intelligence. What matters is that he no longer suffers.

When a person is loaded with early hopelessness, the secretion of endorphins is automatic. It accomplishes two things. First, it kills the pain of the hopelessness of ever being loved. Second, it transmutes the hopelessness into hope. Hope is dope, dope is hope. Someone in terrible primal pain often has no hope left. If they take real dope, like morphine, they have hope—for a time. Or, if they come to believe involuntarily in some imagined agent of fulfillment, the internal dope factory is spurred to greater efforts, and they have hope.

Breast milk contains plentiful endorphins, and there is no

more satisfied look than that of a well-fed baby. Similarly, semen contains endorphins that may contribute to the pleasure of sex. Drink and drugs activate our repressive receptors through various avenues, providing temporary relief from the pain. A belief system does the same thing by using our own endorphins. All irrational beliefs are founded on pain and hope.

JACK: GROWING AROUND THE PAIN

When I was ten, I found my mother staring out of the window at the apple trees with tears running down her face, oblivious to her surroundings. This was about the second anniversary of my father's death, and I'd somehow remained intact and held the family together by an effort of will in the meantime. But in that moment I saw there was no hope of reaching her, and I turned and left the room, split off from my feelings.

It seems like I've had a thousand primals about this scene, saying all the things I could not at the time. I begged, implored, pleaded, and demanded by turns that she help me, love me again, come back to me, and so forth. In these feelings, I couldn't accept her hopelessness because all would be lost, as it was when I quietly turned and left the room.

When it was pointed out to me in tape review that I had completely ignored a patient's hopelessness in a session and pursued a secondary feeling instead, I was crestfallen. For the first time in my familiar scene, I did the inconceivable. I went to my mother's side and stared out of the window with her, despairing, hopeless, and inconsolable. I fell into the blackness of an earlier experience in which there was no air and no escape from an intolerable pressure. The blackness washed over me as I lost my breath. When I came out of the primal, exhausted, many things became clear to me.

I began birth with breech presentation. When my hips were engaged in my mother's pelvis, she was chloroformed and the doctors performed an external rotation, lifting and turning me until I was head down. I felt terror as I lost touch with my mother and then the blackness claimed me. However, she was there when I came around and I "learned" that I would be reunited with my mother on the other side of the blackness.

Years later I concocted some chloroform during a chemistry class and marveled at the familiarity of chloroform intoxication. At fourteen, I found alcohol gave me the same sensation if I drank enough. A couple of drinks made me feel alive, but then I continued to drink until I was practically senseless. My friends mostly had similar problems so we thought it normal, and we all drank heavily together for years.

The more often I felt, the less I felt the need to drink. This is a hallmark of behaviors driven by very early feelings, and the global nature of the triggers—hopelessness, despair, existential doubts, intractable difficulties—confirmed this. Occasional heavy drinking and hangovers seemed to keep things in perspective and kept me from being overwhelmed by hopelessness.

My feeling made clear to me that I have spent my life avoiding the hopelessness I felt when my father died and my mother had a nervous collapse, and originally when I was born. I drank when circumstances resonated with this experience because I "discovered" at birth that things will be better after the blackness passes. In Alcoholics Anonymous, I would have denied my hopelessness by putting my faith in a higher power and avoiding trigger situations by taking life one day at a time. One of the little practical jokes of primal therapy is that one feels worse during down periods because there's more consciousness to suffer and more consciousness of suffering.

I spent my life after age ten trying not to upset my mother so I'd have the possibility of comfort. Breasts were magical, capable of salving my pain by their very shape, although I didn't really know what to do with them and was amazed they didn't matter more to others. The closer I got to a girl, the more uncomfortable I became, so much so that I didn't lose my virginity until I was nineteen. Breasts became erotic because sex is as close to somebody as you can get, and sex provides a legitimate focus and a pain-absorbing reward. Orgasm alleviates pain briefly. Eroticizing my pain was as natural and inevitable as breathing, especially because I didn't have a clue that I was in pain and eroticism is socially acceptable, even praiseworthy. Each new girl was exciting with the possibility of fulfillment.

I had low back pain from arching my back in agony in the crib. Always on my left side, my mouth open impossibly wide, I move upward until my head hits the corner, as I have seen distressed infants do. Nobody came as my body cried out for warmth, touch, and food. When this pain is near, I wake up in the morning with much swallowed air and my back in spasm. I'm sure my diabetes has something to do with this because my blood sugar is usually very high on these occasions, and if I take too much insulin so that I have low blood sugar during the night, it sets off this memory.

The constant nocturnal repetition of the trauma of starving must have put a massive strain on my blood-sugar regulating apparatus.

The incredible thing is that this pain, laid down in such a short time, circumscribes my life. What I find amusing, entertaining, diverting, interesting, and even possible stems from this experience. The course of my life was determined then, for whatever I became had to contain that trauma.

Jack was able to break through his pain, to part the curtain of denial drawn by his alcohol abuse. Ironically, it was primal therapy, not Alcoholics Anonymous or conventional "talk" treatments, that helped him do this. In the next chapter, we explore why most traditional therapies fail to cure.

12

WHY MOST CONVENTIONAL TREATMENTS DON'T CURE

Most people today undergo treatment for either emotional or physical problems. Some go for one kind of psychotherapy or another. Others see physicians for high blood pressure, heart problems, immune disorders, fatigue, allergies, asthma, or migraines. Some do both. In many cases, the treatment seems interminable; it goes on week after week, month after month, with no end in sight. Many people try one approach after another, perhaps receiving a degree of help from some of them, but still wonder how to cure what ails them.

Why is illness so prevalent and cures so elusive? Because those who treat illness often focus on manifestations rather than causes, and fail to realize that healing can occur only at the wound. Most psychotherapies and medical treatments first split the person into the physical and mental selves, focus on one of those selves, and then narrow the focus to a single part of one of those selves. The person is being dissected before any treatment even begins.

We have created a nation of symptom specialists. Today's doctors look at illnesses such as asthma, migraines, or ulcers as separate afflictions when they all may be different versions of the same thing. Drug addiction, alcoholism, overeating, and promiscuity are all considered and treated as separate neuroses when they all may be symbolic attempts to feel warmth and comfort. You cannot take a person apart and put him or her back together without involving the *whole* person.

What generally happens in cognitive therapy, behavior therapy, Gestalt, rational-emotive therapy, biofeedback, hypnotherapy, directive daydreaming, and creative visualization is that the focus emphasizes appearances rather than essences. Very rarely does the specialist ask the question, "Why is a symptom there?" The word *why* is the most neglected in the healing arts.

In Gestalt groups of the sixties and the seventies, we were encouraged to act like chimps and gorillas in order to feel "free." But we were only putting on an act. You don't change from the outside in. The inside of the brain won't allow that. No act on earth can permanently change a reverberating circuit in the limbic system. You are only as free as the feelings that bind you; the neurotransmitter chemicals that shut our gates are resistant. *Acting* liberated is a trap. *Acting* alive and exuberant cannot change the numbness of feelings that are too much to bear.

To ask "Why?" in therapy is to call into question the entire theory and treatment procedure of a given therapeutic system. Instead of employing memory in the service of healing, psychotherapies aim to control the mind and manage it as if it were a business. But the human mind is not an "it"—it is a process. It is not a head without connections to the body. The very term "*psycho*therapy" already tells us what is wrong.

In conventional therapy, the patient is merely encouraged to *talk* about his past, in the hope of gaining "insight." The psychoanalyst acknowledges the role of childhood events (though not the birth trauma or events in the womb), but prefers to discuss the events. That is why it's called a "talking cure." When a patient begins to "understand" his problems, he is seen to be making progress. Meanwhile, whatever lies below remains untouched. Healing never depends on *awareness*, only *consciousness*. This ought to put to rest the notion of an effective insight therapy. "Effective insight" is an oxymoron; insight that does not emanate from a patient's deep feeling is a defense. Insight does nothing to lift repression. Instead, it bolsters it. The use of tranquilizers or antidepressants achieves the same thing. Electroshock therapy is the most obvious example of our failure at therapy and our need to further suppress the pain in patients.

Many psychotherapies operate in the realm of the so-called rational. They deal with such "skills" as goal setting and decision making; they aim to bolster "willpower." People are taught to reason themselves out of their problems. Some therapies involve willfully changing one's thinking patterns. They are based on the idea that through ongoing reinforcement and repeated practice, you can learn new ways of interpreting and reacting to certain troublesome situations, which will enable you to function better in life. This might help resolve some practical problems; you can certainly learn how to breathe deeply and think soothing thoughts in order to calm your impatience while waiting in line to pay for your groceries. But this should not be confused with healing.

As long as a therapy does not help the person plunge into the depths of hopelessness of being loved as a child, it will be endless and unsuccessful, *even while it looks like it's helping, and the patient swears he feels better*! The patient does function better, but that is not wellness.

Suppose, for instance, that you get an anorexic to begin to eat a bit. She will then be considered on the road to health. While this is certainly important, I'm not sure what road she's really on. From our work, we know that talking to oneself, resolving to change, and even forcing yourself to behave differently are ultimately no match for lower-level imprints. These levels are measurable. You can understand food all day long and be starving to death from hunger; understanding and need belong in two separate worlds. You really can't understand your unconscious emotions until you feel them. In fact, trying to understand a childhood need before feeling it usually constitutes an intellectual defense.

This principle is widely misunderstood. In November 1994 the *Los Angeles Times* ran a front-page story on new approaches to crime and criminals. Sexual abuse of a child can be rendered a noncriminal offense in Northern California. If the perpetrator attends a class for child molesters, the crime will not go on his criminal record. However, no amount of understanding of the effects of abuse on children is likely to stop anyone who is loaded with impulses because of the abuse he or she suffered as a child. No matter how many courses such a person takes, he will remain a danger. If knowledge and understanding were so helpful, why do parents keep abusing their children generation after generation?

This is why crash-diet regimes, drug-rehabilitation programs, and twelve-step approaches have only short-lived effects. The person may get off drink, but usually only for a time. The new ideas and understanding learned and resolutions made are merely layered over the still extant feelings and needs. The imprinted power of those feelings can overcome almost any amount of willpower. No adult idea is ever as strong as the alienation a baby suffers just after birth when a sick mother is removed from her child for two months. Approaching this feeling of isolation during therapy usually results in extremely high vital signs. The person's later drinking and drug-taking may be attempts to grapple with very early alienation and loss. The alcohol is only the method she uses. It could just as easily be compulsive eating, or compulsively starving herself to death. There is but one neurosis, any number of manifestations, and only one route to cure.

Even if conventional therapies did recognize the existence of lower levels of consciousness and imprinted trauma, they do not have the techniques to immerse the patient in them, not to mention the rationale for doing so. For a century Freudian therapy has dictated that opening up the mysteries of the deep unconscious would be too unpredictable, a Pandora's box full of shadow forces and demons that must not be tampered with. In most psychotherapies, a self-fulfilling prophecy operates. The fear of tampering with the unconscious leaves the therapist no choice but to reject the very forces that can cure the patient. Instead, these forces must be beaten back and kept at bay with the weapons of words and insights. This notion transfers demonology from religion to psychology; both fear the "mind" as something unknown and possibly dangerous and evil.

In recent years psychologists have found what they thought was a way out of the problem by forgetting there was even such a thing as a mind. In the school of psychology known as Behaviorism, for example, there is no mention of mind; instead, there is simply a stamping-in and stamping-out of behavior, treating people like Pavlov's dog. The standard Behavioral approach for curing a phobia, for example, is desensitization therapy. Someone who is terrified of elevators is encouraged to approach the elevator or to think about it while conjuring up pleasant thoughts and nonthreatening images. Perhaps he'll be instructed to think how safe it is, or to imagine he is floating on a cloud. The therapist urges the patient to come closer and closer to entering an elevator, thereby trying to help him overcome his fears bit by bit. The therapist can only see the elevator and the fear. He can't see the real source of the problem. So he urges the patient to enter the elevator when what he wants is to run from it. By forcing him to submit to this type of "therapy," the therapist is really facing the patient with his past. The patient's body goes into the survival mode and is telling him to stay away from something that can provoke a deep pain and terror. But the patient doesn't know that. All he knows is that he is terribly afraid. Both therapist and patient are convinced that the patient's anxiety is wholly or mostly connected to the present. It isn't. The strength of the phobic's visceral reactions are enough to show that *he may be afraid not of being in an elevator, but of dying from anoxia, and often in the phobia and anxiety are all kinds of breathing problems.*

Because this phobia has nothing to do with words or "negative" thoughts, it cannot be cured by words or new thinking patterns, no matter how reassuring they may be. Even if the therapist tells the patient where the anxiety comes from, it would do no good. Holding a phobic's hand in an elevator and showing him that there is nothing to be afraid of is nothing more than a "holding" action. The terror is still there from primal sources. Changing ideas about one's fears is not curative, it is deceptive—self-deceptive. To say, "I'm not afraid," when terror is circulating down below, is to lie to oneself. It is better to feel the terror.

Anoxia, combined with being enclosed or trapped, as in an incubator after birth, is behind many elevator phobias and other forms of claustrophobia. When the desensitization approach doesn't work, the phobic person may be referred to a doctor who offers tranquilizers. The doctor may think he is helping suppress anxiety through the use of antianxiety drugs, but he is implicitly repressing the memory of pain. The patient now has even less access to his past than he did before. The doctor giving him pills is treating the symptom while putting the cure out of reach. Like the desensitization therapist, he is observing the present but is in reality seeing a reaction appropriate decades ago. He can't see the tiny, terrified infant inside the adult who has come to him. So he gives pills for a current symptom, and the pills also suppress the patient's history, laying the groundwork for addiction. The more life-threatening the original trauma, the more life-threatening the later illness is likely to be, because the pressure on the cells is greater.

An increasingly large proportion of society has taken one of two roads in an attempt to gain relief from their suffering. The first is drugs—nice drugs, legal drugs, prescription drugs, but drugs, nevertheless. The other route, as discussed in the previous chapter, lies in belief systems: astrology, reincarnation, gurus, meditation, channeling, cults, and so on. It seems all roads lead to Rome. If you exclude the believers and the mystics and the takers of legal and illegal drugs (including those who consume tons of aspirin and Tylenol), there would be few people left. So we see our therapists, take our antidepressants, and pray to our different Gods endlessly.

The reason most therapies tend to be interminable is that they involve unconscious hope. The therapist-priest is kind, attentive, and insightful. He cares, exhorts, moralizes, and offers advice. He guides the patient toward clever perceptions and insights, toward reflecting on complex dreams in search of their meaning. The patient cooperates, follows orders, tries to please. This is all part of the struggle to feel wanted and approved of. In general, the therapist and the patient engage in a mutual unconscious pact to avoid pain. The patient needs hope, while the therapist implicitly offers it. The whole setup of the therapeutic office—dim lights, plush furniture, reassuring paintings, a bland and accepting manner—militate toward hope. This form of therapy becomes addictive because painkillers, chemical and psychological, tend to be addictive. To sit down in a chair and have someone listen to you hour after hour, thinking about only you, something your parents should have done, is enticing. The patient is acting out her needs instead of feeling them. That's what "transference" is: acting in the present toward someone with feelings left over from the past. Those needs and feelings do not need analyzing. They need experiencing. Yet who wouldn't seek hope as an alternative to suffering?

There is hope in the pills people take, in the meditation they practice, in the hypnosis they undergo, in the support groups they attend, even in the electroshock therapy they submit to. But healing involves an *either-or* imperative. Either you feel your hopelessness about never being loved as a child, or you're condemned to struggle for it endlessly, even in psychotherapy.

Depression and Electroshock Therapy

Electroshock therapy, or electroconvulsive therapy (ECT), is making a comeback among the Prozac generation. A *New York Times Magazine* cover story by Gene Stone, entitled "When Prozac Fails, Electroshock Therapy Works," begins with the following statement: "ECT is slowly, and very quietly, regaining respectability . . . A *Harvard Medical School Mental Health Letter* (1987) cited evidence that ECT was an important method of treating certain severe forms of depression." In this article it is estimated that between 50,000 and 100,000 Americans are currently receiving ECT. Meanwhile, the April 1994 *Johns Hopkins Medical Letter* chimes in by stating that electroshock therapy is an "effective alternative for treating depression. Refinements have made (ECT) safe, humane and effective."

Yet the *New York Times Magazine* article quotes sources who believe that *seizures* brought on by electroshock somehow seem to help both psychosis and depression. And an American Psychiatric Association task force on the subject recently proclaimed that "ECT is often the safest, fastest and most effective treatment for severe depression." And what is a seizure? A primal turned inside out. The same random massive discharge of electrical energy is involved. One is connected, the other isn't. Electroshock therapy is both unnecessary and unsafe. It is inhumane, ineffective, and can cause brain damage. The effects of electroshock therapy are monstrous.

These sources mentioned above may be respectable, but they support ECT because the patients quickly become "functional" members of society. They cannot see the emotional numbness of patients or the flattening of their affect, nor can they see the lack of access to feelings, because feelings no longer seem to count. Throughout the article there is not a word as to "why" the depression exists—a crucial omission that reflects what is going on in psychotherapy today. Depression is taken as some kind of mysterious "given" and the treatment goes on from there.

What is disturbing to me is that psychotherapy is now a matter of Prozac and its alternative, electroshock. Psychotherapists are eager to skip the talking therapy and try to repress the pain with drugs. If that repression doesn't work, they'll try a stronger repressant. Repression has become the byword of psychotherapy. If you do not probe the unconscious, there is no other way. Either you let feelings up or you push them down.

Seizures produced by electroshock *do* help, specifically because there is a massive discharge of latent primal energy that needs to escape. Electroshock aids that escape, but it doesn't usually last for more than six months or a year. In the meantime the pain is still there. At the one-year mark, fifty percent of electroshock patients relapse, with new episodes of depression and psychosis.

We have the Freudian legacy to thank for the adherence to shock therapy. The Freudians decided that delving deep into the unconscious would disintegrate the mind. They therefore eliminated the most important way to rid patients of deep numbness: experiencing what caused it.

Recently we treated a woman who, after ten months of therapy, began convulsing in a strange way during each of her primals. We thought perhaps it was a kind of birth reliving we had never seen before. It turned out that she was reliving an electrical shock. We discovered that her mother had received a terrible jolt from an electric plug during the sixth month of gestation. The shock happened in Europe, where the electrical output is 220 volts. It is powerful enough to knock someone over and can be lethal. In this instance, it wasn't just the mother who got the shock. So did the baby, and that powerful input had to be relived many times, over many months. One had only to see the terrible convulsions during the primals to realize what was inside this particular patient. This overload had caused a shutdown, the same shutdown occasioned by electroshock therapy given to adult depressives, the same kind of shutdown triggered by massive neglect in the earliest years of life.

Regardless of the source of the message, be it so-called emotional pain or a massive physical assault, all the brain system knows is that there is an overwhelming amount of input that must be dealt with. The fact of our patient's reliving the electric shock confirmed for us how necessary it is for those who have undergone electroshock therapy to relive their shock as well. The fact that electroshock is delivered to someone already unconscious changes nothing. The physiology still experiences the event.

A sixty-year-old woman came to us from a small town in England. She was severely depressed. "What does the depression feel like?" she was asked. "Numb . . . not getting anything out of life . . . despair," she replied. She told us she had been depressed some twenty-two years earlier. She had no idea what had brought it back.

Soon after she started her three weeks of therapy, the Los Angeles area was struck by a major earthquake on January 17, 1994. My patient found herself shaking in a bed that moved across the room. That event reawakened something that changed her symptoms and changed the complexion of her therapy. She reported the following relentless symptoms: a constant hissing sound in her ears, night and day; numbness in the face; a feeling of electricity all over her body (she shook and jerked); and a terrible feeling of discomfort.

In her sessions her face went numb. She lost motor control of her legs. When she tried to stand up while in session, she would collapse. She then began flopping uncontrollably. There were no words to her agony. She had no idea what she was undergoing, had no idea why her body was shaking or why her face went numb, had no insights and seemed blank. She was the picture of a fragmented human being. It turned out that she was reliving the electroshock treatment she had undergone twenty times some twenty-two years before. Her doctor had prescribed it for her previous bout of depression.

When we pressed on her temples (where the electrodes had originally been placed), she arched back and flopped and jerked exactly as though she were again undergoing electroshock. On several occasions, when I put my fingers on her temples, the right side of her face went numb, something that no doubt had occurred originally. Moreover, when I tapped strongly on her right cheek, she reported feeling only pressure on her right cheek but no pain, another indication of numbness in the original experience. When a pencil was put in her mouth at the appropriate time, she clamped down on it as hard as one could imagine, her face grimaced in agony, and she was back in the electroshock experience again. She was reliving the time they put a rubber device in her mouth to keep her from biting her tongue or breaking her teeth during electroshock.

Electroshock is like any shock. It is a trauma that must be relived in its entirety. *What goes in must come out.* It is an extrapolation of the homeopathic notion that if you are allergic and I inject you with a little bit of the antigen over time, eventually you will build up a defense against it.

What does the shock do? It does what any shock or overload does: It raises the level of serotonin, the inhibitory brain chemical that enhances repression. It also alters a number of other neurotransmitters. It therefore does what any state of enhanced repression does; it renders the person ahistoric, bereft of emotional memory for one day, a week, and sometimes longer—a shutdown, pure and simple. In our woman patient's case, the whole shock experience decades later was still rendering her unconscious, blocking memory and preventing deep access. That was the point of the original shock therapy, I presume—to prevent deep internal access, to stop memory in its tracks.

Doctors often resort to electroshock therapy when ordinary tranquilizing pills aren't adequate because the underlying pain is so great that simple medication won't suppress it. The big guns of electroshock are called in to blast the memory out of existence. In a society where results are paramount, electroshock offers a "quick fix." One can see immediate results, which usually last for a number of months. The patient attests to its benefits and everyone seems happy. Meanwhile, churning below the surface is that very shock, doing its damage by stealth. The person is back at work, but part of her has been left back at the shock room in the hospital. Electroshock therapy has helped her be a productive member of society, a robot in the service of results. She is devitalized, desensitized, hollow, and dehumanized, churning out product while her real feelings grind away in the deep unconscious. She is now "superneurotic." She was given shock because her neurosis wasn't working and she was close to her feelings. Afterward she was far from her feelings and her neurosis worked again.

ELLEN: RELIVING ELECTRO-CONVULSIVE THERAPY

It's nice to know that there was a real reason for feeling uncomfortable. I had greatly enjoyed hugging before I had ECT. After the ECT, I still felt the need for comfort but couldn't even begin to make the movement to try to get a hug. Noise, and the effect I feel that my noise (my presence) has on others, is less disturbing. The problem stemmed from very early memories, compounded over the years by my father, who had extremely acute hearing and very low noise tolerance. As I was reliving ECT, my whole body seemed even more sensitive to noise and sound vibrations. My head felt like a tin bucket in which everything echoed. I felt like I was shouting even when I was speaking quietly, and my eyes lost their ability to focus. Now I am much more relaxed and my startle response has dropped from at least two hundred percent to maybe five percent. I can now look at people with direct eye-to-eye contact for more than a split second because I feel they will be able to see somebody in here (me!) and not just the empty container that I felt I was.

Early in therapy, my memory about places in England seemed blank. I felt stupid for not being able to remember my own country. Now I can remember, and when I go out with people after Group for coffee, I can hear and be heard, even when the jukebox is playing! And the "hassle" I used to feel when they were deciding who would drive me back to the hotel is no more; now, it's just some nice people who want to get me home safely discussing how it should be done. I used to be so internally agitated about needing help because making my presence felt and my needs known meant "being a nuisance."

I was always painfully shy before ECT, and was even worse after it because of the memory loss. My memory is improving but I still have a big blank spot around fifteen years of age. What else have I lost? I feel very insecure about making friends—a sort of "Who am I?" feeling makes me cautious. Yet my birth memories and feelings seem very real and make sense of so much that didn't make sense in my life. I feel I can now see and understand the many contradictions in my upbringing and the ever-present sadness that hovered over all the "happy" events.

During many sessions over a period of weeks, our sixty-year-old English patient relived pieces of her electroshock treatment. Its charge value blotted out anything else. Slow reliving of the shock was necessary before she could get to the shocking feelings that lay behind her depression. As long as that event was superimposed on childhood pain, it took precedence in the reliving sequence. Interestingly, as she relived more and more of the shock therapy, she began covering her head and hearing the bombs over London during the blitz in World War II. After that, she began to relive traumas from even earlier. Finally she arrived down deep, to the imprints that caused the depression originally, the very events and feelings that had led doctors to decide that she needed ECT: an early loveless life devoid of any caring beings.

The doctors who had administered electroshock did not talk to the woman about the possible causes of her depression, which is most often unknown by the patient. Observing that she was crying all the time, they decided that there seemed to be no alternative but to shock her.

The electroshock treatment blasted third-line coherence just enough so that the whole meaning underlying her depression would not be apparent. It was the meaning that was catastrophic! And the shocks further concealed that meaning. This meant fragmentation, or not being connected to what's inside of her body—in short, neurosis. Her neurosis fragmented her thought patterns, cut short her attention span, and ruined the ability to concentrate. Such fragmentation kept her from making coherent sense, from getting to the catastrophe underlying her depression. Based on our experience, we did not expect a connected lucidity in this woman until a major portion of the electroshock treatment was relived.

The Problem With "Mock" Primal Therapy and "Rebirthing"

Some people have taken to delving into the unconscious without knowing how to do it correctly. This is what has often happened in "rebirthing" and in "mock primal therapy" (they use the name of our therapy but have the techniques wrong). Practitioners manage to attack repression but without the controls we use, controls that ensure that the system is able to integrate pain little by little. Instead, patients are confronted with the onslaught of pain liberated out of sequence. The system is then forced into desperate tactics to elude consciousness. When this happens, the cortex must stretch itself into all manner of bizarre notions, mystical ideas, and paranoid ideation, all to handle the pain.

Thus, in rebirthing, where first-line pains are abruptly brought to the surface, you find inundation and then wild flights of imagination with delusions and hallucinations. Often you will find a rebirther reporting having lived past lives in faraway places and bygone centuries. In the mystical zeitgeist of the rebirthers, ancient Egypt is a favorite watering hole. That's where many people magically discover they once lived. What has happened is that the person has made a leap into the unreal in order to protect herself from the real.

"Egypt" becomes the symbol because the real past cannot be felt. Not surprisingly, many people discover that they were pharaohs or princesses or wise priests in their past lives. Those who feel powerless conjure up previous incarnations in which they were powerful; those who were not listened to or respected when they were little harken back to a time when they were wise and important and everyone wanted to hear what they had to say. It happens unconsciously; the symbols that arise reflect the specific unmet needs.

Because the chain of pain has been violated, the person being opened up prematurely is now benignly psychotic. She still functions, but with a mixture of coherence and incoherence. She is able to continue working, to solve problems, but in less structured moments the mystical beliefs and delusions take over. What has happened is that the painful information residing in the ancient brain has been abruptly brought to consciousness. This information can't possibly be integrated until months or years of higher-level imprints have been experienced.

In truth, the past lives these rebirthers experience are not in ancient Egypt but from a brain millions of years more ancient, from when salamanders were one of the highest species running around the earth. The patient may have been put close to the memories stored in this part of the brain but has missed the essential connection *because these memories have too high a charge value.*

The therapist may believe in the cosmic ideas, as many re-birthing therapists do, and may even suggest them to the patient. The patient is being made sick in the name of therapy. He is being driven crazy and having his craziness confirmed by the doctor. The patient's cortex has been rushed into service to maintain unconsciousness, with the result being more unconsciousness, not less.

Reliving birth can mean great pain and a life-and-death struggle, and one needs expert help to connect and integrate something of such magnitude. This birth pain cannot and should not be experienced until many lesser pains are dealt with. With a well-timed birth primal, one would never have to linger in some ancient holy place. I have never, ever seen past lives in my thousands of patients over a quarter of a century of primal treatment. It is not because I don't believe in it. It is because I am careful to see that each and every pain is properly integrated so that there is no flooding of consciousness.

Another practice mock primal therapists often encourage is screaming out one's pain. This reminds us of the act we were told to put on in Gestalt therapy. *Screaming for its own sake will not heal anything.* Indeed, screaming comes about or should emanate only out of connection, not as an exercise unto itself. It might even help a little to scream and pound walls viciously, as is done at the direction of some therapists, but it will never heal. In fact, *any direction from a therapist about what to feel dooms the therapeutic process.* Simply stated, the discharge in a real re-living comes from within, on the level where pain occurred, in the proper order, and with the intensity of the reactions that were held back.

No level of brain tissue can do the work of another. No cortical cell network can solve the riddle of an imprint lying deep in the brain. There is a tendency to think that "reliving" is some kind of adult play-acting where adults simulate childhood behavior. This is not what happens in true primal therapy. Adults may simulate childhood behavior, but this can never bring about a lasting cure.

Addressing Symptoms, Not the System

A thirty-eight-year-old woman visits a doctor, presenting with vague physical symptoms. She maintains that she is not under stress. The doctor sees no stress, so he takes the patient's word for it. He may give vitamins and encourage a proper diet, or tell the patient to get more exercise or get more rest. These prescriptions may help. Stress does burn up vitamin and mineral supplies. In fact, diet and vitamins may help so much that vague symptoms disappear. But stress hormone levels will remain high, certain cells of the immune system are still weak or in short supply, and the person needs more and more of this or that to buttress the effects of pain.

It is very difficult to fully understand causes of disease by minutely examining symptoms. This is because *the causes don't lie in the symptoms; they lie below them.* One can see why the doctor searching for objective indicators might be at a loss to understand a certain disease. By looking through a microscope three decades after a traumatic birth or a catastrophic childhood loss, how could anyone possibly know that the trauma of living in a cold, barren foster home between the ages of five and twelve caused this affliction? He can prescribe medication that lowers the blood pressure or alleviates whatever symptom has brought the patient to him, but we can be sure that the imprint will go on producing other illnesses.

When we try to conquer our biology, we fail. So many therapies talk of conquering, subduing, managing, or overcoming our problems and symptoms, or blasting them away with massive jolts of electricity. We may try to neutralize high blood pressure or try to conquer depression with antidepressant medication, but its price includes greater cellular stress. Similarly, you can't hook someone up to a brainwave machine, normalize his brainwaves with biofeedback, and expect to resolve his depression permanently. The biologic question is, "Why are his brainwaves abnormal?" We must probe for the underlying pain to find the answer. Thus, directive daydreaming, in which one imagines that one is hammering the cancer cells away, can help but cannot cure. Cure, I submit, can only be offered when tied to generating sources. Hypnosis cannot cure, nor can acupuncture, meditation, or insight therapy. Any treatment that simply and exclusively attacks the symptoms—therapies of appearances, by definition—cannot be curative. The problem is, they are facile and attractive to the consumer.

Healing the Wound

Most therapies and treatments are only reforming agents. Reform means working within the current structure, trying to improve it. Reform is better than doing nothing. But it is not revolution; it doesn't overthrow a system of interlocking processes. It wants to change this or that and keep the system intact, which means keeping the neurosis intact while rearranging the facade.

Cure is possible if we don't take it to mean that we are going to be some wonderful person of our dreams after therapy. Carefully defining neurosis allows us to discuss cure as the lifting of repression and integrating of the unconscious; no more, no less.

Neurosis is a wound that requires healing according to the same principles as the healing of any physical wound. And, indeed, it *is* a physical wound. Neurosis is a wound that can never fully repair itself until we set in motion those forces involved in the healing process. Psychic wounds, which may cause many physical afflictions, are healed by addressing the wounds on the level on which they occurred and only on that level. This means that if the wound is preverbal, there are no words in the world that can effect healing. You cannot talk your way out of a burn, and you can't talk your way out of the experience of total neglect in the first weeks of life. You cannot heal a wound sustained in the crib at the age of one with words. There is no getting well without the conscious experience of the wound itself, for it is *consciousness* that sends the signals for healing.

I don't mean to discount the importance of counseling, education, child guidance, or family therapy. They help and are important. So is medication for high blood pressure or heart disease. It may help prevent a heart attack or stroke. There is nothing wrong with wanting help, but if you get help while expecting cure, you will be disappointed.

The conclusion is inescapable: Psychotherapies that do not have access to such pain as their ultimate goal cannot help the patient heal and get well in any real sense. If one does not recognize the imprint and engraved memory, it is easy to go astray in the treatment of illness. And I do not mean access to just any pain. I mean systematic access to pain in the reverse order in which it was laid down in the nervous system. Only this process, which is intrinsic to the structure and responses of our nervous system, can lead to any lasting resolution. In brief it is the body which dictates how much pain comes up, in what order, and when it is to be shut down.

If the real wound underlying depression is at the age of one, when you were kicked away with anger from holding Daddy's legs, no amount of verbal processes, insights, discharging tension, or conditioning-style approaches will touch it. You again have to hold (now the therapist's legs) and feel the pain of the utter rejection. Remember the patient I mentioned at the outset, who had cried for his mother in the crib but his furious, angry father came instead? Later in life the patient saw angry eyes all around him. My patient did not want to talk to his mother, or forgive or analyze her; he wanted to be taken in her arms and be comforted. It was a *physical* ache, an ache coded in his arms and shoulders. It wasn't necessary for him to *understand* his need. He had to *experience* it.

The central paradigm of neurosis and its cure is that nothing can come in, nothing from the past can be fulfilled, as long as repression is blocking the way. No insight, exhortation, pleading, or medication can make any profound difference because repression won't allow it. More important, no love from a parent can enter the child's system fully when repression is already in place.

Lifting repression is the basis of the difference between reform and revolution. The more one feels what caused the closure of the system, the more open one becomes. When you change the system, you automatically change the behavior, the brain, and the immune system. The next chapter will talk about the basis of how this can happen; then, in Chapter Fourteen, we will venture into the primal zone to explore how dismantling the barrier of repression opens the door to healing.

13

THE LIMBIC SYSTEM: HOW AND WHERE WE STORE OUR FEELINGS

Emotions are not something to be conquered, suppressed, held in check, or neglected. On the contrary, they are essential to being human and are woven into the fabric of our systems and serve a survival purpose. Without feelings and needs, we would be robots. Feelings give us the ability to reason. They underlie our thoughts, behavior, interests, beliefs, dreams, and obsessions.

Neurologist Antonio Damasio has suggested that feelings are critical in decision making. In most decisions, we imagine a course of action and then judge whether the internal feeling state is a pleasant one. Does it feel good? If so, we do it. But if the feeling state is unpleasant, we don't make the decision to follow through.

When we are shut off from our feelings we have great difficulty making decisions because we don't know what we feel. We may behave recklessly because we cannot *feel* the consequences of our action (or inaction). In general, if not enough emotional stimulation occurs, or if too much emotion drives the thinking brain, then thought processes will be impaired.

By and large, feelings are stored, processed, and expressed in a system of brain structures known as the limbic system.

(See Figure 3 on page 273.) Physiologically, the limbic system acts like a capacitor; it stores the electrical charge of emotional activation, accepting just so much input and "dumping" the excess wherever it can. The model for understanding this is demonstrated in an experiment performed on dogs by Ronald Melzack, as reported by Crichley in *Scientific Foundations of Neurology.*

Each day for several days Melzack gave an electrical zap to the limbic area of a dog's brain. The electrical charge was apparently stored, for the electrical activity of the brain reverberated at a higher level after each zap, until one day the dogs began to have spontaneous seizures. The dogs had developed a form of epilepsy to handle the overload of input.

Since a physical or psychological trauma to the system reaches the limbic system as a "zap" of electrical input, there are then continuing "aftershocks" of electrical activity. Even when the trauma is over, it will still reverberate in the limbic circuitry unless it can reach consciousness. This explains why *every neurotic is under unremitting internal stress.* Recall LeDoux's perspective mentioned in Chapter Three on hidden emotional memory, in which the limbic system "forms and stores its unconscious memories of those events, and that trauma may affect mental and behavioral functions in later life, albeit through processes that remain inaccessible to consciousness." Moreover, as in the above experiment, when the limbic system can no longer handle the storage of pain, the spillover leads to symptoms. (See Figures 4 and 5 on pages 273 and 274, respectively.)

Let us examine some of the limbic structures and see what happens to feelings, how they are processed, gated, translated into symptoms, and finally resolved. The following is by no means an effort at an exact study in neurology, which is not my expertise. Rather, it is an attempt to explain what may happen when we are traumatized early in life, and what happens to the feelings associated with the trauma. Also keep in mind that the roles of the limbic structures overlap; one cannot say that one structure alone is involved in storing while another is involved in retrieving memory.

The Thalamus: Where Pain and Suffering Are Processed

The thalamus is one of the most important structures involved in feelings and a major player in gating traumas that begin early in life. Part of its function is to integrate feelings and help relay them to the prefrontal cortex, where they take on specific context and meaning. Recent evidence in the December 22, 1994, issue of *Nature* has pinpointed a particular thalamic nucleus as a center of the perception and relay of pain. One of the pioneers in neurology, W. J. H. Nauta (together with coauthor Michael Feirtag) describes the thalamus as "a final checkpoint before messages from all the sensoria are allowed entrance to higher stations of the brain . . . At each synaptic interruption in a sensory pathway the input is transformed: the code in which the message arrived is fundamentally changed. Presumably, the data could not be understood at higher levels: translation is needed."

The cerebral cortex is the last stop on the journey of the message. For the message to arrive, it needs to be translated by the thalamus into the language of the cortex. This translation enables the prefrontal cortex to provide meaning to an emotional stimulus. Thus, Mommy's disgusted expression would mean, "I'm bad," or "I am not loved." It enables a person to access and articulate a vague feeling, such as "Mother hates me and makes me feel bad about myself." The thalamus also relays our needs to the cortex for interpretation and satisfaction, such as, "Please be nice to me, Mommy!" With the aid of the prefrontal cortex, the thalamus integrates information about feelings or needs, provided the feeling or deprivation is not too great!

When the information is overwhelming, it becomes a jumble and proper translation cannot take place, nor can proper transmission. One of the thalamus's functions is to *block* feelings from making their cortical connections: "I feel awful—

Mommy hates me!" When the relay ceases to work due to the overload of nerve circuits, we become partially or totally unconscious, unaware of our feelings and needs. When access is blocked so that the cortex cannot define a need, we try to fulfill it symbolically. Also blocked from consciousness is the response: "I'll struggle to be nice to keep Mommy from having a disgusted look on her face." Thus, a person will not know why he constantly struggles to please.

The thalamus is generally activated by imprinted memory. The need for a loving father, for example, activates the system constantly, continually sending messages via the thalamus that the organism is in danger due to lack of love. The need for love then is rerouted and recircuited and becomes a symbolic need, such as the need for attention in the present. (See Figure 5 on page 274.)

Once a trauma is in place, the body goes into its fight-or-flight reaction, which then catalyzes the production of endorphins that attenuate the reaction. Ordinarily, the message must get through to help the person avoid danger and survive. But when there is deprivation, the *message has become the danger* because it creates excessive reactions that threaten the physical system: a very high heart rate, for example, or the oversecretion of stress hormone. If a woman is pregnant, she might give birth prematurely due to the increased amount of circulating stress hormone. The prematurity remains a mystery to all concerned because the underlying imprinted stress has gone unrecognized.

If we return to the example of anoxia at birth, a lack of oxygen can produce lifelong effects to the thalamus and other parts of the limbic system, making integration of pain information deficient. One way this could result is when anoxia impairs the two-way information highway between the thalamus and cortex, creating an inability to shut out extraneous input. (Anoxia can also cause small hemorrhages in the brain that not only can produce seizures later on but also show up as emotional problems as well as physical handicaps.) Repression becomes faulty and stays that way, with the individual suffering from anxiety for the rest of his life, unable to concentrate or sleep well. These patients often have deficient gating, making them, if anything, too aware of their suffering. They simply cannot repress enough. These are the individuals who do not function well or at all. This situation is likely caused by thalamic impairment where there may be insufficient cortical activation. In adulthood, the person may take the stimulant Ritalin to "soup-up" this faulty function. Ritalin assists the cortex in inhibiting lower-level pain, helping to make the person unaware of internal suffering. A busier cortex feels like normalization to this individual. He is "in control" at last.

Energy routed through the thalamus upward to the cortex can stimulate ideation. The third-line thinking brain rushes in with belief systems to absorb the energy. The "unreality" of the idea or belief will depend on the force of the feeling. If no one ever looked after the person, who then never felt safe and protected, the belief might be in a God who is protective and watchful. Getting below the belief system will lead to the feeling driving it, but trying to convince someone of the illogic of the belief is useless since it is logical *in the context of the feeling sequestered in the limbic system*. The real feeling is "unsafe and unprotected." The belief in the protective guru or God makes sense, just as a migraine makes sense when tied to oxygen deprivation at birth. Without connection to cortical consciousness, there will be symptoms, as the energy is dispersed throughout the physical system. Reconnection is the *sine qua non* in therapy. If a patient makes little progress, it is often because there is minimal reconnection. That is why one must tranquilize the patient for a time in therapy to diminish the thalamic load, allowing more cortical input and integration. One must artificially normalize the person and his limbic system until the pain is sufficiently discharged to allow integration without drugs. Until that happens a person can be driven by feelings he cannot recognize because the precise message never reaches conscious-awareness. Worse, the unconscious feelings warp our conscious appreciation of them so that by the time we can "rationally" discuss them, their meaning has been obscured. Now imagine the effectiveness of using insight or "talk" therapy to discuss the feelings that limbic system structures are hiding. The access in insight therapy is not to the feelings but to the results of those feelings on awareness. The lower structures are dealing with feelings long before the cortex is developed and becomes aware. In fact, *many traumas never arrive at consciousness*; lower-level gating sees to that. As LeDoux reminds us, "Emotional learning . . . is mediated by a different system [than declarative learning, meaning left cerebral cortex factual learning] . . . which in all likelihood operates independently of our conscious-awareness." (LeDoux is discussing emotional learning, which comes about through fear conditioning, but I believe the principle holds for feelings as well.)

By sequentially opening the gates, we find the real need, not its symbol. Once we find the need, we always find pain, because it hurts to have one's needs go unfulfilled. As neurosis is reversed in primal therapy, the thalamus will again play a major role in allowing previously disconnected memories to connect with conscious-awareness.

Where Feelings Are Stored:
The Amygdala-Hippocampus Connection

While the thalamus plays a role in the initial coding of information, the amygdala and hippocampus help consolidate the memory once coded.

The amygdalae are a pair of almond-shaped structures lying adjacent to the hippocampus—the tips of the ram's horns—on the inner surface of the temporal lobes, forming a kind of crossroads in the brain (see Figure 3 on page 273). The feeling "I want my daddy!" is coded and stored with the help of the thalamus and concretized by the amygdala and hippocampus. It is sent via the final common pathway to bodily systems—the hypothalamus. There it alters our physical functioning, eventually making us sick (see Figure 6 on page 274).

Much research converges in the understanding that opiate-containing fibers run from the amygdala to the sensory systems, where they serve a gate-keeping function by releasing opiates in response to emotional states generated in the hypothalamus. These structures control access to our emotions, influencing what is experienced and what is not, what is learned and what is not. When the input is too charged, painkillers are released and the message doesn't get through to conscious-awareness. It does get through to various bodily systems, which accept the message uncritically and unabated. They do their best to handle the message but without the aid of conscious-awareness they are helpless to stop the input. The stomach puts out an excess of hydrochloric acid, the adrenals put out too many stress hormones, and the blood system increases its pressure level to dangerous heights. When the message is finally connected, all those effects change and normalize. The message may be, "Why do you hate me? Please, please don't hate me. Love me a little!" When it rises to the top, first there is agony and then the system can finally relax. After such a connection, I've seen blood pressure drop a hundred points. The relationship between pain and blood pressure becomes obvious. Here again we note the dialectic: The structures that organize feeling are also the ones which repress it through the secretion of neuroinhibitors.

Adrenaline and other stress hormones reinforce the amygdalae's recording process, which is why pain and trauma are cemented in the brain so firmly; the greater the fear, anguish, and suffering, the stronger the imprint. Here we see the neurological reason the prototype can have lifelong effects on the structure of the developing brain and personality. Because the amygdalae and other structures that process feelings also secrete repressive hormones, they control access to those emotions, influencing what we are aware of and what we repress. Damage to the amygdalae prevents someone from recognizing fearful expressions in others, another indication of these structures' role in emotional perception. Impaired amygdalae, resulting from a load of pain, can make us less sensitive to how others feel.

The amygdalae plays a key role in emotional speech and crying. When my patients cry "Mama, please hold me!" in a five-year-old voice, we can be sure the amygdalae is involved. Electrical stimulation of the amygdalae creates hypersexuality, and the amygdalae is largely responsible for erection in the male. When there is insufficient holding and caressing very early in life, it is probably the amygdalae that transform stored pain into compulsive sexuality.

Behind the amygdalae, the hippocampus (the word means "sea-horse," which this structure resembles) forms the tip of the ram's horn. One of the most ancient structures of the brain (the amygdalae are even older), the hippocampus is apparently responsible for declarative memory, the context and circumstances of an event as opposed to its emotional significance. If, at five years old, your mother says to you for the hundredth time, "You are useless and stupid. Get out of my sight!" the circumstances and feeling of the event are imprinted by the hippocampus and amygdalae, respectively. Finer meaning is added to the event by the cortex so that the full connection may be, "Mother hates me!" The subconscious logic of the young child is likely to be, "She's angry because I'm bad. She hates me!" But this is intolerable, a devastating realization that the child cannot grasp; so endorphins are secreted by the limbic structures that process feelings inhibiting full connection. The feelings are now gated and kept unconscious. The struggle begins: to make her and then others "like me." The feeling is unconscious and acted out unconsciously. Explaining this to someone who is acting out won't change anything. Feelings, not ideas, are driving behavior. You don't need new ideas; you need connection.

Once Mother is disgusted over and over with a child, that same tone of contempt from anyone can cause the hippocampus to retrieve the memory. This is accomplished by the scanning mechanism: The current event is labeled as to the kind of feeling it is, whose frequency then resonates with a past coded feeling, dredging it up from the limbic storehouse toward conscious-awareness. A torrent of information that activates physical systems is then experienced as anxiety. The anxiety is a danger signal that the original event is approaching consciousness.

It is the right hippocampus and amygdala that produce pictures and images in the brain. They can create illusions, hallucinations, dreamlike states, and dreams. They help transform repressed feelings into the images of bad dreams. Analyzing the dreams won't heal anything, and it is a useless exercise because it attempts to use the cortex to heal a wound lower in the nervous system. The wound has to be addressed on its own level *by that level*, not by the adult "reaching down" to that level.

In a primal, when we go to retrieve the memory, the keys of access to that memory are provided by the hippocampus. In primals dealing with the first year of life, the patient becomes inarticulate as words fade away and emotion takes over. There are then scenes but no words to describe them. The brain's theta waves, which have been found to be associated with feeling states, come from the hippocampus. As a patient approaches feelings, the brain waves often dip into theta. In conditioning experiments with animals, abundant theta rhythms mean the animal is more likely to remember past training. Interestingly, after just a few weeks of primal therapy, we see a statistically significant increase in theta waves. (See Appendix B.)

The hippocampus is heavily connected by nerve fibers to the septum, a pleasure center of the brain. In a classic experiment, rodents given the choice between food and an electrical impulse to the septum chose the electrical stimulus over the food until they died of starvation. This may account for our clinical observation that one must get through pain in order to be able to feel pleasure completely.

How Pain Sent to the Body Produces Symptoms: The Hypothalamus

At the junction of the ram's horn, the hypothalamus regulates hormone production and directs the immune system via the pituitary gland just beneath it. Along with the brainstem below it, the hypothalamus is involved in the body's "homeostatic regulation," controlling body temperature, breathing, heart function, blood pressure, digestion, electrolyte balance, visceral tone, and dozens of other vital functions. As I have stated, the hypothalamus is a final common pathway through which the limbic system sends energy of feelings into the bodily system, exciting the visceral organs. It is what makes a feeling of being criticized churn up the stomach.

In the back of the hypothalamus there is a major center for agony. Whether the pain is from falling down the stairs, a burn, or the perception that "Mommy doesn't like me," the agony is the same. Painful stored feelings such as "I am bad. They don't want me around!" are reflected in bodily reactions: The heart will speed up, more of this or that hormone will be secreted, blood pressure will elevate, and so on.

The hypothalamus has been shown to have a hand in heart disease. Animal studies at New York Medical College show that stimulation of certain centers of the hypothalamus causes major changes in the coronary arteries of rats. The rats chosen for the experiment were not the kind that usually develop heart problems, yet a series of electrical stimuli brought the problems on. I believe this happens with imprinted pain, after Melzack's model noted earlier in this chapter. The electricity "zaps" the hypothalamus, which in turn "zaps" the arteries leading to the heart. This causes constriction and/or a faster heart rate, resulting in the pain of angina. It is a short step from here to arterial spasm and an eventual heart attack. This happens without any conscious recognition of what is going on.

One goal in treating heart problems should be to ease the hypothalamic burden, to decrease the recruitment of hypothalamic pathways in the service of rerouting activation from early pain. The alternative to this—what's usually done in conventional treatment—would be to deal interminably with the symptoms of the malfunctioning heart: giving nitroglycerin to ease the constriction leading to angina, tranquilizers to slow down the activation causing palpitations, and so on.

The System That Alerts Us: The Reticular Activating System

Pain is a warning sign that the system is in danger, that biological needs are going unfulfilled. Pain mobilizes the system like nothing else can, keeping it alert and reminded that there is unfinished business. The agency for activating this vigilance is the reticular activating system (RAS), located in the brainstem. This netlike structure is one of the key areas of norepinephrine concentration, which helps us mobilize the system and make it vigilant. In "The Reward System of the Brain" in *Scientific American,* author Routtenberg explains that "both norepinephrine and dopamine [the activating neurochemicals] send their axons into the cerebral cortex . . . highly complex and intricate patterns of intellectual activity in the cortex are influenced by evolutionarily primitive catecholamine systems." Rather than relaying specific information to higher centers, the cortex "measures" the amount of information passing through and activates the brain sufficiently to deal with that level. Meanwhile, the frontal lobes modulate the activity of the RAS, usually by inhibiting its activity. Thus, we achieve the right degree of alertness for the task at hand, whether it be fleeing from a deadly threat or writing term papers. The RAS matures early, always activating the highest level of neurological functioning available at a given stage of development.

When pain is imprinted, the RAS may continuously overstimulate conscious-awareness. The result may be obsessive thoughts as the frontal area attempts to deal with and suppress the lower-level activation. When this happens, ideas begin to churn. The person cannot "shut off" his brain, as it were. He cannot fall asleep because his mind is working overtime. Sometimes, ideas are enough to shut off the feelings via the descending reticular pathways: "I don't like him anyway," or "She just said that because she's jealous!" But sometimes the feelings are too strong to shut down. Then it seems as though someone opened a valve in the brain and agitation pours forth continuously. This is almost literally true. The gates are open and old feelings rise to the surface, creating a more or less constant fight-or-flight reaction.

In obsessional worry, the thalamus and amygdala, together with the RAS, may be allowing too much input to be released to higher centers, resulting in a cortex that is working overtime. (See Figure 7 on page 275.) It isn't the ideas that are driving the person crazy; it is the feelings that are driving ideas. Fear on its way upward via the thalamus and amygdala can be partially gated but can reach the prefrontal cortex, where it is translated into constant worrying: "What if I have a car wreck?" "What if there is an earthquake?" "What if so and so doesn't call tomorrow?" "What if the economy takes a tailspin?" "What if I lose my job?"

Drugs that work on feeling centers stop the *ideational* frenzy. A number of tranquilizers work on the RAS, suppressing its activation and relaxing the person. Tranquilizers work on obsessions because they quell the pain from below, thereby putting less pressure on the cortex; the cortex, then, no longer has to manufacture worries and obsessions. The barbiturate sleeping pill Seconal promotes sleep by working almost exclusively on the RAS. It is this system that won't let us fall asleep easily, creating idea after idea as stimulation rushes forth when the third-line gate is trying to rest.

It is interesting to note that as feelings have greater access, a person may signal this rise by obsessing about one thing or another. They fixate on a person who they imagine is against them, or concentrate on someone else who they imagine is in love with them. The specific obsession is of little consequence because it goes away as the person drops into feeling. But until the feeling is experienced, even a slight ignoring of the individual is taken as a major insult. The person now is fixated and obsessed with all the strength of the old feeling. If fear is on the rise, he or she may begin to hear noises from the closet at night or see shadows while lying in bed, just as the person did at a young age.

When there is imprinted fear or terror, the center nearby the RAS in a brainstem structure known as the locus ceruleus is active, continuously galvanizing the cortex (see Figure 8 on page 275). It usually isn't felt as terror (that would be a connected primal) but rather is experienced as a racing mind, racing away from the terror. It blasts the cortex with "noise" when one is trying to concentrate. It can involve a cacophony of messages of anxiety and fear in the language of the different levels, all arriving at once at the third line. The result is that the cortex cannot understand the message and can acknowledge only agitation. The message is, "Wake up! Watch out! Trouble is on the way!" So the person is alert against an unknown enemy. No wonder he is wide awake at bedtime!

As soon as the person descends to a lower level in primal therapy, it all becomes clear. The fear becomes the specific fear of one's drunken father, the result of thousands of childhood experiences of abandonment, humiliation, neglect, lack of touch or understanding, or simple kindness. The fear may be that of starting to die from anoxia at birth. The terror one experiences during an anxiety attack is not a property of anxiety, but rather of the original imprint. That is why there are nearly always breathing problems in anxiety, such as shortness of breath and the feeling of impending death. Once connected to consciousness and reacted to, the trauma and pain become a historical fact instead of a continuous force.

Once pain is recorded, it seems to reverberate in loops within the limbic system, spinning out dreams, social behavior, recurrent ideas, and physical reactions (see Figure 9 on page 276). The interconnectedness of the limbic structures is extraordinary, and all of them take part in the reverberation. A key structure for this circulating loop is the cingulum, the body of the ram's horn that forms the top layer of the limbic system.

The danger signal may originate when some present circumstance (that look of disgust, for example) resonates with past trauma in the hippocampus and amygdala, which begin to assemble the memory. It may be that the memory passes along the cingulum, picking up associations from neocortical association areas on the way to the forebrain. But if too much pain is associated with "that look," the strength of the signal will be so great that endorphins are secreted to disconnect the reverberation from awareness. The body is still activated as it was at the time of the trauma, *but the memory never reaches conscious-awareness.*

Where Feelings Are Connected—and Disconnected: The Prefrontal Cortex

The prefrontal cortex completes the limbic loop. Reason and emotion intersect here. In his book *Descartes' Error*, neurologist Antonio Damasio points out that patients with prefrontal damage do not show feeling and seem flat emotionally. These patients cannot evaluate differences between a major tragedy and a minor setback, giving them equal weight. Damasio proposes: "There is a particular region in the human brain where the systems concerned with emotion/feeling, attention and working memory interact so intimately that they constitute the source for the energy of both external action and internal action. This fountainhead region is the anterior cingulate cortex, another piece of the limbic system puzzle."

The prefrontal cortex receives information from all sensory centers concerning our external situation and internal state, and from memory; it is the center for integration of this information. Damasio puts it this way: "Upstairs and downstairs come together harmoniously in the (ventromedial) prefrontal cortices." We need this area to understand the implications of what is going on in the world outside and inside. Feeling means connection of lower-level imprints and feelings to higher levels of consciousness, and connection involves the prefrontal cortex, the integrative center. Do you need to "teach" integration to patients? No. Feelings will do that.

Damasio found that when there is damage to the frontal lobes of the brain, the person is prone to rationalize buried feelings, gathering up snippets of memory and fabricating a story to explain his behavior. Similarly, the repressed person, disconnected from his imprints, fabricates reasons for his behavior which may have nothing to do with reality. For example, a young patient of mine refused to tell her mother about her molestation by the mother's boyfriend; she reasoned that her mother wouldn't be interested. When she got down into old feelings, she discovered her real fear: that if she told her, her mother would become hysterical, fall apart as she had done in the past, and wouldn't be able to take care of her (the child). She needed a strong, protective mother. She only became conscious of it as she felt her needs.

The prefrontal cortex plays a role in the inhibition of emotional expression. When part of this structure is damaged, it is almost impossible to extinguish emotional memory, and when it functions poorly, memory bubbles up to the surface almost continuously. Powerful evidence is found in the fact that murderers who pleaded guilty by reason of insanity showed abnormally low metabolism of glucose in the prefrontal region. When this system is impaired, watch out! It is also underactive in schizophrenia.

Other characteristics of the brain's structure and functioning give insight into the neurotic split in consciousness. They help show how information is sometimes blocked or gated between brain structures, and how disjunction between thinking and feeling and between past memories and current perception is possible.

For example, in a well-functioning brain, the right hemisphere, the major site of second-line consciousness, emotionally evaluates factual information given to the "rational" left hemisphere. This interaction is mediated by the corpus callosum, a nerve network that connects the right (feeling) and left (reasoning) sides of the brain. But this structure does not mature fully until about ten years of age. So a child has a wealth of experience available to the right brain that isn't transmitted to the left side; a good deal of unconsciousness exists before the age of ten simply because the information network isn't in full working order. Until the corpus callosum develops fully, the child can *believe* in Santa Claus arriving in the middle of the night to leave Christmas presents and at the same time *know* that he could not fit down the chimney. Children spend a good deal of time talking to themselves, and they may be literally communicating with their second-line consciousness, describing and explaining things to their feeling self. Laura Berk investigated this in a 1994 *Scientific American* article.

In surgery where the corpus callosum is severed to prevent devastating epileptic attacks—a mechanical form of repression—it is as though one side doesn't know about the other, yet both seem to function rather well. A picture of a nude woman shown to such a patient on the right (feeling) side of the visual field made her giggle and blush. The severing of the corpus callosum served to shield the left side from access to feelings on the right side; the person still reacted to those feelings with blushing and discomfort but without any insight. When asked why she giggled, she rationalized with her left (reasoning) hemisphere that it was "funny." This is exactly what we see in neurosis.

After the corpus callosum has matured and a person's consciousness is integrated, the right hemisphere can clearly evaluate factual information given to the more rational left hemisphere. Its perceptions are often more accurate than those of the more literal left hemisphere, because it is in the second-line right hemisphere where nuances are felt and registered. It can, for example, detect insincerity and duplicity in the words of others. Where the third line may be more likely to believe what politicians say, the second line is better at hearing subtleties in their tone of voice and "seeing behind" their words and promises. But when repression blocks or gates information flow from one side of the brain to the other, in effect disconnecting the two, one may listen only to someone's words and miss the emotional component.

In neurosis, the left hemisphere becomes unaware of the feelings that drive thoughts and behavior. The neocortex gets lost in things intellectual. It imagines, for example, that certain beliefs and the behavior (prayer, meditation, fealty to a religious leader) connected to them are based on a system of ideas, when in reality they are driven by unconnected feelings. The second-line right hemisphere attends to the pain, keeping it away from consciousness by impelling the development of exotic notions. The adult is neurochemically separated from his pain *but is still responding to it*, like the epileptic patient whose corpus callosum was severed. Thus the pain of the intolerable realization that "They do not love me!" repressed long ago drives the dialectically opposite belief that "I am loved by a higher being." This is one role of our "higher-level" thinking centers. They must translate and disguise information reverberating on the lower levels to keep the person unconscious.

How Brain Cells Send and Block Pain

Stimulated brain cells release neurotransmitters. These chemicals stimulate receptors of adjacent cells, which then, according to neurologist Jean-Pierre Changeux in a 1993 article in *Scientific American,* change conformation and alter the flow of information across the cell network. There are more than fifty of these neurotransmitters for which brain cells have receptor molecules at their synaptic junctions. During our development, neurotransmitter release actually determines which pathways persist to grow more interconnections, which will survive and which will atrophy. Thus, the ordinary stimulation of life can enrich interconnection and expand the brain. But the massive overload of information from early pain may actually lessen the capacity to make connections or disconnections.

It is likely that early trauma changes the synaptic weights of nerve cells so that while some are more ready to fire, others are not. Thus, while lower-level imprints facilitate firing, the synaptic weights of the cortex may prevent firing; in this way conscious-awareness remains ignorant of what is going on below. Repression, in short, may be inherent in the cortical synaptic weights, negative or positive, so that the very structure of the nerve cells, altered by trauma, blocks information outflow. What would make neurons fire later on is the regulatory effect of neurotransmitters. If certain cells were more easily set off, it would take more inhibitory chemicals to repress their action. When the trauma is of great magnitude and the neurons easily facilitated, the nervous system may not be able to manufacture enough neuroinhibitors to suppress their firing. The result: a hyperactive, state of anxiety.

A key neurotransmitter that helps transmit messages between brain cells is acetylcholine. It is a facilitator of information flow in the cortex, particularly in the hippocampus. Repression seems to block this neurotransmitter from working properly. If you overexcite nerve pathways with continual supplies of acetylcholine, the receptor molecules lose their responsiveness and shut down. Primal pain seems to be an overexcitatory state which overloads the nerve pathways, causing a shutdown.

The Suffering System

Earthworms can suffer; they writhe and wiggle when they are hurt, but I very much doubt if they feel anxious. Long before we could be anxious, we could suffer.

The suffering system is one of the most ancient in the brain. In the maturation of man, the first nerve cells to mature and deal with noxious stimuli in the brain are those concerned with suffering, and the repression of that suffering. These cells control structures close to the anatomic midline of the body. Some cells in the midline of the brain are also involved in preventing the suffering signal from reaching consciousness (that is, gating early pain). Part of the thalamus in the limbic system conveys suffering toward the cortex. Because it contains many endorphin receptors, it can block information flow to the cortex and keep us unconscious of suffering. Instead, the person may wake up slightly depressed or apprehensive every morning, and the cause remains a mystery to him.

Suffering is the internal appreciation of an unpleasant state and means that somewhere there is tissue damage or the interruption of normal tissue function. In either case, there is an overload of painful information in the transmitting structures such as the RAS and its feed into the thalamus, known as the reticulate core. Parts of the brain network are overwhelmed, which is experienced as suffering. The body reacts with anxiety, the feeling of impending doom. Information about the suffering and malfunction rises from the internal organs and travels via hypothalamus into the ring of limbic structures, and from there to the prefrontal cortex. Then the response returns to modulate the visceral functions in an attempt to alleviate the suffering. Ideas rush in to quell the hurt: "I know they love me." "They didn't mean to exclude me."

Repression effects a neural disconnection between the part of us that knows we hurt and the part that could complete a sequence of healing. What our internally manufactured morphine does is separate the visceral message of suffering from the cortex of the brain, whose physiologic acknowledgment of that message could mediate healing. I'll say it again, because it is the crux of my message: You need connection to heal; you need feeling-acknowledgment to bring about healing. No feel, no heal.

Reconnection and Cure

To address neurosis and its related symptoms, we address the brain mechanisms by which people become neurotic, especially the discharge of excessive lower-level brain activation through connection to higher centers, expressed by crying and distress, leading to the context of the painful feeling. (See Figure 10 on page 276.)

Consciousness must not be confused with insight confined to higher centers in the brain. Such insight is a "cortical" phenomenon, whereas feeling is, as Damasio puts it, an "upstairs to downstairs" event. Insight given by a therapist or offered by the patient without feeling is always guesswork. It is inevitably a matter of "I think that . . . " Intellectual insight cannot be curative because it doesn't reach into the lower centers, where our life's experience and painful feelings live. Conversely, insight is most effective when grounded in lower-level information. Perhaps this is why we speak of "deep insight." Consciousness includes awareness of bodily states and sensations that have existed almost from the womb on; you do not have full consciousness without this fluid internal access and awareness. Insights after a primal are effortless and sure, arriving directly out of the feeling: "The hurt of losing my mother made me drink whenever my wife was cold to me." Primal insights have a strength and certainty we are rarely aware of in other circumstances.

To suffer from claustrophobia is a vague and unconnected phobia, but it continues persistently; to experience being trapped in the womb is a specific connection. The need to wander and keep on the move as an adult is a vague motivation; to feel in a primal that one had to get out of one's home because the atmosphere was intolerable is a specific connection. To scream and yell and cry as a release is not necessarily a connection. This is simply a symbolic discharge of energy from the reverberating limbic loop and therefore is noncurative. To cry about the time one's father gave away one's favorite dog is specific and involves a connection to the cortex, which makes it resolving. *Connection* is the be-all and end-all of healing, the goal of the primal process.

14

THE PRIMAL ZONE: THE ROLE OF REPRESSION IN HEALING

One patient of mine, a forty-eight-year-old woman, relived the abuse she suffered as a child, and the bruises actually *reappeared* during the reliving of the event. Where had the bruises been for the past forty years? They were part of the memory circuit, awaiting release for decades, ready to be triggered and relived, with the horrible meaning, "They don't like me or want me around!" During the reliving the patient fully appreciated this meaning consciously for the first time. As the person reacted with tears and weeping, the cells that sustained the beating finally responded to the insult and completed their reaction; hence the bruises.

In those bruises we see history before our eyes, as though no time had passed since that terrible day decades ago when the child was beaten without mercy. We are also observing healing. *There could be no healing of that pain without the bruises and the sensation of the physical beating*. Furthermore, this particular patient was prone to bruise easily. But when the early trauma was finally felt, this tendency ceased. The cells that were under continual imprinted stress for forty years could finally complete their healing process.

Similarly, if bruises from rough handling at birth were part of the original trauma and repression interrupted their healing, they will reappear during the reliving. This may be difficult to believe, but it is true. The photographs on page 210 show bruises from the doctor's fingerprints that appeared on the ankles of a patient who relived being held upside down right after birth.

Normally, the moment we are wounded, the cells begin repair processes. If we fully experience the wounds at the time of their occurrence, the healing factors (including growth and repair hormones) do their job immediately. But if we cannot, if we must be unconscious to survive, then *the signal for healing to begin is also repressed.* As long as the traumatic memory does not reach cortical consciousness, the signals for healing are not activated.

In a primal, the memory is awakened, and with it all the original reactions. Every structure originally involved reacts again with the complete reexperience of the memory. And indeed, our research confirms that there is an increase in the growth hormones (whose job it is to help repair the body) and enhanced immune system functioning after primal therapy.

Memories: Pure, Intact, Recoverable

Neurophysiologist E. Roy John has noted that humans' brains are in the same state when they recall an experience as they were during the original experience; their brain waves have the same form from brainstem to neocortex. Psychiatrist William Gray has suggested a model for the recall resonance process, which has been elaborated on by Paul LaViolette, a systems theorist. Feelings are encoded as specific neuroelectric wave forms. When something happens in the present that is similar to a feeling in the past, the experience evokes a similar wave form that resonates with the memory of the prior experience. Two of the key structures in the resonance process are the hippocampus and the hypothalamus. The channels are opened from the frontal lobe via the limbic system to the brain stem, reactivating memory traces.

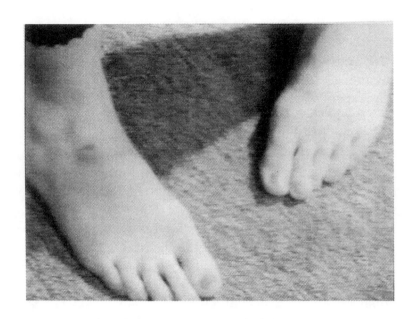

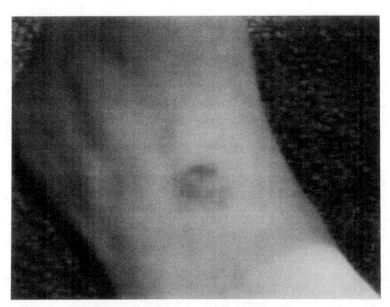

FIGURE 2. Bruises that reappeared when this patient was close to birth feelings in which she was apparently held upside down.

Neurologist Wilder Penfield made clear that memories are imprinted in the brain and leave traces that can be elicited exactly as they occurred. He did this during brain surgery on epileptics (the patient is awake, as the brain does not have sensation) by putting a probe on certain sections of the temporal lobe. A feeling would come up, sometimes with the exact scene from childhood; the patient felt as if he were reliving something from the past. Wrote Penfield: "A young South African patient lying on the operating table exclaimed, when he realized what was happening, that it was astonishing to realize that he was laughing with his cousins on a farm in South Africa while he was also fully conscious of being in the operating room in Montreal." By putting a probe on the olfactory (smell) bulb, Penfield produced a sensation of smell: "It seemed like the manure pile over in the back lot near the short cut." Penfield found that with stimulation of the brain, the patient would often hear songs and music from childhood. The patients who relive these episodes say that they do not see themselves as actors during stimulation; *they just seem to be there.* Penfield discusses the two fields of consciousness (which I call the second and third lines of consciousness) as having independent lives, even though they are connected to each other.

The mark of forceps that sometimes appears during a birth primal shows that there is memory long before there is recall or full cortical consciousness. We can suffer long before we have the means to pinpoint what it means. We recently treated a six-year-old, a victim of satanic abuse. She had been having violent nightmares with symbolic content of the horror she underwent. The abuse happened before she had words, yet there is no doubt that her body remembers.

The problem for professionals who do not believe in preverbal memory is that they are forced to construct current hypotheses to account for symptoms. Thus, adult depressions are termed *endogenous*, meaning they come from inside for no apparent reason. What is forgotten is that for every result there is a cause. That cause can occur long before verbal memory takes place. The organism strives constantly to heal; but the truth must be evident for there to be healing. And if the truth of one's history occurred before the development of words, then it must be experienced without them.

If You Can't Feel the Wound, You Can't Heal

It may be banal to say that skin healing can take place only after a wound to the skin, but when there is an emotional wound, it sets in motion a new need—the need to heal that wound emotionally. We can't fix what isn't broken. The "rub" is that when the body and brain are heavily drugged, the person cannot feel the wound, and the system is saying, "There is no wound," and therefore, there is no healing. Heroin addicts, for example, will heal more slowly than those off drugs, because the sense of the wound is diminished. Both the internally produced painkillers (endorphins) and the external ones administered by someone else (morphine) fool the system into thinking there is no wound. When that happens, the healing forces are deceived and do not do their job.

Some years ago, Dr. Richard Lippin, formerly of the Philadelphia Detention Medical Unit, wrote to us about his experience with addicts. His patients were on high doses of methadone, an opiate that kills pain. One patient was given a skin test for tuberculosis. An antigen is injected into the skin, and the injection becomes painfully swollen as if one has had TB. In this case there was no reaction, giving the impression that the patient had never had tuberculosis (TB). But when the patient was tapered off methadone a year later, a large red, swollen welt appeared. His body was *reacting*. The immune system was able to function normally once the methadone-based repression had been removed.

When a finger is frozen, it begins to hurt. As exposure continues, the suffering reaches a maximum and then numbing occurs. With further exposure there is less suffering and sometimes even a sensation of "warming." When the frozen part is rewarmed, the entire sequence begins again, only in reverse.

The suffering begins again, which, in my opinion, is partly the reexperience of the original suffering; the finger is again warm and suffering stops.

This is the paradigm for primal pain and primal therapy. The thawing process hurts, but that is an unavoidable aspect of healing. Pain is a basic quality of the need state because it helps set in motion the forces of healing. When repression is decreased, there is a return to the potential for full reactivity and healing. *Repression prevents healing; expression restarts it.* Repression is mediated by endorphins, internal opiates similar to the methadone this man was taking. Healing will be inhibited so long as there is deep repression (by drugs internally manufactured or externally administered). In a sense, you need to "know" you're hurt before healing can occur.

Healing involves the memory of health; every cell, once injured, attempts to return to its state of health, a process known as homeostasis. The cell "knows" what normal is because without that memory there could be no healing. In neurosis, unlike the case of the dislocated joint, the only person who can perform the relocation is *you*. The human system has the remarkable innate capacity to return to the exact body and brain state originally present in the trauma, not to think about it or imagine it, but to replicate it exactly. We must go back to complete the unfinished business; approximations do not heal.

An illustration of the principle that "you must heal on the level of the wound" can be found in the therapy of patients who wet the bed (enuresis) as young boys. Invariably, they later became compulsive masturbators, the penis becoming the focus for the discharge of tension. We have seen sixty-year-olds who still wet the bed and who stopped after reliving traumas surrounding birth. *The wound that caused bedwetting and compulsive masturbation is usually on the first line and can be cured only on that line.* This does not mean that machines that shock a child or ring a bell when he wets the bed don't "work." They often stop the symptom; the sheets are cleaner. But now what? What about the child?

CHRIS: A PAINFUL SECRET

I've had birth feelings only recently, but they seem to explain a lot to me. I've caught a glimpse of the answers to a lot of questions I've been asking myself for the past ten or fifteen years. I am beginning to understand why I am the way I am. My birth was cesarean and my mother tells me I didn't want to come out. I feel that I tried my best and hardest to be born, but my mother tensed up and held me back. I must have tried so hard that I think I nearly died. Knowing the way my mother is, I am sure that her body tensed up out of fear and anxiety.

Everything has always been hard for me. The smallest tasks were frequently overwhelming for me (and sometimes still are). Physical situations are always extremely difficult. My body hurts very easily and it recovers from physical stress very slowly. I get overheated very easily. I sweat profusely and I hate it. I feel that my body is already working hard enough in just day-to-day living. When it comes to a job, I am straining myself physically and mentally just to "make it." (Maybe I've never fully recovered from being born.) I wet my bed almost every night until I was fourteen years old. I never understood why I did it or why my mother humiliated me for it.

My body has always felt weak, tense, and tired. I think I am constantly stuck in birth feelings; therefore, I have no energy left to do anything else. There have been times when I feel like an old, worn-out man ready to give up and die. I think I nearly died at birth. I have had a few dreams in which I am suddenly facing certain death. I am usually falling, and the feeling so overwhelms me that when I wake up, my heart is beating furiously and I am sure that what happened in the dream is real.

When I feel my birth, I am struggling in pain to get out. The only way I can relieve the pain is to scream my guts out in agony. I squirm, kick, and shove my body headfirst against the wall and my spine arches and tenses against the pain. I know now why my neck and back are always so stiff and tense. I used to have a dream when I was very young that someone was sitting on my chest. The pressure of my chest comes back occasionally and then I know it is the birth pain coming up. The pain was so great, I used to think I had an ulcer or something.

I can remember as a teenager in high school always wishing I could start everything all over again: class, school days, assignments, school years, relationships with fellow students—my whole life! I wished that I could do it right this time. This hope was the only thing that kept me going. Instinctively, I knew that better parents and better circumstances would have made a world of difference. Unconsciously adopting this attitude, my miserable life was doomed to failure. Everything I tried to do failed miserably. There came a point when I just gave up even trying because I always expected the outcome to be the same. The story of my life is based on the beginning. My birth was hard. My whole life has been hard.

Energy is a key factor involved in healing. One must have enough strength to be able to go back in time and visit the traumas again. The pain trapped in the reverberating circuit of memory seems to deplete the energy of the cells. Repression is a biologically active state, no matter how impassive the person seems to be. The deeply repressed are often chronically exhausted because the body is working overtime to hold down the pain.

The Cells Remember

A fifty-two-year-old patient of mine had nearly died from advanced tuberculosis when she was seventeen. She was severely ill and had an extremely high fever. The doctors had given up hope. One of the treatments back in those days was a drug known as PAS (para amino salicylic acid). During the primal, she relived this experience. She again ran a very high fever and felt she was dying, and she had a bitter taste in her mouth that she assumed was from the PAS.

Many patients reliving anesthesia by ether actually smell and taste the ether during the primals and believe strongly that ether is literally being expelled from their bodies during the reliving. Since the therapists present do not smell the ether, it seems more likely that the memory is so strong as to *seem* real to the patient. And in the memory lie all the original smells associated with the event. Those who were drowning at birth often bring up a good deal of viscous fluid involuntarily during the primal session. Where does this fluid come from? Can so much fluid simply be manufactured during the reliving of the memory? Or is it sequestered somewhere, waiting decades for release? I believe that what is happening in these situations is that we re-create the original situation completely in the primal.

It seems that our cells or cell circuits remember the insults they have suffered through their association with the memory in the central nervous system. When a child is beaten, there is the memory of being hated. That feeling is too much for the fragile child, so it is repressed. The cells record the insult. When repression is lifted, the cells involved in the beating are reawakened. Thus, if the lung and chest cells do not participate in the reliving of the anoxic experience, there will be no healing because an important aspect of the memory has not been relived. Memory, only in the primal sense, is what counts.

In the primal, whatever the individual cell networks did originally to survive they will do again. There may be the beginning of an asthma attack as the bronchioles constrict in response to the memory of the original trauma. The feeling, however, aborts the attack and turns it into the original trauma. The aborted attack is now part of the healing process, just as a beginning migraine may be the beginning of feeling the lack of oxygen at birth. But instead of a full-fledged migraine, the pain is turned into what it was and is: suffocation due to a lack of oxygen at birth.

Sometimes the memory is actually a fever. As one patient was reliving a very early life-threatening fever from meningitis, he again ran a fever. This is clear evidence that memory of a repressed trauma is far more complex than simple verbal recall; it contains the original state of the entire system during the trauma and can be literally relived. In this case, the fever was organized at least partially in the hypothalamus, which regulates bodily states. The tendency for a high fever was no doubt always there but repressed. As we got down to the exact memory, he developed a fever.

We must keep in mind that the complete biological memory of a toxic state (i.e., the imprinted trauma) must be the same toxic state as the original event. Once the patient integrated the memory of his fever, with all its toxins, it no longer reverberated below consciousness. His experience is a paradigm for all other kinds of imprinted memories and their resolution.

The Memory of Health

Why is the pain constantly surging upward? Why doesn't it just relax and stay put? It is because full consciousness, with easy access among all levels, means connection and integration. The energy of repressed pain, not fully blocked by lower-level gating, moves upward and outward to be absorbed by ideas, logic, and rationales. Consciousness is an evolutionary survival mechanism, the new cortex, or neocortex, being the level where the highest functions take place—discrimination, selection, accurate perception, flexibility of choice, sensitivity, anticipation of future events, and the ability to plan ahead. To be unconscious is to be bereft of all these qualities and thus to be a victim of one's environment instead of in control of it. It is to have only the capacity of a lower animal form. Since consciousness of pain is a sensuous state, it acts like one of the senses. Being unconscious is equal to being blind or deaf. It is to be helpless before events. In neurosis one is still guided by pain and need; in wellness one is in control of one's behavior. For traumatized people, however, consciousness early on became a danger to its own coherence, and thus unconscious (repression) became the survival mechanism. Now we have to liberate the person in adulthood from the primitive survival mechanism of repression so that she again may be more highly adaptive to the present environment instead of constantly reacting to the past.

The body is always trying to heal, and that is what consciousness is about. We are a self-healing organism, not in any mystical sense, but in the fact that every organism has self-healing agents. One burns one's hand, and the healing forces begin their work. Crust and scars develop. Phagocytes move in to clear up debris. I have found that consciousness is the ultimate agent of healing for the whole organism because neurosis is not a local wound, ever. It involves the whole organism. Human consciousness is energy efficient. It directs and channels. In the case of being scattered by early pain and using one's energy in helter-skelter, unorganized ways, one sees neurotic inefficiency. Nothing gets done because the person cannot concentrate and focus on one thing for any length of time. Or someone runs around joining this group and that, expending energy until he feels the basic need to belong. His family was scattered and chaotic. He needed an anchor, a place to feel at home and comfortable. He was never comfortable until he felt what he was doing.

When do our patients become conscious? When they have *felt* lower-level pain, and not just been made aware of the unconscious by a therapist. One of my patients was acting out her dependency on others. Her former therapist told her, "You still need your mother, and that is why you act the way you do." She agreed. End of session. Now what? No change. The need is still there and will not change.

Awareness without feeling is a disconnected state. Intellectual insight therapies, therefore, enhance disconnection. We can see how our patients come from the deep unconscious (the primal coma) back into conscious awareness. They slowly open their eyes, blink a few times, and look as though they just came from far away. And they have, from years of their own history, and from millions of years of phylogenetic history. They have been residing on deeper levels of consciousness during the session. Consciousness is survival. Those who were most conscious in history were the smartest. They survived and passed on their genes. Thus it became elaborated and refined over the millennia. At the same time, to make sure that consciousness would not be too threatening and overwhelming for awareness, repression also sprang into being and that, too, was passed on. The two combined to make neurosis, the current adaptive mechanism.

Why does consciousness heal? Because consciousness means that the pain is within the zone of full reactivity, which is the *sine qua non* of healing. *The feeling zone is the healing zone.*

Consciousness is the final evolutionary accomplishment of humans. Repression, then, is an evolutionary force that protects consciousness in general, but it is antievolutionary for the repressed individual, stunting development. In the feeling zone there is neither too much nor too little stimulation or stress, comfort, or discomfort. There is access to pain, but neither too much nor too little. The feeling zone applies not only to primals but to any feeling state. One can experience just so much pain at a time. Beyond that boundary, there is a cut-out mechanism that limits our perception and response.

Inside every traumatic imprint is the memory of normality, a history of wellness. To reenter the memory is to begin to return toward the normal biological state. Psychotherapy can help but can never truly heal. Similarly, drugs and body therapies that work on muscle groups can help but not heal. Patients hurt and cry in deep body therapy; but not in depth and not in methodical order. They travel in the right direction, but not far enough. The missing elements? *Memory, context, pain.*

What are the elements of healing? First, general suffering must be linked with specific early pain and brought into the primal feeling zone. Second, one must heal in neurophysiologic order, taking the most recent, less powerful pains first and then moving progressively to the pains of higher valence. You can't start healing at the end, such as with rebirthing methods. In this way, we develop consciousness of past unmet needs and feelings, acknowledging them and turning their power away from symbolic channels and toward health, allowing less energy for the neurotic process. Finally, with the old pains linked to current symptoms and behavior, we may use this new and enlarged consciousness for different behaviors that *we* consciously choose, rather than being compelled to act out as before. One of my patients could never say no to anyone, whether it was someone who wanted sex or someone who wanted to borrow money. She went to counselors and "discussed" this inability to say no. The counselor would tell her all the reasons why she should not lend money to so-and-so, pointing out in all reality how irrational it was. And the counselor was right. Until she felt how her tyrannical, demanding, and unyielding father had taken her "no" away, the tendencies were always there, advice from therapists notwithstanding. Advice was nonhealing third line; the feeling was second line.

Why do we see wisdom teeth dropping into place in a person age forty after primal therapy? Why do beards suddenly develop in men in their thirties? Because when our personal evolution has been arrested by repression, we block maturation on every level of functioning. What repression seems to do is block healing because the forces of healing are themselves repressed. Clearly, repression is a global event and is not a series of mental mechanisms, as Freud imagined. That is why after primal therapy, when early pain is connected to consciousness, we not only see symptoms abate but also observe significant changes in the output of all sorts of hormones affecting healing processes, from growth to stress hormones. We see signs of physical maturity, such as growth of breasts, hands, and feet and redistribution of body hair, that had been arrested due to pain—and that indicates that the genetic code is finally finding its proper expression.

15

PRIMAL RESEARCH: MEASURING HEALING

When a microbe intrudes into the body, one of many reactions is elevated body temperature. The same reaction is seen when one approaches early imprinted hurt.

It is a constant in our therapy that when someone starts to reexperience early pain, there are radical swings in body temperature and other vital signs. Just before a deep feeling the body temperature can rise three or four degrees. The thermostat for temperature regulation lies in the hypothalamus, where pain is also regulated; it is packed with opiate receptors. Under attack, the hypothalamus helps raise body temperature. But the attack doesn't have to be a bacterium. It can be a feeling that is reacted to exactly as if it were an invading bacterium. The body and brain treat the feeling—"I am all alone and no one cares about me!"—as something to defend against and to reject. The system reacts to those feelings as it would to an incompatible skin graft: as something alien. It does not differentiate between an alien bacterium and a painful feeling; they are both strangers and threaten the integrity of the organism.

I count neurosis as a wound because it involves the deformation of biologic processes, fever, and the release of "toxins" (in the sense of noxious information), which is as real as pus stored in an abscess. The deeper the wound, the more extreme the fever, just as in the reaction to a virulent bacterial infection. The earlier and stronger the trauma, the more likely there will be high fever during the reliving. In some patients temperature rises by several degrees. It is not surprising that the least-gated, first-line pains cause the greatest fever. (The only exception we have observed is when massive doses of painkillers are given to the mother at birth; the birth struggle is chemically aborted and the temperature rise is slight or may drop.)

Why does temperature rise when feelings rise? Because the feeling, treated as an invading organism, has never been part of the self and never been integrated. The system recognizes it as a wound and mounts its healing forces for it. It will do anything to keep that wound out of consciousness because somehow the system believes that it is still the baby who cannot take the pain. Pain can shatter consciousness, and pain can liberate it.

There are two ways that patients run a fever in primal therapy. One way is when they relive the memory of a fever. Since this memory is almost always, at its heart, a life-and-death struggle with massive sympathetic activation, temperature rises. Remember that a second-line trauma compounds underlying first-line trauma. The more common way is when a deep, early feeling is on the rise, and the body begins its defense. Normally during the preprimal phase, when the pain has escaped repression sufficiently, the body reacts to the memory, and the system heats up. The person perspires profusely, rips off sweaters and shirts, and seems to be "roasting."

Fever is an excellent defense mechanism because it tends to deplete pathogenic, disease-causing agents. Many bacteria cannot thrive in higher temperatures. To inhibit the growth of pathogens, there is a reduced level of iron and an increase in zinc during a fever. Meanwhile, chemicals are pouring into the bloodstream to fight the intruder. The cells, now under heat stress, defend themselves in several ways. They increase their metabolic rate, and they manufacture protective proteins (such as Heat Shock Protein 70). These proteins are an integral part of the immune system. In experiments with lizards injected with bacteria, infection consistently drove them to seek warmer areas in order to raise their temperature. When they were forced to stay in cooler areas, only twenty-five percent of them survived. Elevated temperature is no doubt one of the body's premier defense mechanisms to combat disease. One of the ways it does this is by speeding the flow of white blood cells to the areas affected.

Does this mean that the healing mechanisms for both a virus and a feeling are identical? Except for the site of healing, I believe the answer is yes. A cut on the finger is healed there. Neurosis is laid down as *experience*, not an idea. You can't point to a behavior or an organ and say, "Yes, there lies neurosis." You must treat the person as a whole.

The experience of early pain in primal therapy can bring down the temperature three or four degrees in minutes. Once the pain is integrated, it is no longer an alien force to be defended against. It is now conscious; therefore what lies in the unconscious is no longer a threat. It is common in our therapy to see how a parasympath patient will come in with low vital signs and go out after the session with much higher, or normalized, signs. This is all accompanied by feelings of doom and hopelessness at the outset and far less of such feelings at the end. In short, the organism is of a piece; one can see attitudes follow inexorably the vital-sign configuration. The patient comes in feeling terrible and doesn't know why. Her vital signs tend to be low, as they were in the original trauma. These vital signs and the psychologic attitudes mean that the old event is close to consciousness. Feeling the despair in early context changes those feelings and alters the vital-sign configuration toward higher readings. After a session, when we do the measurements, we can usually tell what the psychologic attitudes will be. If the readings are higher, we generally see less despair and more optimism.

DAPHNE: PAIN AND BLOOD PRESSURE

An amazing thing happened to me. After a few months of therapy, while at my doctor's office, my pulse was read at 72. For me this was amazing because I have a history of a fast pulse. My pulse had never been read below 80, and it was normally in the 90s; even 100 to 106 was not an uncommon resting pulse for me. I would often lie in bed at night and feel my pulse, which would sometimes rock my entire body.

After this reading of 72, I at first figured it would not be repeated. However, on four subsequent visits to the doctor, the low reading continued. Once it was read at 64, about 30 beats lower than what it normally had been. Furthermore, for the past ten years my blood pressure had been at 135/85, and suddenly it had gone down to 110/80.

I am truly excited and relieved about the drop in my pulse and blood pressure. I can hardly believe it's true, except that it matches my overall feeling of having had a tremendous burden removed from inside of me. I can't believe how much all those feelings were continuously agitating my body. So much repressed anger, it was literally killing me, and feeling is reviving me.

The average temperature of advanced primal patients is in the low 97s. Why does the body temperature drop as a result of consciousness? Because energy is no longer being used (creating heat) to defend the organism. Part of the alien force has been discharged, and the memory residue is now part of us. That is healing; *only the hurt contains the seeds of cure.*

If we take the symptom of high blood pressure, we note that the early trauma continuously stimulates the blood pressure system, keeping it elevated. The hypothalamus in part is responsible for high (or low) blood pressure. But when the patient relives the imprinted, prototypic reaction of high blood pressure *in context*, then this symptom will diminish and will eventually be eradicated. Just before a primal, the blood pressure may be as high as 220/110. But within hours of the primal it can drop dramatically. We have noticed that in some cases, the blood pressure may take some hours to fall after a primal, although we find the pulse and core body temperature to be below their baseline values immediately after the primal. This is a key point, since trauma-originated high blood pressure is so widespread and potentially life-endangering. Reliving the prototype high blood pressure means consciousness and integration of the memory. The rise in blood pressure during the start of a primal shows us unmistakably the relationship between blood pressure and hidden pain. Low-salt diets and special medication certainly are helpful but are not curative where pain is the underlying problem.

Locomotive Breathing and the Cure of Disease

Now we return to our patient, described in the introduction to this book, whose reliving of the lack of oxygen at birth included "locomotive breathing"—heavy, deep, rapid breathing for a twenty-minute period. This was part of research in blood gases we undertook at the UCLA Pulmonary Function Laboratory in association with Dr. Donald Tashkin and his associates Dr. Eric Kleerup and M. B. Dauphinee. We took frequent blood samples during the primal episode and again during voluntary hyperventilation to measure blood oxygen and carbon dioxide levels as well as core body temperature, heart rate, and blood pressure. The primal and the simulation were as close as we could make them in terms of strenuous physical activity and deep, rapid breathing.

During the simulation, the blood carbon dioxide and oxygen levels were what one might expect. There were clear signs of the hyperventilation syndrome after a little over two minutes of deep breathing, including dizziness, tingling hands, bluish lips, and loss of energy such that the subject could barely exert himself.

In the primal of oxygen deprivation at birth, however, there was no hyperventilation *syndrome*. Despite twenty minutes of locomotive breathing, there was no dizziness, puckered lips, or tingly or clawed hands (which are caused by the alkalinity of the blood from exhaled carbon dioxide). The UCLA researchers could not account for the lack of hyperventilation syndrome in our subject: "There has to be some other factor at work," they offered. *I submit that factor is memory.* Why did being in the birth memory inhibit the hyperventilation syndrome? And what importance has that for the cure for neurosis?

We know that the automatic, saw-tooth (that rough, raspy sound) locomotive breathing such as we saw in the primal is organized deep in the brainstem by the medulla. It seems likely that the locomotive breathing is part of the memory of anoxia, and when that memory is triggered, with it comes the associated locomotive breathing. By contrast, deep breathing when done by *an act of will* is regulated higher in the brain, which accounts for the effort it takes to breathe and the resulting fatigue. Voluntary deep breathing is a *decision* that has cortical or third-line components.

Being enveloped by the imprinted memory makes breathing automatic and effortless and does not lead to fatigue. Indeed, an act of will (from higher in the brain) prohibits the medullary response, and it is the medullary reaction with its locomotive breathing that prevents hyperventilation syndrome. Voluntary simulation of such breathing does not cure; it relieves tension, as would any other form of exercise. I emphasize this because there are schools of deep breathing now which claim to cure a variety of ailments. *Only being in the memory is curative.*

In the birth primal, a different set of muscles is employed, namely, the muscles of the newborn: the axial-spinal muscles working in alternating fashion against the abdominal muscles, generating the dolphinlike motions of the newborn. The work is gigantic and produces a great amount of lactic acid which normalizes the acid-alkaline balance of the blood and prevents hyperventilation syndrome from occurring. It is akin to a marathon runner breathing hard and not passing out because the lactic acid generated by the anaerobic respiration of his muscles balances the alkalinity of his blood caused by the carbon dioxide he breathes out with each pant. During a simulation of a primal, the subject cannot exert himself sufficiently to prevent the hyperventilation syndrome. The subject does not pass out because he exerts himself harder than the marathon runner. How can you exceed the level of effort of a marathon runner? Only under life-and-death circumstances *such as those experienced during the original primal trauma.*

The absence of the hyperventilation syndrome during the protracted locomotive breathing of our subjects (there were two of them at UCLA, both filmed) demonstrates that they were in the grips of the memory. This means, according to my former colleague, neurologist Dr. Michael Holden, that *the memory of a brainstem reaction is itself a brainstem reaction.* The memory is anoxia and the muscles that grind and produce such enormous energy are midline and infantile—precisely the ones which were part of the original event. Deep-level pains are constantly agitating the system in terms of hormone displacement, cellular processes, and other visceral reaction. The memory of lack of love at age four is held in the emotional centers, not predominantly in the cortex.

As soon as there is a decision or desire or will, the hyperventilation syndrome will appear. Sex is a good analogy. You can try to simulate orgasm, but it is never the same as when the impulse comes from within. It is a completely different feeling, all-encompassing. It is the same as in a primal, where the impulse to breathe comes from within and is a response to a specific trauma. It cannot be simulated.

It would seem that no factor other than memory could account for the near-normal acid-alkaline balance in the blood during prolonged heavy breathing. *No voluntary effort can produce enough lactic acid to do that. Hence, life-and-death efforts were involved in the primal in the absence of a current life threat.* That life-and-death threat was a memory that was real! This has important implications for the current controversy over recovered memory syndrome; it is strong evidence that memory awaits in a pristine state to be recaptured intact. If the subject in our experiment were faking in the slightest degree, he would have suffered from hyperventilation syndrome! His physiology was controlled by the memory.

The variable to account for the difference between the non-curative simulation and a curative one is a neurologic circuit deep in the brain that sends the person into "automatic" survival mode. The newborn musculature used in a primal is controlled by a memory. It is impervious to experience. Nothing will change the memory, not even shock therapy, because the memory involves survival. Another way of looking at the event is that there is no hyperventilation syndrome because the oxygen debt in the cells is being restored. The cells need the oxygen now because they needed it then. During the primal the patient is in the "then" mode. "Then" and "now" are identical. The lower-level imprints do not have a time code. The patient, therefore, is not discussing his self; he is the self. Feeling the memory finally allows the neurotic to separate past from present.

There is a curious paradox. During the primal, despite the fact that the blood oxygen is normal, even saturated, the brain is sending a signal of the *lack* of oxygen. That signal coming from the imprint determines the system's reactions. It is the internal environment that one always reacts to first. That is the essence of neurosis: reacting first to one's history, being dictated to and driven by the past despite one's best intentions to the contrary. *The imprint is indifferent to any reality except its own.* It attends only to its own truth and overrules anything contradictory. It just won't listen to any other reality because it is too busy trying to survive its own. Don't try telling the system to give up sleeping pills when the body is out of kilter and needs to normalize its serotonin levels. The body knows more about its reality than any outside expert. That means that psychotherapy can be of no help except on a superficial level, no matter what the doctor and patient think. No advice, counsel, or exhortation will make any difference. In short, you can't tell anyone anything. The body uses drugs to normalize, to get normal. How can anyone combat that?

Feeling and Healing

In primal therapy we systematically perform vital-sign testing on our patients before and after sessions. These objective physiological measurements show whether or not there has been connection and resolution of feeling. Let's take an example. A patient gets caught in a traffic jam and can't move for thirty minutes. He first gets furious, then anxious. He arrives at our clinic terribly agitated. In his session he feels blocked, and he says, "They stopped me, those bastards. I can never do what I want!" He is talking about traffic and unconsciously meaning his parents. He gets into the feeling, starts to thrash and pound the walls and complain that his parents blocked him whenever he wanted to go out. He starts to cry, "I could never do what I wanted!" He moans and cries for a half hour and relives a scene when he wanted to play football after school, but his mother insisted he come home and take his regular nap, even though he wasn't tired.

The therapist is silent. Suddenly the patient's knees come up to his chest, and his arms cross in fetal position. His back arches, and he begins butting his head against the wall. No more words, just grunts without tears. He thrashes and butts for over forty minutes. He then comes out of it as though he has been far away. He rests, and then the insights start: "I got stuck. *That's* why I can't stand to be stuck in traffic."

Let us look at what has happened with our instruments. The first stage was essentially an anxiety attack. The patient was nervous and restless, had butterflies in his stomach, and felt a sense of dread, doom, and a premonition of death. His vital signs started to skyrocket, his pulse going to 175, core body temperature from 98.7 to 103.5, blood pressure from 125/90 to 200/100. His EEG (brain wave) amplitude rose by fifty percent. (See Chapter Seventeen for a detailed discussion of mapping the brain.) This is the preprimal state. Note that as he responds to the present, his vital signs are responding to his past. Then he recollects the blockage by his parents; he is dropping into the second line. As he cries deeply, his vital signs drop. Forty minutes later he drops into the birth sequence.

For a time the vital signs rise abruptly. As he gets locked into the feeling of being blocked, unable to catch his breath and coming close to dying, his vital signs fall radically. Within minutes, his core body temperature is 95 degrees, his blood pressure 95/55 and falling. We look at him on the floor and see him as he was forty years ago, a tiny creature trying to get born. We are observing the depths of his unconscious. We see his struggles as he seems to be about to die, yet he has an expressionless fetal face. Expression will come later.

Eventually, it is over. He has gone back decades to undo his history by fully experiencing it *for the first time*. It was never fully conscious before, but it's part of his conscious-awareness now, part of his conscious history. He feels good and relaxed. What a relief!

The patient has been somewhere else, in a "conscious coma," a lower level of consciousness where only the next breath has meaning. Later, the experience will be recognized as underlying and giving the tone to dozens of other, later experiences, particularly those involving despair and futility. Those later experiences compound the original one through an elaboration of the nerve networks. That is why a current stress can set off early terror and anxiety. The person was locked into a birth sequence, fully conscious on a lower level of consciousness that we often call the unconscious. He was more conscious than he has ever been. Now he knows what the sensations belong to. He has the context: anoxia and helplessness at birth. A current helpless situation follows the nerve tracts down to the origins. From this fundamental connection comes consciousness of his motives in dozens of baffling act-outs.

A primal is a vivid psychophysiological reexperiencing of a painful event from infancy or childhood. It has a biphasic response pattern that starts with an escalating sympathetic nervous system crisis. It is no surprise that it is a fight-or-flight, sympathetic nervous system crisis that begins the feeling. The vital signs rise to a peak *in concert* and then fall during the crying, the parasympathetic recovery phase. In a completed primal the vital signs fall *in concert* to below-baseline values at the end of the therapy session.

In the preprimal phase, one suffers and experiences a crescendo of anguish. This reaches a maximum level when defenses give way and the early painful event breaks through to consciousness. There is a vivid memory, sometimes with visual, auditory, or olfactory components, or all three, from early life experience. At the end of the primal sequence, one is lucid and profoundly relaxed, and insights connecting present behavior with the trauma just experienced flow easily. "When I feel hated by anyone in the present, I act like I want my mother to love me like she didn't in my childhood. Then I start acting obsequious and desperate for love." Previously, when someone was cold to this patient, he felt tense. It made him gnash his teeth at night and produced a stiff neck. After his feeling is connected, the tension in the muscles of the forehead and neck (measured with an electromyograph) drops significantly. The energy has been appropriately connected instead of neurotically rerouted.

The earlier the trauma, the more global the insights. Many patients report that such insights carry more conviction than almost anything else they have ever learned. One patient remarked: "I know these things more surely than I know anything else in this whole stinking mess of my life!" This quality of surety is a second major indication of a true primal experience.

Abreaction: The Noncurative Release of Feelings

We have distinguished the primal response from the physiological changes occurring in abreaction and uncompleted primals. Abreaction is an emotional outpouring, sometimes with tears, in which an individual cries *about* his suffering without ever actually descending into the actual memory. It is simply the discharge of the energy of the feeling. The difference between an abreaction and a primal can be recognized by whether resolution occurred in physiological terms, whether the vital signs followed the characteristic pattern caused by trauma.

In rebirthing and mock primal therapy centers, patients may abreact for years and get nowhere, thinking that they are having primal therapy. Making patients scream, pound walls, and cry for Mommy has nothing to do with primal therapy. Abreaction has been rampant in every mock primal therapy I have investigated. You cannot *make* a patient feel, nor can a therapist decide what the patient should feel. Further, the therapist must know the sequence of rising pains or resolution cannot take place. Because the mock therapists are not driven by precise theory and technique, because they have no research control of the session, and because their own therapy has usually gone awry, they don't know what they are getting with the patient, and the patient will suffer. Scientific controls are essential in any psychotherapy because humans have stopped knowing what is going on inside them.

Using our vital-sign testing, we know immediately if there is abreaction, the release of the energy of feelings without real connection, and we move to correct the situation. Abreaction often looks like a primal, except the vital signs change erratically during the session and do not fall below their baseline values afterward. It takes an experienced therapist to discern the difference.

What happens neurologically in abreaction? Just what always happens in neurosis: Usually, the energy of a feeling from one level of consciousness is discharged on another level. The energy from the reverberating limbic circuit is released in non-connected, helter-skelter fashion, through crying, pounding, and screaming. *There is no cortical connection.* When the patient has distress *about* an event rather than being *in* the event reliving it, he is not in the feeling zone, not on the level where the wound is, and no healing can take place. "My mommy always hated me!" when accompanied by adult tears is very different from "Mommy, please don't hate me!" in a tearful, five-year-old voice. In the first case, pain from below powers a third-line behavior. In the second, pain finds its connection to consciousness. Or, birth pains intrude on a feeling of, "It's so hopeless to ever be loved;" the feeling is driven by the birth pains that are not felt for what they are.

What is deceptive about abreaction is that one does feel some relief afterward, just as in a primal. And there are often complaints in mock therapy centers about primal therapy when the complaints should be about the mock therapist. There is much more true relief in a primal, but in abreaction the release of tension does feel good for a short period of time. Abreaction can happen very easily and is dangerous to the individual if allowed to go on, because a "groove" develops so that each time a feeling comes up it is rerouted into specific, symbolic channels. Soon the person will just discharge energy of the feeling automatically, believing he is getting better. The problem is that like jogging and meditation, one has to keep on doing it to get relief, whereas with a primal, once a piece of a feeling is felt and connected, it never has to be felt again. Once the message gets through to consciousness, there are signs of healing everywhere: more growth hormone, less stress hormone, improved immunity, and the resolution of symptoms. We have studied capillary blood flow in the face with infrared cameras, and patients show greatly increased blood flow after a year of therapy. They have warmer faces and extremities. I believe that repression restricted blood flow throughout the body, perhaps as part of the original effort to conserve oxygen. Restricted blood flow represents a crisis for the affected tissues, because the cellular anoxia and the accumulation of waste products are what cause aging. With the resolution of trauma, it may be that "natural" aging is slowed.

What we see in our research is how repression is truly the one key biologic defense. When repression is faulty, secondary defenses come into play: meditation, acupuncture, drinking, drugs, smoking, confession, masturbation, talking constantly. They take up the slack, absorbing and discharging the escaping energy. Repression is quantifiable and can tell us about the level of pain involved. We can not only "see" primal pain in our therapy, we can also measure its processing and its effects.

16

PRIMAL THERAPY AND THE NATURE OF HEALING

The memory of oxygen deprivation remains as a state of deprivation in the same way that deprivation of love early on remains as a constant lack. Countless times in primal therapy I have seen the memory of anoxia rise to the surface in pure form, seemingly unchanged since the time of birth. That is why patients during a primal breathe in locomotive style (deep, rapid, forceful breaths) for some twenty minutes. A primal patient in a room full of oxygen relives the *lack* of oxygen at birth and looks as though she is dying. The memory is an overarching reality. Where was this lack-of-oxygen memory all these years and decades? It may have been temporarily neutralized by drugs or alcohol, but it was always there, making the person anxious, creating asthma or shortness of breath or migraines, or perhaps forcing him to smoke compulsively. If it were not an ever-present reality, the person would not have such continually high stress hormone levels, levels that drop after the reexperience.

The lower brain dealing with anoxia or feelings will never respond to reason *because it has no reasoning capacity*. When someone tries to get well through insights in psychoanalysis, they are trying to use a recently developed neocortex to handle an experience from millions of years ago. Reasoning with our lower brain is like trying to reason with a salamander (see Chapter Four). And it is why anxiety, for example, is so widespread and so impervious to cure in "talking therapies." Its source is deep and ancient. Anxiety afflicts us in epidemic proportions not specifically because of forces in the present but because its underlying imprint is permanent, and because the experience has yet to be lived completely. We inherited the reptilian brain and we must learn from what we experienced while at the salamander level of development. It is this lower brain that mediates our reaction to anoxia at birth, and it is that brain that is constantly doing what it can to survive, by speeding up the heart and agitating the viscera. Churning stomach, palpitations, and other effects, plus the feeling of dread and doom, characterize the anxiety state.

You can't just decide to have a slower heart rate any more than you can decide to "calm down." The memory is waiting its turn to meet with consciousness. It takes its place in line below the higher-level, less catastrophic pains. *The only thing that will make anxiety disappear is to live for a time on the level in which the imprint occurred; writhing, moving without the aid of limbs, slithering in a fashion very much like a reptile,* experiencing the terror in all its "glory." To finally know the source of the terror is most relieving. It is no longer displaced fear of the unknown.

Anxiety may be said to be part of the pre-primal phase, the forerunner of a feeling to come. Suffering is moving upward, battering against the repressive gates and making us fearful, first of the unknown, then of the known. The unknown phase is called anxiety. The known phase is called a primal. What we do in primal therapy is provoke the pain to rise while holding back the elaborate intellectual defenses. When suffering moves upward and finally connects with cortical centers, it becomes specific pain. The full extent of the imprint is now conscious. The first-line *sensations* of anxiety—a state that some experience as butterflies in the stomach, losing one's breath, and a tightness in the chest—are experienced. With the resulting explosion in a primal, the anxiety turns into feeling. To feel pain is to feel again. When you have seen thousands of wordless primals in which patients squirm on the floor for an hour or two, you know for certain that a primordial force is at work.

JESSE: THE SALAMANDER SPEAKS

My mother told me that my birth took a long time. I started to be born around 11 P.M. My mother said that she was very sleepy (evidently drugged), and the nurse had to keep waking her to tell her to push. It is not surprising that I have had feelings about never getting any help from my mother from the very start of my life, and that I gave up trying in the birth because of this. Ever since then I seem to have been waiting for something to happen. Now that I have felt my birth, it seems like waiting was the only alternative I had to forging ahead and feeling the pain of not being helped. My first neurotic shutdown happened before I was born.

I feel like I finally found out about the origin of several of my symptoms, including vertigo, nasal congestion, and bronchitis. Along with getting rid of those symptoms, I have finally discovered why I hesitate and stand back all of the time. I've always felt like it's easier to get things done by being good and waiting patiently. Ever since my birth, I have been afraid of any conflict that would arise if I were assertive.

I am usually led to my feelings by specific symptoms that start to come up. One time I was working in a tall office building, thirty stories high, and I had to run errands on different floors by using the elevator. I had always felt uneasy about elevators, but now the feelings became overpowering. I would imagine the chute of dark air under the elevator and feel afraid that I was going to plunge down all the way to the bottom. I was afraid I would get so dizzy and sick that I would have to hold on to the sides of the elevator.

I began to feel the fear was coming from somewhere else. One day in therapy I began to feel alone when I remembered being left in a mental hospital by my father. The feeling went back to my being a baby and screaming with terror. My body was rigid and awkward as though it were expressing the terror, too. I then began to feel like I was falling backward into a black void. I was dizzy and totally disoriented, and I cried and screamed until finally the feeling subsided. During the feeling my legs went up over my head, and when I finished I was practically upside down.

I knew then what the feeling was. After I was born, somebody held me upside down. My fear in the elevator was the same feeling.

A few months later I began feeling something slightly different. I developed a huge swollen gland in my neck that was so painful I had to go to an emergency ward. The doctor didn't know what had caused it, but a week later I began feeling like a tiny baby and I relived having fluid in my throat that was suffocating me. I cried and retched; there was something in my throat that shouldn't have been there. Then the mysterious lump went away. I now know why I would get an immediate bronchitis attack under times of stress in my life, like when my brother died and my father left home. I guess these experiences triggered an old birth trauma in which I was trying to keep from dying with all that fluid in my windpipe.

Primals tend to normalize one's blood pressure and hormone levels because the trauma that dislocated those functions is being addressed. Once the trauma connects to consciousness, there is no longer a frantic infant and conscious adult in one body, walled off from each other by repression.

There will be insights (the perceptions arising out of a primal feeling), but healing doesn't depend on insights; rather, insights are a sign of healing. It is the primal feelings that provide true insight. *Connection, not insight, is the vehicle of healing. Disconnection is what the wound is about.*

Primal therapy is not a disintegrating experience. On the contrary, it is a broadening experience that removes the bars of the neurotic prison, integrates the levels of consciousness, enlarges one's emotional range, and sets physiological healing in motion.

PHILIP: ROCKING IN THE CRADLE

My birth was a long, eighteen-hour struggle. I felt that there was no way out, but I could not stop struggling because to stop would mean never getting out.

I was born angry. My head was misshapen and bruised at birth, and I've always felt sore in my neck and upper torso. I was always afraid of physical hurt, but I still played sports in order to get attention. I could not play well due to my fear of being hurt (again).

I was a head banger and a crib rocker. That was because I had been banging my head to get out from the start. Whenever I was frustrated, I just resorted to what I did originally to find relief and freedom. In order to stop my banging, I was tied with a sling under my chin to immobilize my head so I could not bang it. This way I had to relive, again and again, the original pain of my birth of being caught by the head. I've had pain in my joints all of my life, I guess from trying to get free. I had treatment for rheumatoid arthritis starting at age thirty-four. I've also had reliving sessions in my feelings where a hand is grabbing at my face and two fingers are in my eye sockets. Once I felt this pain, my lifelong headaches just above the eyes disappeared. If I get an occasional headache, I know that feelings are coming up; and when I feel, the pain goes away.

My married life was crazy. I always felt "tied down" and wanted to be free, yet I did not want to be alone. The act of going to bed alone in a dark room was always painful, and I always fought it. I needed to drink in order to fall asleep. Again, that primordial aloneness must have left me with a memory or terror that I never got over.

Now I can enjoy a good night's sleep, and anyone who has had sleep problems knows what a blessing that is. It is so nice to wake up and enjoy the mornings.

Reversing the Chain of Pain

The reliving process always works in reverse to how memory is laid down. Memory is first in, last out, and reliving is last in, first out. We relive memory bit by bit, first the most recent, benign imprints, and over time to the most heavily charged, early lethal ones. This descent in therapy is called a 3–2-1. Each reliving on a higher level allows the patient to go deeper.

As further evidence of the prototype, therapeutic sessions with our patients are analogues of birth. In the case of a para-sympath, the patient usually comes in deadened and has to be stimulated by the therapist; otherwise, she may just lie there inert. Then she tries a bit, falls into despair, feels hopeless and powerless, and gets nowhere. She gets nowhere because that is the early feeling re-created exactly. The therapist has to be careful not to fall into the trap of the imprint with the patient, who is acting out getting nowhere. She has to feel getting nowhere in original context so that she'll get somewhere—in therapy and in life. Until the patient feels "stuck" in context (stuck in the canal; stuck in a dysfunctional home), she will act out being stuck in therapy.

My notion of the prototype—the representation and the re-representation of trauma in the nervous system—provides a road map for the therapist. When a patient presents himself with a distressing, overwhelming reaction, the therapist can be confident it is a re-representation of an earlier trauma *because it is neurologically impossible for it not to be.* Re-representation gives rise to the chain of pain: The feelings and sensations are the link between the levels of consciousness, growing stronger as one descends. By eliciting details of the present distressing event, the therapist causes the present to resonate more strongly with the past, thus provoking anguish as the memory moves toward conscious-awareness. Certain techniques at the critical moment allow the feeling to break through and the patient spends the next two hours riding down the memory-feeling to its origins.

We often see patients who feel as though they are going crazy as they begin to gain access to very early imprints. What is actually happening is that the original terror and frenzy are mounting. Because the memory was laid down before there was a rational cortex, there is no conceptual handle on the terror. The feeling simply is of going crazy; everything is mixed up, confused, and out of control. Brainstem cells, where early terror is imprinted, send signals of panic and approaching death upward so that the limbic circuits recognize a feeling of impending doom, while the cells of the cortex might be saying, "I don't know what's happening to me. This doesn't make any sense!" The patient cannot say what he is terrified of. The person has no idea why he suddenly feels as though he is dying. It's because too much or too little reactivity originally meant death. Of course, they didn't die the first time, and they don't die during the reliving in therapy. This is reassuring for both my therapists and my patients. They won't die because they are no longer frail fetuses facing life-or-death trauma. They are physically strong adults whose system monitors and adjusts the pain during the session. They will feel it over many months, bit by bit, so it can be fully experienced, reacted to, and integrated.

Someone with claustrophobia, for example, may need to go through the incubator experience perhaps a hundred times over a period of months. During this process, it is entirely possible that she won't know what she is going through until months after the primals have started. This is because she will only feel a piece of the original trauma at a time, just enough to be integrated. Later, the trauma will begin to make overall sense as more and more of it is experienced. It is like putting the pieces of a puzzle together.

As the pain is felt, patients find that they have less "need for" alcohol and drugs. They no longer have to rely on the dope of belief. Nightmares and delusions are resolved. Many are surprised by the new degree of feeling they experience in sex, having previously thought that they were having a good sex life, while in reality a universe of sensation and emotion had escaped their notice.

Since you can only feel what you can feel, and cannot feel what you cannot feel, you will never know if you're fully feeling unless you feel what you previously could not feel. You do not become free until you fully feel being trapped in the past. Feeling caged in a depressing childhood home is liberating. You are courageous when you have felt fear from your childhood. You are independent when you have felt your total, frustrated dependence on indifferent parents. You come alive as you feel your deadness. Primal therapy isn't only about repressed pain. It's about suppressed joy as well. Suppressed joy leads to pain, too. The joy and the impulses toward wild abandon have to be expressed as well.

The Power of Tears

An integral part of getting well, we have found, is weeping. The history of neurosis is the history of misery, and the natural response to misery is to cry it out. Psychotherapists who feel uncomfortable with weeping may try to cut off these displays with explanations and insights and take the patient out of crucial feelings. We know that there is nothing more powerful therapeutically than releasing the tears of the child. Tears wash out the internal painkillers—the endorphins—and dissolve repression, breaking down the barriers to consciousness. They help soothe one's irritability and lift depression. Tears are not just a "nice" objective in psychotherapy; they are a *sine qua non* of healing. A therapy without profound tears is not therapy but an intellectual exercise using a brain that is a stranger to feeling. We have found in our research that the deeper the cries, the more profound the changes that occur.

ROSEANNE: THE NEED FOR A FATHER

I used to be assaulted by terrible anxiety attacks. Since the age of fifteen, I have lived in the dreaded fear of having a heart attack. Every time I had the anxiety attacks I would feel panicky, weak, and sweaty. I would become pale and sometimes faint. There are no words to describe the loneliness and helplessness I felt in those moments. Those attacks became the symbol of my hopelessness.

I don't have the attacks anymore, and the reason is simple. I don't build up overwhelming stress and anxiety. If something hurts me now, I cry or get angry. I react to it and let it out instead of keeping it in like before. My chest used to be a pressure cooker. My unexpressed feelings would create so much pressure in my chest that I would actually experience the symptoms of a heart attack. All those feelings inside me were trying to get out, pushing against my chest and making me feel "I'm going to die without love."

Now I let the stream out. It has felt so good to cry about my father—the need for him to talk to me, to touch me and help me, all the things I had been deprived of. Every time I cry about my needs I get more in touch with myself and I become less tense. It sounds strange, but the truth is that feeling the pain actually helps me to reduce the stress, strain, and awful anxiety in my life.

Although weeping is essential in psychotherapy, primal therapy is not and never was about making people cry and scream. People react differently to pain. Some scream, some cry and sob, others moan. The central point is connection. Connection means feeling what happened to you a long time ago. You cannot and should not objectively discuss the rage engendered by years of beatings and neglect. You cannot decide to forgive the perpetrator or understand him. Rather, you must feel the rage in all its fury, over and over again. Beating the walls and pounding the mats should come not at the direction of a therapist, but from deep within *yourself*.

A patient who uses swear words while reliving an event he experienced at the age of four is having an abreactive rather than a real experience. Most four-year-olds do not say, "Shit!" During a primal, a patient who, on his knees, raises his arms up to "daddy" to be held, tears pouring forth, is having a real experience. Whatever explanation is needed will be provided later by the patient. The cries were held back by the musculature. As soon as the exact gestures were made as they were originally, the pain comes up. The memory, in this case, was coded in the arms as well as elsewhere.

Need and pain, pain and repression are a dialectic unity. Look for the need and you will find the pain because it is need not fulfilled that turns to primal pain. Look for repression and you will find pain, and vice versa. The awareness of the hurt of early deprivation is gated, while the unmet need is preserved in pristine form for later connection. Hence, it is not enough to feel the hurt; one must go further and feel the basic need. A patient who is able to feel about a parent, in context, "Why do you hate me so much?" still has not reached the core need: "Please love me!" *This* is what healing is about. Without this step, the distress and tears are never-ending because the basic unmet need, the agonizing trauma that is the reason for repression in the first place, remains intact.

So many will cry out their pain of neglect, of an erratic, undependable father or a weak, ineffective mother for weeks or months. Then, when I say in session, "Ask your father to be nice. Say it like a little girl, with the little girl's voice." At first it is an effort for her to mimic a little girl. Once locked into the feeling, however, the baby talk comes out naturally. It has a different sound; the child's brain is now in charge. The pain gushes forth again as the patient is suffering the agony of a need left unmet years ago. Most often, it is not necessary to help guide the patient into being the little child. The current feelings themselves become a vehicle to carry the person back in time to childhood.

TIM: THE SEARCH FOR WARMTH COMES TO AN END

Before entering primal therapy, my life had been a bad and sad one. There had been incest and molestation by both my parents and by a neighborhood boy as well. My father abandoned us when I was three. I was improperly brought up by my mother, who was often not around, and by my grandmother, who was severe and tyrannical. My sister despised me, was jealous of me, and essentially did not speak to me until I was in my twenties. On top of this, everyone referred to me as "spastic" and fed me Valium all day long.

As a kid, I was constantly looking for love and attention. What started out as a benevolent search for affection and affirmation was soon transformed into act-outs of the garden-variety sort. Early on, sex became a compulsion. As early as six years old, it pains me to say, I was marauding for sex with both genders. Bloodhounding, especially for girls, became my favorite pastime. Being without a girlfriend made me literally sick inside, yet my relationships with them never seemed to work. I was always ending up wounded beyond repair. The girl I loved most delivered the last and decisive blow. There was nowhere else to turn but to men. I was not able to halt my relentless search for sex and love. The compulsion to act out sexually augmented with each advancing year.

To thwart this self-destructive hunger, I turned to religion and also poured myself completely into my work as a poet and writer. Yet no activity could quell the tremendous energy that sought to consume me. Now I see that my defenses had reached a saturation point. My defense system was not able to dam back the mounting pain that found outlets in my lower back and legs, as well as a whole host of complicated psychological symptoms. Furthermore, my days were severely hampered by torturous, sleepless nights replete with nightmares, a ceaseless liturgy of worries, endless trips to the toilet, and eight long years of painful all-night erections. Then I contracted a mild skin disorder, vitiligo, which saps the skin of its pigment. Enter primal therapy, and just in the nick of time.

For months I relived the incest, molestation, and the agonizing feeling that nobody loved me. My therapist, who had been incested too, was able to guide me effectively through some pretty turbulent waters. It's nice having someone there who has experienced similar traumas and who really cares. Empathy seems to be a requisite in this line of work.

The crystallizing moment of healing came in a session when the reliving of the incest was accompanied by a defining birth primal. At the time, I didn't realize that as a result of this session my life would change forever. The session commenced with my telling and crying to my therapist about how much I missed her and needed her. The next stage began with what I call fragmented memory floats, an experience that occurs when I am about to go into a deep feeling. Bits of significant memory break off from the unconscious to guide and help the feeling find its way to resolution. When I told my therapist about them, she said, "Well, they're not accidental." These particular fragments were all associated with feelings of needing and missing my father: nights at baseball practice, when other kids' fathers were there to help and encourage them, and I was left to stand by myself, figure out things for myself, and draw on my own energy for courage and strength. Other memories flooded my mind as well, priming me for the feeling and insight that would heal and change me.

Suddenly I went into a powerful first-line feeling. My body took the fetal position. The all-too-familiar sense of feeling stuck, paralyzed, immobile, and wanting to give up struck me. I realized from whence came my primary act-out to run away. I resented being impelled to move forward. My legs seemed frozen and disconnected from my upper body. This phenomenon filled me with frustration and confusion.

Next I was gagging and choking on phlegm and mucus. I began to move like an inchworm, nudging my way forward. Sometimes I would completely lose my breath and the terror that I would die suffused my whole body and mind. At these times my face felt that at any moment it would burst its thin veil of skin and gush forth a flood of blood. But it didn't, and I made it, just like the first time. My movements continued to be fluid and snaky. No coughing or gagging intruded. To my surprise, my legs moved in sync and harmony with the rest of my body.

Tears for my mommy and daddy accompanied my emergence from this birth primal. Then another memory pried loose and caught my attention. Heeding my therapist's instructions that it was not accidental, I began talking about it, albeit uncomfortably and hesitantly, as I instinctively knew it contained great primal pain. Sometimes, though, you have to push and see if you can handle it.

The memory concerned a time soon after my father had deserted us and we had moved in with my grandmother. There was this corner, this nook of darkness situated in the far background of the schoolhouse near where we lived and which for some reason always grabbed my attention. I was fascinated and terrified by it and was forever staring at it. For some reason, I said to my therapist, "He's not there." She said very firmly, "Yes, he is." Immediately I became frantic. It was as though someone was chasing me and trying to kill me. I began frantically wailing, "Don't let him get me, please don't let him get me." My legs automatically locked together as if in a vise. My leg injury began to hurt and throb. My whole body quaked and trembled like someone who has just seen a ghost or whose very life is being threatened. My legs, which were squeezed together and shaking, began drawing up as a unit verging toward my chest and then they opened in spread-eagle fashion. I was in too much pain, tears, and shock to even recognize what was happening when my body began moving in jabbing motions, like someone ramrodding me piston-fashion up the ass. (Just the other day, months after this experience, I finally felt actual painful sensations around the anal area. It is true: The pain comes in stages and according to what the body can handle.)

When I finally realized that I was in the position of being fucked "military style," I collapsed in tears and humiliation. I turned away from my therapist in utter embarrassment and began sobbing uncontrollably for myself and for what my body had done and revealed to me. After sobbing for a long time, I began emitting hitherto-unheard-of sounds out of my voice box, full-throated animal sounds bellowing forth. It occurred to me right there and then why people end up "possessed" or institutionalized. After this wild and strange scene went on for fifteen minutes, an onslaught of bile began forcing its way to my throat. This was followed by vomiting. The whole event was just so far out of my control that I was stunned.

In the postsession I began to work out what this all meant. My feeling started with missing my therapist, then progressed to missing my father, to the disconnection between the lower and upper parts of my body caused by problems with my legs, to feeling stuck and then exploding into a free-flowing birth primal, to missing my father and searching for him in the dark recesses of the school playground, to the rape, and finally to the animal convulsions and bile expulsions. I saw that, somehow, the key to comprehending those stages lay in understanding the role my legs played first in the birth primal and then in the rape.

All my life my legs have given me problems or been a sort of focus. As a swimmer my legs would often give out in a race for no apparent reason. After a leg injury some years ago involving a weak femur, I entertained an obsession for several years that one day I would be crippled. Often, waking up in the morning, my legs have been absolutely numb, as though I were "cut off at the hip." I suspect that my weak femur is either congenital or birth-related and contributed to my leg never really healing. On the second line, the role of my legs is blatantly obvious; I used them to fight off my father.

After that day of experiencing more major feelings than ever before, several huge changes occurred in my life. Immediately my leg and back problems subsided completely and remain nonexistent today. Two brief flare-ups have occurred, but as soon as I felt the feelings associated with incest or first-line trauma, the pain has gone away. It is such a relief and really a joy to be free of constant leg pain.

The second wondrous change is that I sleep soundly and sometimes straight through the night. To me one of the great joys in life is a good night's sleep! Only occasionally will I have a relatively sleepless night, with nightmares, an overactive bladder, or back pain. I take this as a sign that a feeling is on the rise and/or I have been unconsciously triggered.

Another major benefit is that I no longer believe that people are "out to get me." After feeling these feelings, the fear of people fell away. On the contrary, it was my parents who committed terrible acts and instilled in me a deep horror, who planted the seeds of my paranoia. I am now able to tell people in a calm manner what's on my mind. I have stood up to people at my job for the first time in three years, including my boss, who would unfairly push me around.

Furthermore, my skin condition has been clearing up. My doctor was amazed. Three small spots spontaneously regressed. One large spot—I won't say where—went away, too. Of the depigmentation on my face and neck, which was present when I began primal therapy, 95 percent is gone. The only three new spots which have appeared since I have been in therapy came right at the beginning of a new feeling.

I have also seen significant improvements in my sex-drive orientation. My desire for men has greatly diminished and my attraction to women is slowly returning. Suffice it to say that the more incest I feel, the more I am repulsed by men. Yet I still need love from my father and to be touched, so I am sometimes drawn to men. Some of the therapists and patient friends of mine help me by hugging and touching me.

Now there is a lot of hope left for me. I always wanted a wife and family. I am thirty-five and I am grateful it is still in reach if I choose it. Today, when feelings powerfully arise, I am able to feel them and get on with life and not be paralyzed. I can say what I need to say and do what I must do. Hallelujah!

Recovering One's Humanity

Primal therapy is a revolution in psychotherapy. At the Primal Center, our usual procedure is to take in one patient per therapist for three weeks. The patient stays as long each day as necessary; the fifty-minute "therapeutic hour" is not practiced here. Our patients decide when their sessions are over. We give the power of treatment back to the patient; that in itself is therapeutic. It is called self-determination. Our patients are not passive recipients of a process, and our therapists do not "own" the patient's symptoms. Primal therapy does not revolve around the therapist's wisdom, nor does it adhere to the therapist's unconscious agenda. Instead, we recognize that each patient carries his own truths and wisdom within. Everything the patient is going to learn is already waiting inside her or him. This relieves the therapist of the burden of having to know more than the patient. Although we use symptoms to lead us to where the pain lies and on what level, we leave knowing about symptoms to the specialists, as it is a very necessary part of the therapeutic program. For instance, we often send alcoholics in our therapy to AA for a time. They need the support they can get there. We do not expect them to be strong and independent at the start of therapy. The difference is, however, that once they get deeply into feeling they no longer need that outside support. They are not alcoholics forever because their baby needs do not go on forever once they are felt.

At our clinic we treat causes, not symptoms. We work in reverse of the classical medical approach. Our job is simply to help the patient gain access to a memory that already exists. We join the patient in the scanning process, looking ever deeper into the unconscious until we arrive at ultimate causes. The patient is the chief archivist of his history. History is to be trusted; the entry code is "feeling." The task is not to understand history but to change it. The very same feelings that caused the problem will be the ones to resolve it. *Our job is to teach patients how to gain access to feelings so that they can acquire the tools to do their own therapy. They leave formal therapy with the therapeutic tools that are theirs for the rest of their lives.*

I am often asked whether primal therapy is spiritual. I never know what the question really means. Perhaps it means spiritual in the religious sense. What we don't want is for patients to make therapy their religion. Therapy should not be a search or a quest or a route to salvation. If spiritual means having decency, kindness, and generosity and being loving and caring, then to be spiritual is to be fully human, which means fully feeling. The more feeling the patients become, the more human they will act. Unfeeling people hurt others mostly unintentionally. Repression makes people hurt others because it makes them unaware of the effects of their acts. They can't feel what they do to their children, for example. A parent acting out being helpless will make a child grow up too fast, so that he can take care of the parent soon. A depressed parent cannot be spiritual with her child no matter how hard she tries. One of the recurrent results I see in our therapy is when after patients come out of a feeling they suddenly realize the kind of harm they've done to their children. Once they have rediscovered their own humanity they will do less harm. That doesn't mean that the graduate patient will be perfect.

What we do produce are individuals who are no longer driven by unseen forces. Does this last? Yes, because once the pain is gone it is gone; it cannot be brought back by any force of will, assuming someone would want to do that. The follow-up studies we have done show that the changes, both physical and mental, do last. The extent and nature of these changes, though, differ from person to person. (Please see *Primal Man*, T. Y. Crowell, 1975.) We do not produce a group of homogeneous robots. Indicators of what is "normal" will be different for everyone. Normal is not a specific pulse rate or blood pressure. We are born with different metabolic rates, so a blood pressure of 120/75 might be normal for one person and a lower-than-normal reading for someone else. We do not use psychological testing to find out who is normal because, by and large, psychological testing simply gives the person back what he just fed into the questionnaire, only in more sophisticated language. Being normal just means being yourself. "Being yourself" is such a seductive phrase and generally tends to be meaningless. But in our biochemical research we found years ago that those males who began therapy with high testosterone had lower levels after therapy, while those with low levels tended to move upward as a result of our therapy. Thus, "being yourself" meant two different things to two different individuals. Perhaps a better word is "normalize." When people normalize, their systems are in balance, and that balance may be different among different populations. There are general standards, however. In our brain research, by and large, a slower brain means a healthier one.

I believe most of us have the capacity to be normal at birth, but adversity complicates things. Based on our observations of patients who, after reliving very early trauma, no longer suffer from lifelong severe and debilitating symptoms, we can assume that there is a causative relationship. When someone re-experiences anoxia at birth and then finds migraines lessening and finally disappearing, the connection is evident. It is no great detective job, nor did it come from a complex theory. I constructed the theory around what we observed in thousands of patients so as to understand the phenomena and make our work systematic and predictable. The theory came after the fact, just as insights should not precede a feeling experience. Insights are tantamount to a personal theory about one's state. Neurosis is not built on lack of insights and is not reversed by adopting them. During a session, a patient who was constantly humiliated early in life will come out understanding the hidden motivation behind his desperation not to be criticized. Evolution has coded all the instructions and information into the feeling.

Can any professional do this therapy? Professionals are not better off than lay people when it comes to practicing primal therapy. Too often they are "in their heads." To learn our techniques, a psychiatrist's or psychologist's previous education is marginally helpful. The problem is all the intellectuality that goes with higher education; it is the opposite of what is needed to practice our therapy. Conventional approaches try to construct defenses; primal therapy dismantles them. Therapists need to feel their own pain or it will interfere with the therapy they are doing. This is one of the requirements someone must meet in order to participate in our training program. Because we recognize the inherent dangers of a powerful therapy that delves into the deep unconscious, we must insure that primal therapists are properly trained. It is open-heart surgery of the mind. When the unconscious is laid bare, it must be treated with great care. Our therapists need to know what to do when patients are open to their pain. They need to know how to avoid forcing patients into feelings, how not to circumvent the order of pain (the chain of pain), which will produce flooding, overload, and abreaction.

The primal therapist's skill involves knowing how to remove the defenses carefully and allow the pain to rise slowly to consciousness, a small piece at a time, until the whole pain is felt. He or she must be able to distinguish between proper context and the motions people sometimes make to simulate feeling.

The therapist needs to be able to identify the difference between connection and abreaction, because the former heals while the latter doesn't. Cure means an ordered sequence of feeling pains, from the lowest valence to the highest, from the most current to the most remote.

We use objective measurements to determine whether or not feelings are real, whether pains are arriving in proper sequence, and whether or not integration occurs. We watch vital signs to know whether deep pains are arriving in a timely fashion or are surging prematurely toward consciousness. In a primal session, the patient typically first defends against the feeling before dropping into the feeling, going from a sympathetic to a parasympathetic mode. This pattern reflects the vital-sign changes of the original trauma, since we always respond to threat with fight-or-flight signs. Furthermore, if one has had a big feeling, but the instruments indicate that the vital signs remain high, it means that the feeling has not been properly integrated. If, after the session, there are not characteristic changes in brain maps, we have another objective indicator that integration has not taken place.

Mixing primal therapy with other approaches dilutes the therapy. Our therapy is the only one that follows the patient's neurophysiology, works with biological principles, and takes into account access to the levels of consciousness. There is no need for other therapists to use a trial-and-error process on their patients to experiment with other methods when we have already done that, made mistakes, and honed our techniques. If social manipulation in the treatment of patients is necessary—such as moving them out of their homes into halfway houses and giving them job training—then that would be an adjunct to the individual therapy. There is a definite place for family therapy, counseling, supportive therapy, child guidance, and the other more conventional approaches. We must be clear about their limitations and not ask too much of them. Not everyone should get to his or her pain. There are those too fragile to do that. They need to sit up and talk, to have a helping hand and emotional support. "Fragile" is another one of those facile words we use in psychotherapy. But it is clear that when a person has had a poor work history, has tried suicide, and has been in mental hospitals, we have clues. But in our pre-therapy interviews, we learn more about the patient. If they have pain constantly bursting through, if they cannot concentrate or focus, and report that they do not function in the present, we consider them fragile.

Neurosis and other forms of mental illness almost always involve unconsciousness. Consciousness means full reactivity and full reactivity could have meant death early on. Yet, paradoxically, it is only consciousness itself that is finally liberating. It rights the system, producing normal cellular function. When there is neurosis, part of the past is forever in the present; the unconscious continually intrudes. The only antidote for neurosis is consciousness. *The only antidote for pain is to feel it.*

In the end, cure means nothing more than recapturing our humanity which has been dormant for far too long—a humanity buried so we could function in a non-feeling way. Primal Therapy can help us liberate feelings.

We are free to decide what to do with our lives. We can choose to feel or not to feel; to find relief in consciousness or to be driven by unconscious forces for the rest of our lives. But there *is* a choice. Suffering humanity has good reason to feel encouraged. We know that every wound carries with it the seeds of its own healing. That is what the human system needs to do: find again one's unique history of wellness and become whole. No one has to be taught to feel or integrate pain. The body does it all for us. All we have to do is to give in to our needs and feelings. History will do the rest.

AFTERWORD

Primal therapy is not just about making people scream. It was never "primal scream therapy." Those who read the book *The Primal Scream* knew that the scream is what some people do when they hurt. Others simply sob or cry. It is the hurt we are after, not mechanical exercises such as pounding walls and yelling "Mama!" This therapy has changed what was essentially an art form into a science.

There are hundreds of professionals practicing something they call primal therapy without having had a day of training in it. Many unsuspecting patients have been misled and seriously damaged as a result. Of the hundreds of clinics in the world using my name and falsely claiming to have been trained by me, I have rarely seen the therapy practiced correctly. We spend about a third of our time treating patients who come from other practitioners of our therapy.

I must emphasize that this therapy is dangerous in untrained hands. It is important to verify the qualifications of your therapist by contacting us.

Dr. Arthur Janov's Primal Center
1205 Abbot Kinney Blvd.
Venice, CA
(310) 392-2003
Fax (310) 392-8554
EMail.primal@PrimalTherapy.com
Web page: http://www.PrimalTherapy.com/welcome

Once a person has been opened up to his or her pain, they are vulnerable to manipulation. Great care must be taken not to control the patient or take him or her where the therapist needs to go. Those therapists with needs for control might lead the patient astray; or they might miss the fact that the patient needs to lose control and go to places unimagined by the therapist, who himself has not been there. The possibilities for abuse are limitless. The only protection is to go to a therapist who has felt many feelings on his or her own. My therapists have had many years of intense training and are now practicing at the Primal Center. Others are practicing elsewhere. Check with the center regarding therapists' qualifications.

I'd like to offer primal therapy to the world, but I am limited by the number of years it takes to train therapists and the funds for doing so. We have started a new training program for those who live outside the Los Angeles area and who cannot stay for long periods of time. Our library has literally hundreds of videotapes of our work that we use in training.

The therapy works. The patients know it. And I hope through this book to make it known to those unhappy, lost, and suffering souls. But primal therapy isn't only about neurosis and suffering. It is a way of looking at the world, a way of understanding ourselves and those around us. It isn't only a method of therapy. It is a way in which feeling becomes a style of life.

MAPPING THE BRAIN— DIAGNOSING AND PREDICTING THE COURSE OF THERAPY

Brain maps are one of the most important tools for understanding personality and psychopathology and for measuring progress in psychotherapy. They objectively verify for us the existence of the three levels of consciousness and tell us who has access to deep feelings and who doesn't. We can see who is the most anxious and needs medication, and we can spot signs of borderline or prepsychotic states. This tells us that we are not just dealing with an abstract mind, but neurologic processes as well.

Our brain maps tell us about the patient's prognosis. They help us determine, with some accuracy, how fast a patient will progress and is progressing in the therapy. They provide objective data on whether our therapy is working or if the patient is abreacting. It is so easy to fall into abreaction in primal therapy that measurement and surveillance are critical.

Over the years we have done four separate brainwave studies of our patients: one at the UCLA Brain Research Institute, another at Copenhagen University, a third at Rutgers University, and a fourth at our Brain Research Laboratory under the direction of Dr. Michael Holden. The studies have shown how reliving pain changes brain maps. They reveal changes in brainwave frequency and amplitude after the patient gains access to and resolves traumatic memory. They indicate that the brainwave patterns of advanced primal patients are less repressed and less busy. The brain waves are better synchronized and slower, and the amplitudes are more evenly distributed over the whole brain. We also see a better balance of activity between the right and left hemispheres. Results of brain studies on our patients have been reported in the *UCLA Brain Research Bulletin* and in *Acta Scandinavia*.

Measuring Brainwave Activity

The electroencephalogram (EEG) is a measure of the electrical activity at the surface of the brain. On many of our patients we measured brainwave activity by using nine leads attached to the scalp in the key areas of the brain. We took the measurements before and after sessions and before and after the therapy. These measurements take place about every six months. They have enabled us to print out maps of the brain's activity in color. The maps help us construct a diagnosis and prognosis of the patient to aid in his therapy. An introduction to brain mapping appears later in this chapter.

Through our brain maps, we see that the development of and access to the levels of consciousness are represented by variations in specific brainwave patterns and frequencies:

- *Delta waves* are the signature frequency of the brainstem or first-line consciousness. Patients on the verge of first-line pains will suddenly develop long, slow delta brainwave patterns. The patient is wide awake and alert yet is in touch with a level of consciousness ordinarily found only in infancy and deep sleep.
- *Theta waves*, generated by the limbic system or the feeling level, are faster than first-line delta waves. They predominate in children up to the age of six. In our therapy, when patients are near second-line feelings, their EEG shows the appearance of these theta waves, which tells us stored suffering is on the rise.

- *Alpha waves* appear as the third line develops with the maturation of the neocortex or thinking brain, at age twelve or thirteen. At this age, we see the theta waves of second-line consciousness replaced by faster alpha waves. This indicates maturation of the frontal lobes, greater cortical organization, and greater capacity for repression. Alpha is considered the normal frequency range and usually indicates an alert, relaxed state.
- *Beta waves*, faster than alpha, are also emblematic of cortical activity. When the brain is excessively busy, thinking and scheming, obsessing with delusions, then there may be beta-1 and beta-2 activity. Beta-2 betrays a racing mind, the kind that occurs at night when we worry and can't fall asleep.

Frequency and Amplitude

The *frequency* of the wave is the dominant frequency, or pulsing of the brain, in each of the areas studied; it basically tells us how fast the engine is running. The *amplitude,* or height of the wave, indicates the total number of neurons at work on a problem or feeling at any given time. If we visualize a surfer riding a wave, frequency is the speed he is going; amplitude is the height of the wave he is riding. Amplitude is related to how much power is being fed into the engine.

Frequency is divided into five bands:

1. Delta—0.5 to 4 cycles per second (cps)
2. Theta—4 to 8 cps
3. Alpha—8 to 13 cps
4. Beta-1—13 to 20 cps
5. Beta-2—20 to 40 cps

With regard to *amplitude,* the higher the wave, the more likely that repression is failing; 200 microvolts or more indicate active suffering.

With the EEG, we are able to tell which level of consciousness the patient is operating on, based on the configuration of the wave. We can see how busy his brain is in the service of repression. We can see whether feelings from deep unconsciousness are threatening to break through to consciousness. The EEG gives us a method for knowing about the intrusion of lower-level pain.

When deep pain bursts through into conscious-awareness, it is indicated by (1) a slowing of frequency, usually into the theta range, and (2) a sudden increase in amplitude. This is often accompanied by a subjective feeling of discomfort and anxiety. This is particularly true *when the frequency dips into delta and the amplitude rises dramatically—a sign of first-line intrusion.* We can see the intrusion clinically (there are several key signs) and can usually judge by the EEG signature whether it's birth or later childhood pain. For example, while testing a patient before a primal session, we noticed delta waves suddenly appearing. In her session, she quickly slipped into a deep primal, reliving a birth sequence. This sequence seemed to be presaged by the high, slow waves we saw initially. These are the same waves that we see in deep unconsciousness—deep sleep.

In the normal awake adult, one is not supposed to see delta waves, but we do see them in some primal patients. This indicates two possibilities. Either the subject has faulty gates with breakthrough of deep material that threatens the defense system, which we call "intrusion," or he is an experienced patient with good access, able to integrate first-line material, who is on the verge of deep, early sensations and feelings.

Repression as Reflected in EEGs

In our brainwave studies we are able to see the gating system at work. People who have a low-amplitude EEG with little alpha activity and whose frequencies tend to be mixed seem to be those who are shut off from their feelings. We call this a "flat" EEG and it is not a good sign for the prognosis of the patient. Flat EEGs show a bit of almost all the frequencies, with nothing predominating. The person is "zeroed out." This is a sign of global repression where the patient lives largely "in his head," dealing with symbols and abstractions. It is a fragmented state, disconnected from feelings. A flat EEG is never seen in infancy or early childhood. It takes the maturation of the frontal cortex and its repressive capacity to achieve that.

This kind of person is below the primal zone. Depression sets in when repression is lifting, but there is still no access to feelings. He then feels the effects of repression without knowing the pain that engenders it.

A repressed person who is not overtly anxious will have a resting EEG with an amplitude of 20–40 microvolts and a frequency of 11–15 cycles per second. A less repressed individual who is clearly anxious may have a higher voltage, perhaps 50–150 microvolts at 10–13 cycles per second. Gating here is failing. Those who are actively suffering often can have an EEG of 200 microvolts or more; their gates are breaking down. Faulty gating occurs when the gating system has been overwhelmed by too much imprinted pain and ceases to function properly. The gates are like dams, holding back primal energy. As each lower-level gate gives way, the energy travels to higher levels, finally meeting and possibly overwhelming the cortex and its third-line gates.

Brainwave amplitude and frequency and the vital signs rise in tandem when the defense system falters. All signs, including body temperature, move up with deep pain as the body fights against consciousness. Anxious patients who first come to us with defective gating will often show high-amplitude alpha and beta waves. One of the ways that we know that anxiety stems largely from first-line trauma is that amplitude is very high where gates are faulty, allowing very early, highly charged trauma to rise.

Weakened gates occur for many reasons. Current events— the loss of a mate, a severe auto accident, failure in business— may compound old pain. Or someone takes drugs such as marijuana, LSD, ecstasy, or speed, all of which challenge the gates. The combination of impulses breaking through with severely compounded childhood pain can be deadly. In these cases, what we see on the EEG at first is a good deal of alpha and then a decrease into the theta/feeling range with increasing amplitude. This, together with other indices, may put the patient on suicide watch.

If first-line birth trauma is exceptionally strong in someone who has also had a horrendous childhood, the combined charge value of those traumas can shatter the gates. It is then that we might see delta in a new, disturbed patient, meaning that very early trauma has wended its way unobstructed to third-line consciousness. We sometimes see such patients going into birth sequences in their first three weeks of therapy, assuming the fetal position, grunting and contracting, something we almost never see in well-structured patients. The maps plus the clinical evidence indicate the necessity of medicating the patient immediately. They tell us about what traumas to steer away from for the moment, since we do not want the patient to be further overwhelmed. On the contrary, we want to make sure that small pains are felt and integrated for many months to come in order to strengthen the gates.

We can use our brainwave patterns to help us judge what kind of medication, if any, should be used to separate out levels of consciousness so that each level can be felt without intrusion of another level. For example, prepsychotic states and borderline personalities show a great deal of intrusion from the very start of therapy.

If the intrusion is very strong, it may be that the patient is ready to feel first-line pain. This may call for second-line blockers such as Prozac or Valium. We have seen amplitudes of over 300 microvolts in the resting EEGs of some of our patients. One patient with this reading could swallow a handful of Valium and feel only slight effects. The amount of underlying neuronal activity was so strong that it took Herculean amounts of drugs to calm the brain. In severe neurosis, when the pain-killing repressive chemicals are diminished in the brain, one can take enormous amounts of tranquilizers without being rendered unconscious. When beta frequencies are evident and the person cannot concentrate, is confused by impulses surging into consciousness, and has a short attention span, we need to use third-line drugs such as Dilantin and Ritalin to normalize neuronal transmission. These drugs can activate the third line so that it can better repress.

As unconscious feelings approach during a primal session, the EEG frequency decreases and the waves become slower and higher in amplitude. Once locked into a feeling, the frequency, amplitude, and temperature normalize. When pain is relived, the patient's voltage may drop to 10–20 microvolts and 7–10 cycles per second; the gating system is now working effectively again. The drugs that primal patients use are not designed to calm them. They are used to help them into the primal or feeling zone where connected feelings can take place. A blood pressure of 220 and a pulse of 130 with beta-2 brain waves means the patient is above the primal zone. Medication will lower the signs so the person can experience feelings with the right help.

Brainwave Signatures

One recent depressive we saw had an amplitude of more than 230 microvolts, about five times the normal level. His frequency was around 7 cycles per second, with almost constant migraines. Because he couldn't feel, he developed symptoms. Nevertheless, the slow, high waves indicated the possibility of access to feelings, meaning that they were moving toward top-level conscious-awareness. This was even more evident as we watched his frequencies often drop into the theta range. Thus, he was dealing with early feelings and the brain was doing its best to repress. Feelings were moving out of their hidden caves but were not strong enough to be felt and connected. He had an "agitated" depression.

When amplitude moves upward while the frequency remains in the alpha band there will be little or no possible access to feelings and the subject may report depression. This tends to confirm my notion that depression is nothing more than deep repression. There is another factor to consider, and that is the synchronization of the brain. When the brain is focused, it tends to be synchronized, with all parts working in close harmony. It tends to build amplitude as electrical potentials from each neuron summate. A desynchronized EEG can mean disharmony, with different areas of the brain each doing their own thing, and less amplitude because all of the neurons of the brain are no longer firing in synchrony.

Those with a racing mind and fast beta activity are usually the obsessive types. There is a constant flight of ideas going on in their heads. The pain is coming up, the lower gates have given way, and the third-line gate is only moderately effective. Consciousness is then busy fabricating worries, preoccupations, rituals, and obsessions to handle the upsurge. Worries absorb some of the energy, or at least focus it. Beta usually means that repression is failing so that consciousness is flooded from below and frantically searches for thoughts to help out. The result is an explosion of activity. Painkillers that work on lower structures of the brain can ease obsessions, which tells us what is driving them. When we take away deep-lying pain, the higher-level cortex slows down, indicating how deep unconscious imprints activate the mind.

It seems that those who took many hallucinogenic drugs have permanently damaged gating systems. Some of these people can no longer sleep without sleeping pills because their energy is on the rise all the time. Thus, drugs such as LSD can drive a person over the primal zone. What often happens in this case is a leap into an ever-continuing loop of mystical notions and "far-out" ideas such as UFOs or pyramid power. Every idea becomes part of the defense and must be unreal and far from current reality. As the gates weaken, obsessiveness gives way to more serious "mental" illness such as paranoia. Then, as the gates weaken further, the brain flees into pure bizarre ideation. If there is defective gating on the first line, the second-line gates are pressed into service. At night, this can mean lengthy, convoluted, symbolic dreams. If the second-line gates are defective, the cortex is sure to become involved and will start building amplitude for defense, which may be translated into rumination and obsessions.

Amplitude almost never goes as high as when birth traumas are involved. These traumas are invariably life-and-death. It is one key way that we know that the birth trauma is real and that it has a charge value higher than almost any other life event, the only equivalent being incest. In prepsychotics, we see a strange mixture of frequencies of the theta and beta variety and a drop in amplitude, meaning that cortical defense has been blown apart. The brain gets into the feeling level and then uses the cortex to race away from it. The fact that we observe significant feeling frequencies with a breakup of amplitude tells us that the patient is in danger and should be medicated to help in the gating process. This kind of patient cannot build up a strong defense; LSD or shattering life circumstance has literally cracked the defense system. It is why I believe that the hallucinogenic drugs are the most dangerous drugs of all, with lifelong deleterious effects.

Impulsives are those with high amplitude, which is an almost exact measure of primal pressure pushing from below toward cortical consciousness, and therefore, of how much pressure the person is under. This is a precise state since primal pains and their energy are literally electrical impulses. Visually, it looks the same as when one puts a handkerchief over a fist and raises it abruptly. The shape of the handkerchief looks like our graph; exactly as though the feeling were thrusting upward, driving the amplitude wave ever higher. When there is connection in a primal, EEG frequency will usually increase slightly while amplitude is diminished. It is one of many ways we know whether a feeling has been connected and integrated. As feelings are on the rise and amplitude rises, the person has no choice but to feel the feelings or develop a symptom ranging from a delusion to a migraine. And when the amplitude rises, the system does what it can to defend and repress. It is at the end of this process, when endorphin supplies have been exhausted in the battle to hold down pain, that migraines, delusions, or dissociative symptoms (a feeling of being distanced from oneself) may occur.

Brain Waves and Sex

Sexual excitement sets off a high level of emotional reactivity and therefore triggers the equal, original emotional level of the prototypic trauma. The brain may then literally reproduce a wave shape that is identical to the primal event. As neurophysiologist E. Roy John reminds us in his *Mechanisms of Memory*, there is "an oscillation with a characteristic wave shape" produced during recall.

One of our therapists took part in our EEG research. We were curious about his symptoms as they related to EEG patterns. Previously, whenever he got sexually excited he suffered from violent migraines. He volunteered to masturbate while hooked up to the EEG. As he got more sexually excited, his brain waves sped up, and the amplitude of the waves mounted. But then something curious happened. As his sexual excitement peaked, we found slower and slower frequencies in the right temporal lobe, eventually in the delta range, with skyrocketing amplitude of over 300 microvolts. These large, slow waves are peculiar to the newborn. They occur on the deepest level of consciousness, and we find them only in those who experience birth primals. He began to experience shortness of breath, similar to the anoxia feelings he was familiar with from birth primals. The result: a terrible migraine following his orgasm.

Let's review what happened. At first the sexual excitement sped up his brain waves until a certain level of intensity was reached, then they slowed down as an old survival mechanism as he descended to the first line. In a seeming contradiction, he showed *deep-sleep brain patterns while being sexually stimulated.* He was dredging up first line, together with its anoxic imprint. The memory of the lack of oxygen at birth came up, and with it the migraine. *The memory of anoxia produced anoxia and the symptom*. Instead of enjoying the experience, the brain defended against it.

When the level of sexual excitement comes close to that of the birth trauma, it will be interpreted and reacted to by the brain as danger. Incidentally, the drop of frequency down to 3 cycles per second in the right temporal area during the buildup of sexual stimulation is a rather astounding finding because one would expect under stimulating conditions to see the brain speed up. The answer seems to be that he was in the grip of an ancient brain with long, deep, slow waves, the kind of waves that would lead you to believe he was deeply asleep. Sex here released first-line pressure. It confirms my theory that for convulsive pain of the first line, one needs an equally convulsive release, and sex fits the bill.

I saw a patient recently who complained of "going dead" in the heat of passion. He relived being anesthetized so heavily just before birth that he literally almost died. The level of activation in sex set off the original deadness and was eventually resolved by feeling it. We measured the resolution of his entire system by changes in his vital functions. During the session his core body temperature dropped to 95 degrees (an extremely low figure) and his other vital signs also dropped radically. Although the instruments indicated serious physical disturbance, he was actually running off the original trauma in the session, exactly the way he did in sex. After these primals, he had very different brainwave patterns.

Real-Time Studies of the Brain During Primal Sessions

Computer software is just now being perfected in Denmark to allow us to measure the brain during a session. Previously, we could not do so because any muscle movement (known as artifact) interfered with the brainwave reading and gave us false information. Now we are just beginning to suppress muscle artifact and obtain accurate readings. What we are starting to do as a pilot study is hook up selected patients during sessions while we are being monitored by a video camera in the therapy room. The software provides us with a split computer screen displaying eight channels of brainwave signals on one side of the screen, and three colored brain maps on the other side showing the distribution of the brain in alpha, beta, and theta activity. We receive four to sixteen brain maps per second in real time. Following the session the EEG data and the video will be replayed and studied in order to correlate the behavior during a session with the EEG recordings.

Real-time brain mapping will give us more insight into the relationships between brainwave patterns and states of consciousness. We will also know more about brainwave patterns and the various levels of consciousness. In this way we can see when a patient is close or far from a feeling, when he is anxious or depressed, and what it looks like on our maps. We will know more about the characteristics of defense. We want to know where the pain is, what happens in the brain when it is resolved, and where the pain goes. We want to establish norms for what a resolving session should look like, and to see what abreaction is like in brainwave patterns so that we may avoid this error in primal therapy. Finally, we shall see the brain correlates of certain psychologic states and have additional data to confirm our hypotheses. Thereafter, when a patient says he is fine, we can check our brain data for corroboration. It is a most useful tool in our therapy.

Our preliminary data indicate that initially the patient will show beta (fast) activity in the temporal lobe, which seems to mean resisting upcoming feeling. As feelings push harder, alpha and theta (feeling) amplitudes tend to increase in certain areas. A doubling or tripling of alpha amplitude is often observed in the back (posterior) areas of the brain accompanied by increases in theta and beta amplitudes. Some advance patients can drop effortlessly into a feeling, and according to Dr. Hoffman, our researcher, as they approach very highly charged pain their amplitudes can reach 200–300 microvolts; this is accompanied by very slow waves between theta and delta frequencies. To put it differently, as the patient dips into lower levels of consciousness where high valence pains reside, the amplitude can shoot up enormously. It is our experience that the amplitude rises in accordance with the rise toward conscious-awareness of feelings. Real time maps show vividly the intense theta activity shooting up at the exact moment when the patient has dropped into a feeling during a session. This pattern is repeated over and over again, confirming our assumptions. Thus, slow brainwaves signify feelings on the rise, while amplitude tells us how close to consciousness they are. In a resolving session where feelings are integrated, the slow waves give way to more alpha activity, usually indicating integration. A skilled therapist now has one more tool to control and understand the primal process. We can now see an incipient anxiety attack and can tell from our instruments that the closer to consciousness a feeling is, the more anxious the patient is, with characteristic brainwave signatures.

We have also completed a two-year follow-up study of fourteen of our patients. Alpha activity is enhanced throughout and moves toward the frontal part of the brain. After two years there are higher alpha frequencies in the frontal area, which may mean better integration and control of feelings.

Maps of the Internal Universe

We hope through our brain maps to discover more and more about what is on the various levels of consciousness and what techniques help most with each level. It is daunting to consider that we are measuring the activity of a level of consciousness dating back hundreds of millions of years and seeing how events on that level affect brain function and present-day behavior.

I consider the EEG responses part of the vital sign group. As EEG frequency drops and blood pressure and heart rate decrease we begin to see signs of normalcy. Too often in other psychotherapeutic approaches or in meditation, the patient thinks himself normal when all physiologic measures betray him. It matters what the patient thinks about himself, but it matters a great deal what his body is saying, too. Thus, when amplitude rises we see characteristic changes in body temperature and blood pressure. Sometimes the blood pressure will compensate for rises in amplitude; sometimes they work in conjunction with one another. When all vital signs work in harmony, rising and descending together during a session, it is a sign of an integrated feeling.

Over years in primal therapy, we see fewer busy brains, a decrease of peak EEG frequency. Based on previous brainwave studies done on my patients, we also note a more harmonious brain with the power more evenly distributed between the right and the left hemispheres and between the front and the back part of the brain, as made clear by Dr. Erik Hoffmann's previous work and the UCLA Brain Research Institute study.

Whoever said we use only 10 percent of our brains was sorely mistaken; we use far too much of our brains in the service of repression. As pain and its repression diminish, we use far less brain power. The postprimal brain is a quieter, more focused brain. We see it in our patients who report having a longer concentration span, less distractibility, and clearer thought processes after primal therapy.

Psychological behavior always has its material counterparts in the brain. Psychologic processes cannot be reduced to simple brain function, but it cannot be separated from it. This has been a great problem in the field of psychotherapy until now: judging psychological phenomena on their own as a measure of sickness or progress without regard to neurophysiologic processes. Psychology has been measuring the third line, neglecting at least half of the human being. When a person operates smoothly on all three levels of consciousness smoothly, he can perceive the world objectively; that is, he has felt enough pain subjectively so as to be no longer subject to it. All three levels contribute to our total experience. If a person is connected to all of his levels, he is going to have a more profound experience, whether it be in sex, joy, or sadness. Brain maps will inform us about how well connected a person is to himself.

Primal therapy is the first psychotherapy to show permanent

changes in the brains of patients. Unlike meditation, biofeedback, and talking therapies, which must be repeated over and over, primal therapy is permanent simply because it attacks the imprint. It is clear that one cannot defeat imprinted memory permanently through temporary conventional measures; that would be tantamount to trying to erase one's physiology.

APPENDIX B

THE LIMBIC SYSTEM

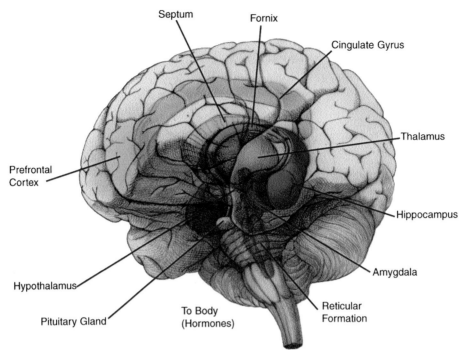

FIGURE 3. The structures of the brain that process feelings. From the outside, the limbic structures look like ram's horns in the middle of the brain, underlying the neocortex. The hypothalamus and the pituitary gland ultimately send the messages of feelings to the body, where they are translated into hormonal and vital sign changes.

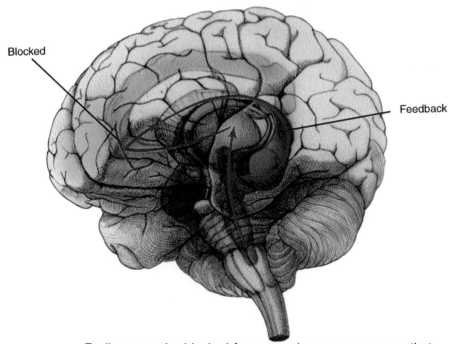

FIGURE 4. Feelings may be blocked from conscious-awareness so that they reverberate in the limbic system without connection, perhaps for a lifetime.

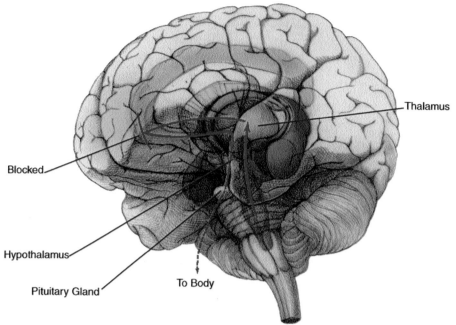

FIGURE 5. Feelings are blocked, sent back to the limbic system, and ultimately steered into the body, where they are experienced as anxiety, disturbed intestinal processes, elevated blood pressure and heart rate, and so on.

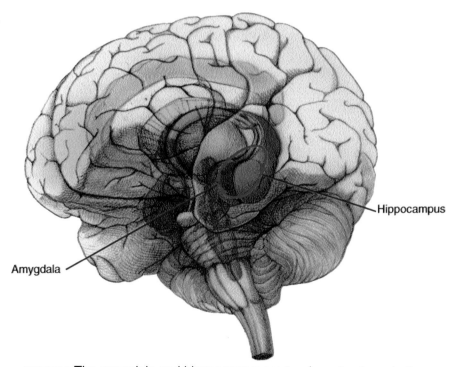

FIGURE 6. The amygdala and hippocampus are two key structures in the imprinting of feelings, particularly feelings from early childhood.

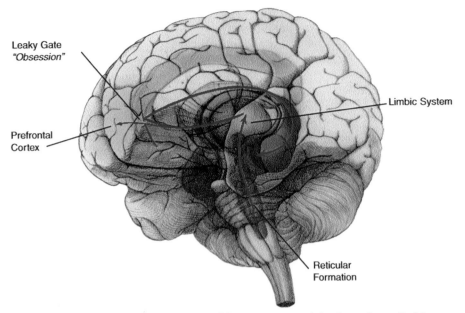

FIGURE 7. A figurative depiction of how repressed feelings from limbic structures break into conscious-awareness without full connection. The result is a liberation of primal energy into the cortex, which may find expression in obsessions, insomnia, disturbed ideas, the inability to concentrate, and so forth.

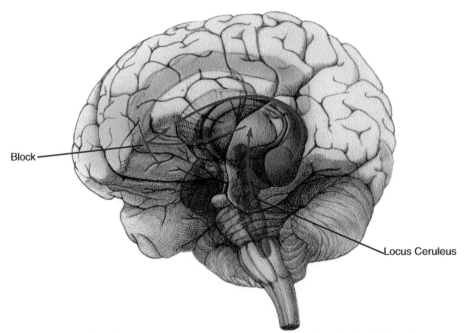

FIGURE 8. The locus ceruleus is a terror center of the brain. This structure, with the RAS, rushes messages of fear up toward the cortex. When the specific information about what is feared is gated by limbic structures such as the thalamus, the person may experience great discomfort without knowing why.

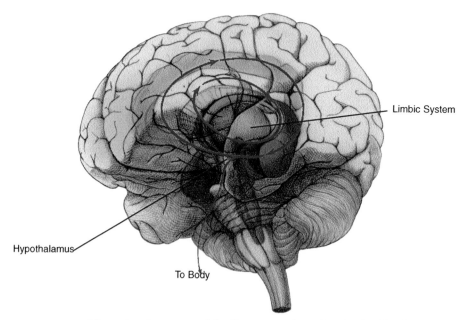

FIGURE 9. The primal energy of feelings reverberating in the limbic circuits travels upward to produce aberrant ideas and perceptions, and downward to produce biochemical and physical changes in the body.

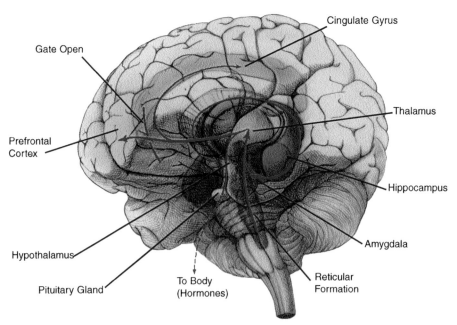

FIGURE 10. A graphic of the normal processing of feelings. As the limbic structures make final contact with the prefrontal cortex, we see full access to feelings.

BRAIN MAPS

An Introduction to Brain Maps

Dr. Erik Hoffmann, research director at the Primal Training Center, has written a detailed explanation of the brain graphs. Figure 11 displays the six types of brain maps. There are three color scales ranging from the lowest (bottom) to the highest. The ovals represent the shape of the head as you look down on it. The little protuberance at the top is the nose position.

The top left-hand picture indicates the frequency or speed of the brain in all of the major lobes. The darker colors indicate low frequencies largely in the delta range. Purple and blue show theta frequencies of 4–8 cycles per second. Green colors extending to the yellow involve alpha of 8–13 cycles per second. Orange, red, and white indicate the faster frequencies in the beta-1 and beta-2 range. This is a very fast brain.

Ideally, we would want to see an even distribution of a blue/green, indicating alpha mixed with some theta. This kind of person is both alert yet relaxed and in touch with his feelings. When the person is attentive, he is in the alpha range. When he becomes drowsy and sleepy, alpha tends to disappear. To the extent that he shows theta frequencies, he is likely to be near his feelings.

The map just under the top left, on the bottom quadrant, shows the power, which is related to the amplitude or the voltage of the brain waves. (Power here is the sum of the square of the voltage in each frequency band—delta, theta, alpha, and beta.) It shows how well the cortex is integrated. If many neurons work in synchrony, the amplitude is likely to be high. When we see a flat EEG of low amplitude, it could mean severe repression at work low in the brain; the energy is blocked before it mounts toward conscious-awareness. That energy, now diverted, will be absorbed in an "act-in" with physical symptoms occurring.

As ascending pain approaches consciousness, the frequencies are forced down, slowing considerably while the amplitude rises. In order to compensate for this slowing, the cortex recruits more neurons and drives up amplitude. High-amplitude slow waves mean close access to old feelings. If the amplitude is high (100 microvolts or more), it would mean that the person is close to feelings and may be actively suffering.

Individuals with extremely low power levels have well-functioning repression, are not suffering, and often don't even know they are repressed. The only time they are aware of their repression is when it is extremely high, pushed by unconscious feelings; here the sensation of repression creates discomfort.

If you refer to Figure 11 you'll see the absolute distribution of power within the five major frequency bands. The circle on the lower right quadrant indicates delta activity. Next to it on the lower left is the graph for theta range. We find the alpha range in the middle and upper right and left, respectively, are beta-1 and beta-2 range. We like to see the top right and left (beta) in the dark-blue areas meaning little fast activity, since fast activity is often correlated with anxiety. Lower right should be dark blue because we don't want any very slow wave activity during alert waking states. If we do see a good deal of delta, it could mean either brain dysfunction or access to very early, powerful imprints.

Optimum readings would show the lower left image as blue-green, often veering toward yellow, indicating the presence of some theta. This person was in touch with his feelings. A child would show a great deal of theta, and in most children under the age of ten the theta graph would show maximum activity. In an adult during the waking condition, the alpha graph should always be more emphasized than the theta map.

If theta is evident, it can mean good access to feelings without overload. Too much theta and delta showing concurrently with rising amplitude can mean the person is being swamped by old early feelings. This is often indicated by periods of high-amplitude slow waves (theta and delta) appearing synchronously in different areas of the brain.

In the middle oval of the chart, the optimum pattern would be predominantly alpha, evenly distributed (green and yellow). This would mean all parts of the cortex are equally active and attentive. This is a "democratic" or harmonious brain. Too often we see a frontal area with low amplitude and fast activity, meaning more repression and a busier brain. This we call a LVF pattern, or low-voltage, fast activity. This is synonymous with what we call a desynchronized or "flat" EEG.

In borderline individuals we see a split in the spectrum: some slow-wave activity mixed with fast waves. Here the cortex is trying to cope with upcoming deep pain and speeds up, almost as if it is fleeing the pain. If the brain "stays and faces reality," it would increase amplitude and would not speed up its frequency. The mixed frequency pattern is a "flight" pattern away from the pain.

We have chosen some different kinds of maps to give the reader an understanding of what I have been discussing. The legend below each map in Figure 11 explains further. In Figure 12 we have included brain maps showing changes in brainwave patterns following a single therapy session, three weeks of intensive therapy, and one year of therapy. Finally, the graphs in Figure 13 compare changes in frequency after both three weeks and one year of therapy.

Legends for the Six Types of Brain Map

IA. Normal, low-frequency alpha. Monorhythmic low-frequency alpha activity with a rather even distribution. Almost all the activity is within the alpha band. This is a patient with a coherent defense system. Low beta activity indicates the absence of anxiety in this patient. A peak frequency of 8 Hz and the presence of some theta (green) reflect that this subject has access to his feelings but is not overwhelmed by them.

IB. Repressed, "flat" EEG. This poorly synchronized, almost "flat" EEG with almost no alpha activity indicates a rather repressed individual with poor access to feelings. Lower-level activation is not reaching the cortex, indicating that gating is effective deep within the brain.

IC. Borderline, "split-frequency" pattern. Fast beta-2 activity is extremely high in the frontal areas of this patient, while the rest of the brain is predominantly low-amplitude alpha. The defense system here is fragmented and not holding together well. This patient is a borderline personality suffering from almost continuous pain and anxiety.

ID. First-line, slow-wave intrusion. Spontaneous bursts of high-amplitude delta waves mixed with theta are seen in all areas of the brain. Here we see someone with pronounced intrusions of deep unconscious (first-line) material pushing for conscious integration. This is from a patient with good access to early pain. The dark blue color of the beta ovals indicates an absence of anxiety.

IE. Overload: a high-amplitude, slow-wave pattern. Very high alpha amplitude waves are mixed with considerable theta and delta activity. This is a patient with a strong third line (signified by the plentiful alpha activity) who is constantly close to first- and second-line pain. She has too much access to early feelings and becomes easily overwhelmed by them. This is a patient who is prone to depression.

IF. "Open access" hypersynchrony. This pattern is sometimes called hypnagogic hypersynchrony. The patient was deeply relaxed but not asleep during the recording. We see that theta is predominant, mixed with alpha and delta; this pattern indicates continuous second-line intrusion. The patient has a fragile third line (indicated by the high ratio of theta to alpha) and is hypersensitive and extremely vulnerable.

Legends for Brain Map Changes after Primal Therapy

IIA. Changes in EEG following a session. This patient shows a slight decrease of peak frequency and almost a doubling of power following a single therapy session. There is a substantial increase of both alpha and theta activity, indicating that the subject is more open with better access to feelings after the session.

IIB. Changes in EEG following three weeks of intensive therapy. These maps, from a new patient, show a doubling of theta activity. There is a decrease of peak frequency of approximately 1 Hz, while power has increased considerably. This patient has gained considerable access to his feelings.

IIC. Changes in EEG following one year of therapy. Peak frequency has decreased and power has increased in this subject. Most of the change is seen within the alpha band, where amplitude doubled and there is a more even distribution of the alpha rhythm.

IID. Changes in EEG following three weeks of intensive therapy in a borderline patient. This patient initially showed high beta-2 activity in all areas. After three weeks of therapy, the mean EEG frequency was considerably reduced, from 15 Hz to 11 Hz. Beta-2 activity was halved, while alpha increased between 100 percent and 150 percent in the posterior areas. Following therapy, this patient reported feeling much more relaxed and in touch with his feelings.

IIE. Resolution of first-line pain in a therapy session. Following a session in which the patient relived very early traumatic feelings, delta activity was greatly reduced (by 65 percent in the posterior areas), reflecting resolution of first-line pain. At the same time, alpha increased by 30 percent to 60 percent, indicating a strengthening of the patient's gating and third-line or cortical control.

IIF. Changes in EEG following three months of therapy after withdrawal from Valium. This patient was in devastating emotional and physical pain after withdrawal. The EEG amplitudes were extremely high, especially in the theta band. After three months of therapy, power has dropped by 75 percent and peak frequency is up by approximately 1 Hz. Amplitudes are still high, but now most of the power falls within the alpha band, indicating a strengthening of the third line. The patient reports feeling better but there is a long road ahead.

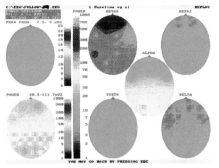

I A. Normal, low-frequency alpha

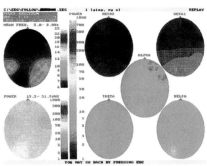

I B. Repressed, 'flat' EEG

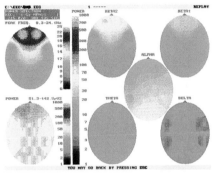

I C. Borderline, 'split frequency'

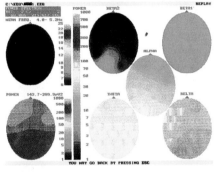

I D. First-line slow-wave intrusions.

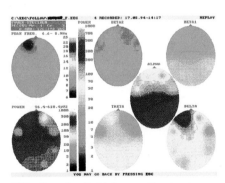

I E. Overload, high-amplitude slow

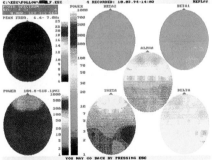

I F. 'Open access' hypersynchrony

FIGURE 11. The six types of brain maps.

II A. Changes in brain wave patterns following a single therapy session.

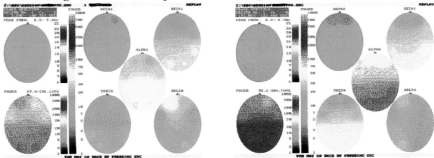

II B. Changes in a new patient after three weeks of intensive therapy.

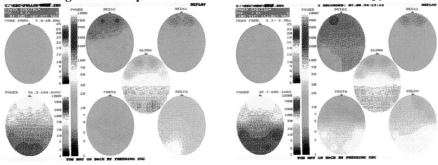

II C. EEG changes in a patient following one year of therapy.

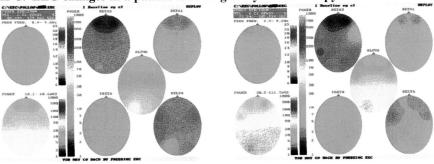

FIGURE 12. Brain-map changes in EEG following primal therapy.

II D. EEG changes following three weeks of intensive therapy.

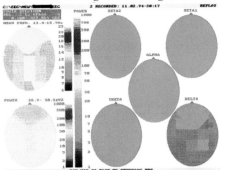

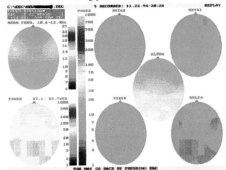

Beginning of therapy

After 3 weeks

II E. Resolution of first-line pain in a therapy session.

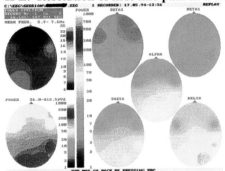

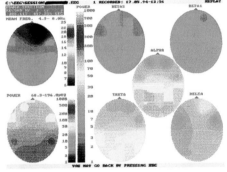

II F. Changes following 3 months of therapy after withdrawal from valium.

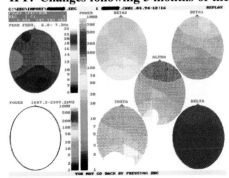

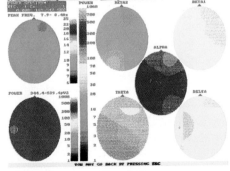

Time of withdrawal

After three months of therapy

FIGURE 12.

Legends for Graphs of Frequency Changes after Primal Therapy

Graph I. Percent Increase of Mean Theta, Alpha and Beta Amplitudes

A) Following one year of therapy (n = 20)

B) After 3 weeks initial therapy (n = 14)

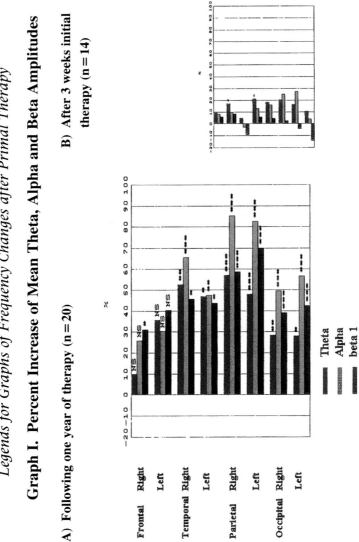

Graph I shows the percentage increases of mean theta, alpha, and beta amplitudes following a year and three weeks of primal therapy. These increases are statistically significant at one year in all but the frontal area.

Graph II. Changes in Right/Left Temporal Alpha Asymmetry

A) Following one year of therapy (n = 19)

B) After 3 weeks initial therapy (n = 14)

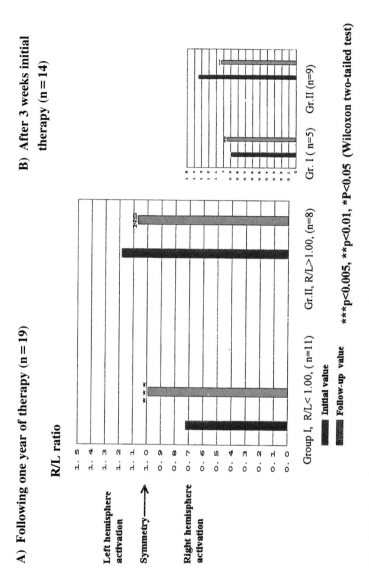

Graph II shows that the patients investigated fall into two groups: those for whom the right/left ratio achieves parity at one year and those for whom it doesn't. The difference between the groups is that the "responders" appear to have underactive right (feeling) hemispheres at the beginning of therapy, while those in whom the change is not significant have underactive left (third-line) hemispheres at the start of therapy; in this group, the change is still toward parity but has not yet reached significance.

BIBLIOGRAPHY

Andreasen, N. C., et al. "Thalmic Abnormalities in Schizophrenia Visualized Through Magnetic Resonance Image Averaging." *Science News* (1980): 279.

Blakes-Lee, Sandra. "Theory on Human Brain Hints How Its Unique Traits Arose." *New York Times*, Science Section, November 8, 1994.

Alkon, Daniel, M.D. *Memory's Voice*. New York: HarperCollins, 1992, p. 159.

Anand, K. J. S., and P. R. Hickey. "Halothane-morphine Compared With High-dose Sufentanil for Anesthesia and Postoperative Analgesia in Neonatal Cardiac Surgery." *New England Journal of Medicine* 326(1992): 1–9.

"Beyond Prozac." *Newsweek,* February 7, 1994.

Berk, Laura E. "Why Children Talk to Themselves." *Scientific American* 271(1994): 78–83.

Bolon, B., and V. St. Omer. "Biochemical Correlates for Behavioral Deficits Induced by Secalonic Acid D in Developing Mice." *Neuroscience and Biobehavioral Review* 16(1992): 171–175.

Changeux, Jean-Pierre. "Chemical Signalling in the Brain." *Scientific American* 269(1993): 58–63.

Cleary, J. P., M.D. "Etiology and Treatment of Alcohol Addiction." *Journal of Orthomolecular Medicine* 2(1987): 166–168.

Critchley, M. J., et al. *Scientific Foundations of Neurology*. London: F. A. Davis, 1972.

Dalens, B. "Acute Pain in Children and Its Treatment." *Annales Françaises d'Anesthesie et de Reanimation* 10(1991): 38–61.

Damasio, Antonio. *Descartes' Error*. New York: Putnam, 1994.

Davis, J., L. T. Giron, E. Stanton, and W. Maury. "The Effect of Hypoxia on Brain Neurotransmitter Systems." *Advances in Neurology* 26(1979): 219–223.

"Early Violence Leaves a Mark on the Brain." *New York Times,* October 3, 1995.

Fishman, R., and J. Yanai. "Long-lasting Effects of Early Barbiturates on

Central Nervous System and Behavior." *Neuroscience and Biobehavioral Review* 7(1981): 19–28.

Gazzaniga, M. S. "The Split Brain in Man." *Scientific American* 217(1967): 24–29.

Goleman, Daniel. "Studying the Secrets of Childhood Memory." *New York Times*, April 6, 1993.

Herbst, K. R., and E. S. Paykiel. *Depression: An Integrative Approach.* London: Heineman Medical Books, 1989.

Holden, E. Michael, M.D. "Anaesthesia and Consciousness." *Journal of Primal Therapy* 111(1976): 220–229.

Hooper, J., and D. Teresi. *The Three-Pound Universe.* Los Angeles: J. P. Tarcher, 1986.

Janov, Arthur. *The Feeling Child.* New York: Simon & Schuster, 1973.

Janov, Arthur. *The New Primal Scream.* Wilmington, Del.: Enterprise Publishing, 1991.

John, E. Roy, M.D. *The Physiology of Memory.* New York: Academic Press, 1967.

Kovelman, Joyce, and Arnold Scheibel. "Biological Substrates of Schizophrenia." *Currents*, September 1985.

Lagercrantz, H., and Theodore Slotkin. "The Stress of Being Born." *Scientific American* 254(1986): 100.

LaViolette, Paul. "Emotional-Perceptive Cycling; A Link Between Limbic System and New Brain." *Brain-Mind Bulletin* 7(1982).

Leboyer, Frederic, M.D. *Birth Without Violence.* New York: Knopf, 1975.

LeDoux, J. E. "Emotion, Memory and the Brain." *Scientific American* 270(1994): 50–57.

"Letters." *Nature,* December 22, 1994.

McGaugh, James. "Stress Hormones Hike Emotional Memories." *Science News* 146(1994): 262; from *Nature,* October 20, 1994.

Mednick, Sarnoff A. "Birth Defects and Schizophrenia." *Psychology Today* 4(1971): 49.

Mishkin, Mortimer, and Tim Appenzeller. "The Anatomy of Memory." *Scientific American* 256(1987): 80–89.

Nauta, W. J. H., and Feirtag, Michael. "The Organization of the Brain." *Scientific American* 241(1979): 104.

Neziroglu, F., and J. A. Yaryura-Tobias. *Over and Over Again: Understanding Obsessive-Compulsive Disorder.* New York: Lexington Books, 1991.

Nolen, Willem, et al. *Refractory Depression.* New York: Wiley, 1993.

Penfield, Wilder, M.D. *Epilepsy and the Functional Anatomy of the Human Brain.* Princeton, N.J.: Princeton University Press, 1954, p. 109.

Penfield, Wilder, M.D. *Mysteries of the Mind.* Princeton, N.J.: Princeton University Press, 1975, p. 55.

Raine, Adrian, Patricia Brennan, and Sarnoff Mednick. "Birth Complications Combined With Early Maternal Rejection at Age One Year Predispose to Violent Crime at Age Eighteen Years." *Archives of General Psychiatry*, 1994 December, 51 (12):984–8.

Routtenberg, A. "The Reward System of the Brain." *Scientific American* 239(1978): 161.

Saal, Vom, D. M. Quadagno, et al. "Paradoxical Effects of Maternal Stress on Fetal Steroids and Postnatal Reproductive Straits in Female Mice From Different Intrauterine Positions." *Biology of Reproduction* 43(1990): 751–761.

Salk, L., et al. "Relationship of Maternal and Perinatal Conditions to Eventual Adolescent Suicide." *The Lancet* 1(1985): 624–627.

Schoendorf, Kenneth C., M.D., M.P.H., and John Kiley, Ph.D. "Relationship of Sudden Infant Death Syndrome to Maternal Smoking During and After Pregnancy)." *Pediatrics* (1992): 905–908.

Snyder, Solomon. "Opiate Receptors and Internal Opiates." *Scientific American* 236(1977): 44–67.

Stone, Gene. "When Prozac Fails, Electroshock Therapy Works." *New York Times Magazine,* November 14, 1994.

Stolberg, Sheryl. "Fears Cloud Search for Genetic Roots of Violence." *Los Angeles Times*, December 30, 1993.

Warburg, Otto. *The Metabolism of Tumors.* London: Constable and Co., 1930.

Weber, Tracy. "Doing Time by Mail, Not Jail." *Los Angeles Times*, November 28, 1994.

Welch, W. J. "How Cells Respond to Stress." *Scientific American* 268(1993): 56–81.

Werner, Emmy. "Children of the Garden Island." *Scientific American* 260(1989): 106–111.

Windle, W. F. "Brain Damage by Asphyxia at Birth." *Scientific American* 221(1969): 76.

INDEX